THE USBORNE
CHILDREN'S
ENCYCLOPEDIA

Researched and written by

Holly Bathie (History, How Things Work), Felicity Brooks (Our World), Fiona Chandler (History), Phillip Clarke (Facts and Records), Anna Claybourne (Science, How Your Body Works), Liz Dalby (Maps of the World), Ben Denne (How Things Work, Our World, Animals and Plants), Paul Dowswell (Animals and Plants, Space), Rachel Firth (Science, How Your Body Works), Laura Howell (Animals and Plants), Sarah Khan (How Your Body Works), Anna Milbourne (How Things Work), Kirsteen Rogers (How People Live), Caroline Young (How People Live)

Illustrated by David Hancock

Designed by Francesca Allen, Laura Hammonds, Nelupa Hussein, Stephanie Jones, Joanne Kirkby, Susie McCaffrey, Keith Newell, Susannah Owen, Ruth Russell, Karen Tomlins, Candice Whatmore, Helen Wood

Edited by Felicity Brooks, Anna Claybourne, Anna Milbourne, Kirsteen Rogers, Judy Tatchell

This edition designed by Stephanie Jeffries and Tom Lalonde
This edition edited by Holly Bathie and Alice Beecham
Americanization by Mara Alperin

Art Directors Mary Cartwright and Karen Tomlins
Cartography European Map Graphics Ltd.
Digital manipulation Roger Bolton, Keith Furnival, Fiona Johnson, Mike Olley, John Russell, Mike Wheatley
Picture research Ruth King, Valerie Modd, Ehimare Ogona
Internet research Jacqui Clark and Emma Danes

Consultants Craig Asquith (Maps, Flags), Stuart Atkinson (Astronomy, Space), Dr. Samraghni Bonnerjee (History), Dr. Emma Curtis-Lake (Space), John Davidson (Geography), Liza Dibble (Farming), Professor Kate Dossett (History), Dr. Wendy Dossett (Religions), Oliver Grant (Engineering), H.M. Hignett (Ships, Boats), Professor Michael Hitchcock (How People Live), Sinclair MacLeod (Science), Dr. David Martill (Dinosaurs), Dr. Anne Millard (History), Eileen O'Brien (Music), Alison Porter (Technology), Professor Michael Reiss (Science), Dr. John Rostron and Dr. Margaret Rostron (Biology, Natural History), Dr. Kristina Routh (Human Biology, Medicine)

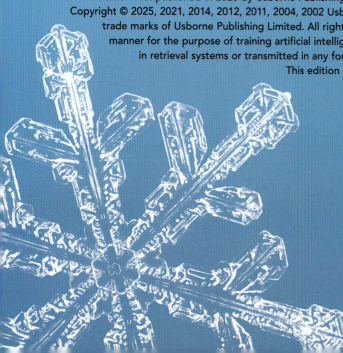

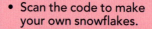
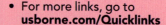

- Scan the code to make your own snowflakes.
- For more links, go to **usborne.com/Quicklinks**

THE USBORNE
CHILDREN'S
ENCYCLOPEDIA

Contents

Science

How Things Work

Space

Maps of the World

Usborne Quicklinks

Throughout this book you'll see QR codes, like the one below. Scanning these takes you straight to specially selected websites where you'll find videos, experiments, quizzes and other online activities related to the topics in the book.

- Scan the code for a video of pandas feeding on bamboo.
- For more links, go to **usborne.com/Quicklinks**

If you don't have a smartphone or tablet to scan the QR code, simply go to **usborne.com/Quicklinks** and type **CE2** into the search box.

Even more to explore

At Usborne Quicklinks you will also find links to **over 800 websites** where you can:

- Take a virtual tour of our Solar System.
- See how Egyptian mummies were made.
- Follow food on a journey through your body.
- Visit a coral reef and see what lives there.
- Discover how science can explain why flamingos are pink.

You can also download many of the pictures featured in this book for home or school use (but not for commercial purposes).

How to scan a QR code

Most smartphones and tablets can scan QR codes through their built-in camera app. Open the app, point the camera at the QR code and tap the banner that appears.

If your smartphone or tablet does not have this functionality, you can download a free QR code reader app.

Links to external websites

Usborne Quicklinks are links to content on external (non-Usborne) websites. These websites have been selected by Usborne editors to enhance the information in Usborne books and are regularly reviewed and updated. However, Usborne does not control and is not responsible for the content or availability of these websites.

Online safety

Parents – children should be supervised online and follow our three basic rules:

- Always ask an adult's permission before using the internet.
- Never give out personal information, such as your name, address, school, or telephone number.
- If a website asks you to type in your name or email address, check with an adult first.

You don't need a smartphone or tablet to use this book.
To explore links to over 800 recommended websites for this book,
go to Usborne Quicklinks at **usborne.com/Quicklinks**
and type **CE2** into the search box.

Our World

Our planet

Our planet is called the Earth. It is the only planet where we know that plants, animals and people live. The large areas of land are called continents. Each continent is divided into smaller areas called countries.

This is a house...   in a town...   in a country...   in a continent on planet Earth.

Planet Earth travels around the Sun. It takes one year to go all the way around.

As it travels, the Earth spins around. It takes 24 hours to spin around once.

Below is what you'd see if you went up in a spacecraft and looked at the Earth.

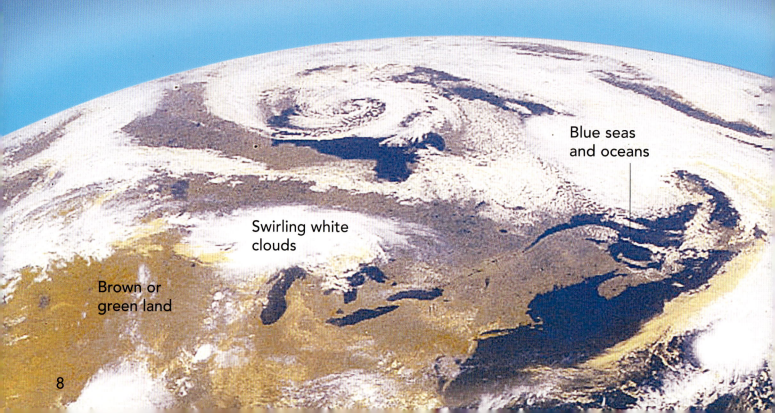

Blue seas and oceans

Swirling white clouds

Brown or green land

- Scan the code to see what Earth looks like for astronauts in space.
- For more links, go to **usborne.com/Quicklinks**

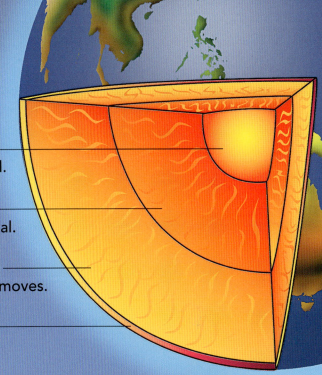

What's inside the Earth?

The Earth is made of rock and metal. If you could cut it open, you would see different layers inside. The picture on the right shows you what's inside the Earth.

In the middle, there's solid metal.

Next there's very hot, soft metal.

Then there's hot, sticky rock which moves.

On the outside, there's solid rock.

The atmosphere

The Earth is protected by an enormous blanket of gases, called the atmosphere. It stretches from the surface of the Earth up to 391,000 miles (630,000km) into space. The sky you can see is part of the atmosphere.

The light, hazy blue on this photograph shows part of the Earth's atmosphere.

The atmosphere helps keep the Earth warm at night.

In the daytime, it helps protect you from the Sun's heat and light.

Day and night

When it is day for you, it is night for people on the other side of the world. When it is their day, it is your night.

Sunlight can't reach this side of the Earth, so it's night here.

The Sun is shining on this side of the Earth, so it's day here.

Sunrise

When your side of the Earth turns to face the Sun in the morning, the Sun is said to rise.

Sun rising over a field

Sunset

When your side of the Earth turns away from the Sun in the evening, the Sun is setting.

Sun setting over the sea

Turning Earth

Day changes to night, and night to day, because the Earth turns. As it turns, different parts face the Sun.

The part of the Earth with the USA on it is facing the Sun, so it's day in the USA.

USA

A few hours later, the USA has turned away from the Sun, so it's night there now.

The Earth keeps turning all the time.

The Earth travels around the Sun this way.

After 24 hours, the Earth has turned all the way around, so now it's day again in the USA.

USA

Solar eclipse

The only time it is dark in the day is when the Moon blocks out the Sun. This is called a solar eclipse. A total solar eclipse doesn't happen very often, and it only lasts a few minutes.

- Scan the code to find out more about solar eclipses.
- For more links, go to **usborne.com/Quicklinks**

This picture shows why an eclipse takes place.

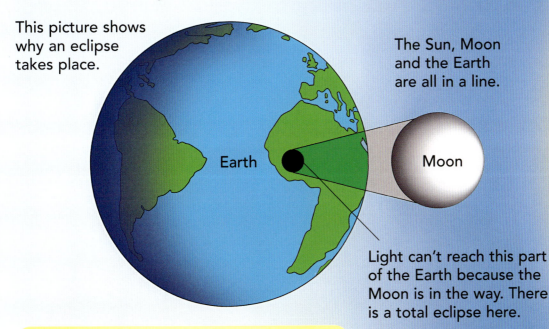

Earth

The Sun, Moon and the Earth are all in a line.

Moon

Sun

Light can't reach this part of the Earth because the Moon is in the way. There is a total eclipse here.

Make a shadow

On a sunny day, you stop some sunlight from reaching the ground. This is what makes your shadow.

Try looking at your shadow on a sunny day. You will see that it always points away from the Sun. As the Sun rises higher in the sky in the morning, your shadow gets shorter. As the Sun sinks lower in the afternoon, your shadow gets longer.

Cloudy days

Even on a cloudy day, the Sun is shining on your part of the Earth. You just can't see it because the clouds hide it.

Clouds like these may hide the Sun, but it is always there above them.

11

The weather

There are lots of different kinds of weather, such as rainy, snowy, sunny and windy weather. The three main things that cause the weather are the Sun, the air and water.

The Sun gives out heat.

The air moves to make wind.

Water makes rain and snow.

4 The water droplets bump into other droplets and join together to make clouds.

Rainy days

There isn't any new water on the Earth. The same rain falls again and again. This is called the water cycle. Follow the numbers to see what happens.

3 Up in the sky, it's cooler, so the water vapor turns back into tiny water droplets.

5 As more water is added, the droplets get bigger and heavier and fall as rain.

2 The water turns into water vapor, a gas which we can't see, and rises up into the sky.

6 The rain falls down to the ground where it flows back into seas, lakes and rivers.

1 The Sun heats up the water in seas, lakes, and rivers, and even snow on the tops of mountains.

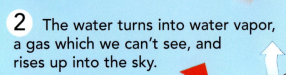

Windy weather

When it's windy, it's because the air is moving around. You can't see the wind, but you can see it blowing leaves around and feel it on your face.

A gentle wind is called a breeze. It can help dry wet clothes.

Gales are much stronger winds. They can blow tiles off roofs.

Hurricanes are very strong winds that can do a lot of damage.

Rainbows

Sometimes it rains even though the Sun is shining. Raindrops split sunlight into different colors. When this happens you might see a rainbow. From the ground, it usually looks like an arch, but from an aircraft, it might be a circle.

Make a rainbow

You can make your own rainbow even when it's not raining, as long as the Sun is shining. You will need:

a plastic tray or bowl; a piece of paper; a mirror

1. Fill the tray with water and place it somewhere sunny, such as on a windowsill.

2. Put the mirror in the tray so the Sun can shine through the water onto the mirror.

3. Hold the paper above the tray. Tilt the mirror until you see a rainbow on the paper.

Icy snowflakes

Snowflakes are made when it gets so cold that the water in a cloud freezes and turns into ice. Snowflakes all have six sides or points, but they form millions of different patterns.

Every snowflake has a different shape.

- Scan the code to find out about clouds and the weather.
- For more links, go to **usborne.com/Quicklinks**

Storms and floods

In a big storm, the wind blows very hard. There's usually lots of rain or snow. There may be thunder and lightning too.

Types of storms

The pictures below show some of the things that can happen during different types of storms.

Lightning is a big spark of electricity in the sky. Thunder is the noise that the spark makes.

A tornado is a spinning funnel of wind. It whirls along, sucking up anything in its path.

A hurricane is a huge storm with lots of wind and rain. It can destroy towns and forests.

The swirling clouds on this photograph of the Earth are a hurricane.

Storms at sea

At sea, violent storms and huge waves can appear suddenly and cause terrible damage. Tornadoes, called waterspouts, sometimes pull sea water up into a spinning column. This sucks up anything in its path as it moves across the sea.

Giant sparks of electricity zigzag through the air during a lightning storm in Arizona, USA.

Floods

If a lot of rain falls in a short time, or if it rains for a long time, rivers get too full and spill onto the land. This causes floods, which cover land that is usually dry.

A flash flood is a sudden rush of water. It happens when a lot of rain falls in a short time.

Some floods happen when snow and ice melt. The soil is still frozen, so water can't soak into it.

Huge waves can cause floods. They are made by storms, undersea volcanoes or earthquakes.

Monsoon floods

A monsoon is a wind that blows one way all summer and the other way all winter. In Asia, the monsoon in summer brings very heavy rain from the oceans.

Each year, homes and villages in southeast Asia are flooded by heavy monsoon rains. This photograph was taken in India.

- Scan the code to see hurricanes and find out how they form.
- For more links, go to **usborne.com/Quicklinks**

Rocks and fossils

There are lots of kinds of rocks. Some are formed by heat from inside the Earth. Others are made from sand, mud and pieces of dead plants and animals.

This is a fossil of a sea animal called an ammonite.

Rocky layers

Sand, mud and pieces of plants and animals that sink and settle at the bottom of the sea are known as sediment.

Layers of sediment

Layers of sediment build up slowly. Over millions of years, the bottom layers get squeezed and stick together to become sedimentary rocks.

Fiery rocks

Volcano

During a volcanic eruption, hot, sticky rock from inside the Earth breaks through the surface.

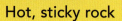

Hot, sticky rock

When the hot, sticky rock cools, it becomes hard. This kind of rock is known as igneous rock. Igneous comes from the word for "fiery" in Latin.

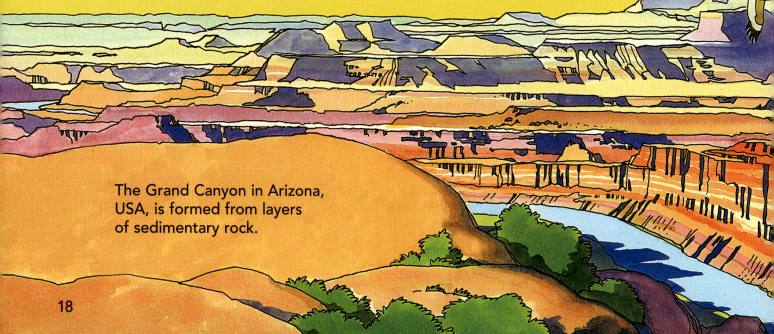

The Grand Canyon in Arizona, USA, is formed from layers of sedimentary rock.

This is a fossil of a sea animal called a trilobite.

This is the fossil of a sea creature called a sand dollar.

Fossils

Fossils are the stony remains of animals that lived millions of years ago. Most fossils are found in sedimentary rock.

- Scan the code to see how people dig up fossils.
- For more links, go to usborne.com/Quicklinks

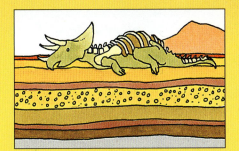

When an animal dies, its soft parts rot away leaving its bones. If they sink into mud, they get covered in sediment.

Over millions of years, the sediment layers slowly harden into rock. This keeps the shape of the animal's bones in it.

Millions of years later, people sometimes find fossil bones or shells inside rocks. They have to dig them up carefully.

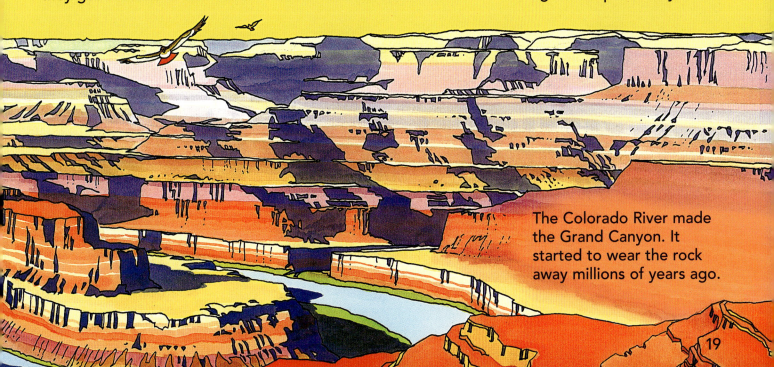

The Colorado River made the Grand Canyon. It started to wear the rock away millions of years ago.

19

Earthquakes

An earthquake happens when huge rocks deep under the ground slip and push against each other. This makes the ground above shake.

The red dots on this map show where earthquakes are most likely to happen.

Start of an earthquake

The place underground where an earthquake starts is called the focus. The effects of an earthquake are strongest on the surface right above the focus.

- Scan the code to find out more about earthquakes.
- For more links, go to **usborne.com/Quicklinks**

Earthquake effects

Most earthquakes are too weak to be felt by people, but some can cause great damage. The pictures below show some of the effects of an earthquake.

In a weak earthquake, hanging things swing from side to side. Windows and dishes may start to rattle.

A stronger earthquake makes walls crack and pictures fall.

In a very strong earthquake, buildings and trees fall down.

This house fell down in a big earthquake in California, USA.

Staying safe

In countries where there are a lot of earthquakes, people are taught ways to stay safe. Children have earthquake drills at school.

Indoors, it is safest to shelter under a table.

Outdoors, you are safest in a big open space.

Earthquakes at sea

An earthquake that happens under the sea shakes the seabed. This sometimes creates a series of huge waves, called a tsunami (say "soo-naa-mee").

In the deep ocean, a tsunami is not dangerous and may pass under ships without anyone noticing. It only becomes enormous if it reaches shallow water. Then it breaks and crashes onto the land.

As the seabed moves, the sea above forms long, low waves.

If a tsunami reaches the coast, it is squeezed up into a huge wave.

Earthquakes can cause a huge wave, like this one. The biggest wave ever recorded was 1,720ft (524m) high.

Volcanoes

A volcano erupts when hot, sticky rock called magma from deep inside the Earth bursts through the surface. The liquid rock is called lava as it pours down the sides of the volcano and over the land.

This photograph shows a fountain of lava shooting out of a volcano.

Volcanic eruption

When a volcano erupts, lava comes out of a vent (opening) in the volcano's top or side. Rocks may shoot up into the sky, and thick clouds of ash and gas may billow out. Sometimes a vent is in a hollow at the top, called a crater.

Lava is so hot it destroys everything it touches. The heat of the lava has set this wooden house on fire.

Volcano shapes

The lava cools and hardens into rock. Layers of lava and ash build up each time the volcano erupts, giving the volcano its shape. Some volcanoes are tall cones with steep sides, and some are fairly flat with gentle slopes.

Many volcanoes are tall and steep. Their thick lava does not flow far before it hardens.

Some volcanoes are flatter. Their lava is runny. It spreads out quickly before it hardens.

Sea volcanoes

There are lots of volcanoes under the sea. When one gets tall enough to appear above the waves, it makes an island.

This photograph shows clouds of steam and ash billowing from Surtsey, a volcanic island near Iceland.

Lava often moves very slowly, so people usually have time to escape.

Alive, asleep or dead?

A volcano may be active (alive), dormant (asleep) or extinct (dead).

An active volcano erupts quite often.

A dormant volcano hasn't erupted for a long time, but may erupt again in the future.

An extinct volcano hasn't erupted for at least 10,000 years. Some towns are built on extinct volcanoes.

- Scan the code to see volcanoes erupt and watch lava flowing.
- For more links, go to **usborne.com/Quicklinks**

Following a river

A river starts high up in hills or mountains. The water comes from rain or melted snow. It flows downhill until it reaches the sea. Follow this river to see how it changes.

1 The start of a river is called its source. This may be where lots of streams join together.

- Scan the code to follow the journey of a river.
- For more links, go to **usborne.com/Quicklinks**

2 The water wears the rock away to make a valley shaped like a V.

3 Other smaller rivers called tributaries may join the river and make it bigger.

The sides of the river are called riverbanks.

People sometimes put big, flat stepping stones in a river. You can step on them to cross it.

4 Here the river flows fast over rocks and stones.

These anglers are trying to catch fish that live in the river.

This is a waterfall. The water flows very fast here.

Waterfalls

A waterfall forms where a river flows from hard rock to soft rock. The water wears away the soft rock faster than the hard rock. This makes a big step.

This photograph shows water flowing over the Kachanh Waterfall in Cambodia.

9 The place where a river joins the sea is called the mouth of the river.

Lots of birds feed on the little animals that live in the sand.

Bank of sand

7 The river carries lots of sand and mud to the sea.

8 The river drops most of its sand and mud when it reaches the sea.

6 The river is deeper and wider on the outer edge of the bend.

5 Here the river starts to flow in big loops called meanders.

You can cross a river on a bridge.

Mountains

Mountains form over millions of years. Vast pieces of rock on the Earth's surface push against each other and force part of the land up into mountains.

A group of mountains is known as a range. These mountains are part of a range called the Rocky Mountains in Canada.

Parts of a mountain

Some mountains have snow on their peaks (tops) all year round. The level where the snow ends is called the snowline.

A gap between two peaks in a range is called a pass.

Peak

Treeline

Pass

Snowline

This picture shows the parts of a mountain.

Trees often grow on a mountain's lower slopes, but it's too cold for them to grow above a certain level. This is known as the treeline.

Glaciers

On the coldest parts of some mountains, snow builds up and turns into ice. Solid rivers of ice, called glaciers, move very slowly downhill.

Glaciers like this one carry stones and rocks downhill. As it warms up farther down the mountain, the glacier melts, forming streams.

Mountain life

Some plants and animals can live on mountains. They need to be able to survive in very cold temperatures and strong winds.

Mountain flowers such as purple saxifrage grow in short, round clumps.

Conifer trees have tough, narrow needles instead of broad leaves.

Golden eagles build their large nests on mountain rocks and ledges.

Mountain hares have thick fur which turns white in winter.

- Scan the code to take a trip and explore some mountains.
- For more links, go to usborne.com/Quicklinks

In the desert

Deserts are the driest places in the world, where it might not rain for many years. Most deserts are very hot in the day, but cool at night.

AFRICA

Sahara Desert

Kalahari and Namib deserts

Deserts cover about a third of the Earth's land. About a third of the continent of Africa is desert.

Desert homes have flat roofs, and small windows to keep out the Sun.

Palm trees

An oasis is a place where there is water so plants can grow.

Camels can go a week or more without water.

Euphorbia plant

Antelopes

Most deserts are rocky and bare. Only parts of them are covered in sand.

Jerboas hop along like miniature kangaroos.

Sandgrouse

Desert plants

Many desert plants have long roots, and stems which can soak up water. Some, like the barrel cactus, can store water inside.

A barrel cactus swells with water when it rains.

Before rain   After rain

A giant saguaro cactus may live for hundreds of years.

When the wind blows, the sand piles up into hills called sand dunes.

Lanner falcon

Desert-dwellers live in groups and move from place to place. They keep sheep, goats and camels.

- Scan the code to see how animals survive in the desert.
- For more links, go to **usborne.com/Quicklinks**

Fennec foxes have huge ears which help them lose body heat.

Saw-scaled vipers slither along with an S-shaped wiggle.

Grasslands

Plains, or grasslands, are big areas of land covered in grass. Bushes and some trees may grow there too. The picture below shows part of a grassland in Africa.

Grasslands, shown in orange on this map, cover over a quarter of the Earth's land.

Baobab trees can store water in their trunks.

Ostriches

Rhinos

Elephants

Thousands of insects called termites make these big mounds.

Baboons live in large groups called troops.

Lions live in family groups called prides.

Weaver birds make complicated nests.

Wildebeest

Tourists come in trucks and buses to see the animals.

Hyenas

Zoologists in a
hot air balloon

Vultures

- Scan the code
to see animals in
African grasslands.
- For more links, go to
usborne.com/Quicklinks

The dry grass catches fire easily.
It grows again when it rains.

Giraffes

Lots of animals come
to a waterhole to drink
and stay cool.

Antelopes

Warthogs

Cheetahs

Zebras

Prairies and steppes

There are many names for grasslands
around the world. Grasslands in
Russia are known as steppes.

Grasslands are also known as
prairies. Most prairies in North
America are now used as farmland,
as wheat grows well there.

Huge fields of wheat stretch across the
grasslands of North America.

In the rainforest

Thick, green rainforests grow in hot, wet places near the Equator. It is warm all year there, and it rains nearly every day. Rainforests are home to thousands of different plants and animals.

SOUTH AMERICA

Amazon River

The biggest rainforest is the Amazon Rainforest in South America. The Amazon River runs through it.

- Scan the code to watch animals in their rainforest home.
- For more links, go to usborne.com/Quicklinks

Rainforest trees grow very tall.

Spider monkeys

Morpho butterfly

Lichen

Poison dart frog

Jaguar

Hummingbird

Orchids

Plants on trees

Many rainforest plants grow on the branches of trees. This is because there is more light up there than on the ground.

Scarlet macaws

Ferns

Toucans

Howler monkeys

Bromeliad

Lianas are plants with long stems like ropes.

Sloths move very slowly.

Capybaras look like large guinea pigs.

Caiman

These big buttress roots hold the tall trees upright.

Giant armadillo

Scarlet ibis

Matamata turtle

Anacondas are huge snakes.

Giant water lily leaves

Seas and oceans

More than two-thirds of the Earth is covered with water.
This makes the planet look blue from space. The water
is divided into five large areas called oceans, and lots
of smaller areas called seas, bays and gulfs.

Watery world

It is like a different world under
the oceans. There are deep
valleys, huge mountains,
forests of seaweed
and many amazing
sea animals.

- Scan the code for
  fascinating facts about
  oceans and ocean wildlife.
- For more links, go to
  usborne.com/Quicklinks

Oil platform

Coast

Divers only go down
to about 500ft (150m). The
deepest parts of the oceans
may be more than 70 times
deeper than this.

Most oceans have a shallow
area near the coast.

Oil gets trapped
between layers of
rock under the sea.

People drill
holes into the seabed
to get the oil out. See
page 44 to find out more.

At the bottom of
the sea is the seabed.

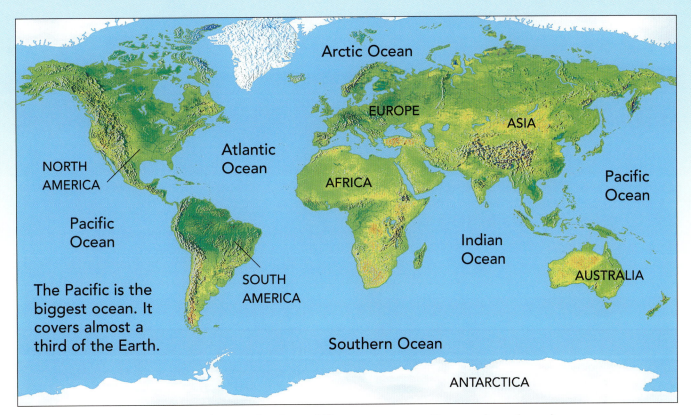

This map shows the five different oceans. Remember that the world is round, so the two parts of the Pacific Ocean join up.

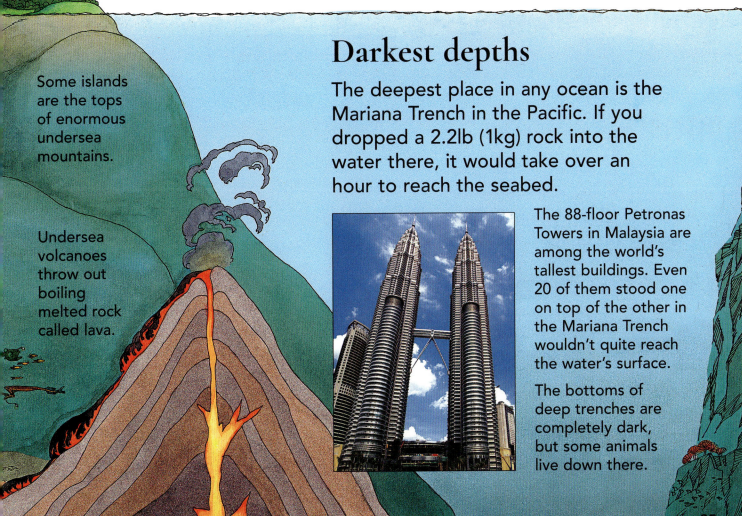

Darkest depths

The deepest place in any ocean is the Mariana Trench in the Pacific. If you dropped a 2.2lb (1kg) rock into the water there, it would take over an hour to reach the seabed.

The 88-floor Petronas Towers in Malaysia are among the world's tallest buildings. Even 20 of them stood one on top of the other in the Mariana Trench wouldn't quite reach the water's surface.

The bottoms of deep trenches are completely dark, but some animals live down there.

35

Waves

Waves are made far out at sea by the wind. They sometimes travel enormous distances across the oceans before finally crashing onto the seashore.

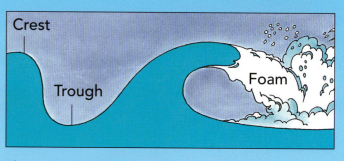

This picture shows what the different parts of a wave are called.

Making waves

Wind blowing across the sea makes ripples on the water. If the wind continues to blow, the ripples will get bigger and bigger, until they turn into waves.

When the wind blows across the tops of waves, it creates foam on them and makes them grow.

Breaking waves

The shape of a wave is affected by the depth of the sea. This makes waves change shape as they get closer to the coast.

- Scan the code to watch huge waves breaking near the coast.
- For more links, go to **usborne.com/Quicklinks**

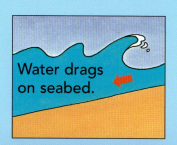

As a wave gets closer to land, the water gets shallower. The bottom part of the wave starts to drag on the seabed and slows down.

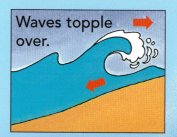

The top of the wave now moves faster than the bottom. This makes the top of the wave fall forward and topple over. This is called breaking.

Currents

Ocean currents are like big rivers which flow through the world's seas. Different currents flow at different speeds. Some move as slow as 6 miles (10km) a day, others as fast as 100 miles (160km) a day. These patterns of moving water affect weather patterns around the world.

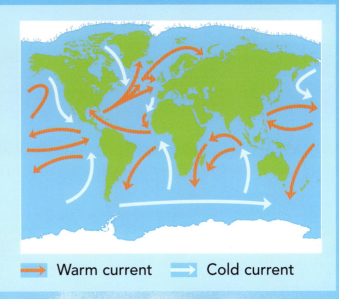

➡ Warm current   ➡ Cold current

Monster waves

The size of a wave depends on how strongly the wind is blowing and the distance it has covered. During storms at sea, strong winds create huge, powerful waves, which are big enough to sink a ship.

In some places, waves can be over 40ft (12m) high. That's higher than a two-story house.

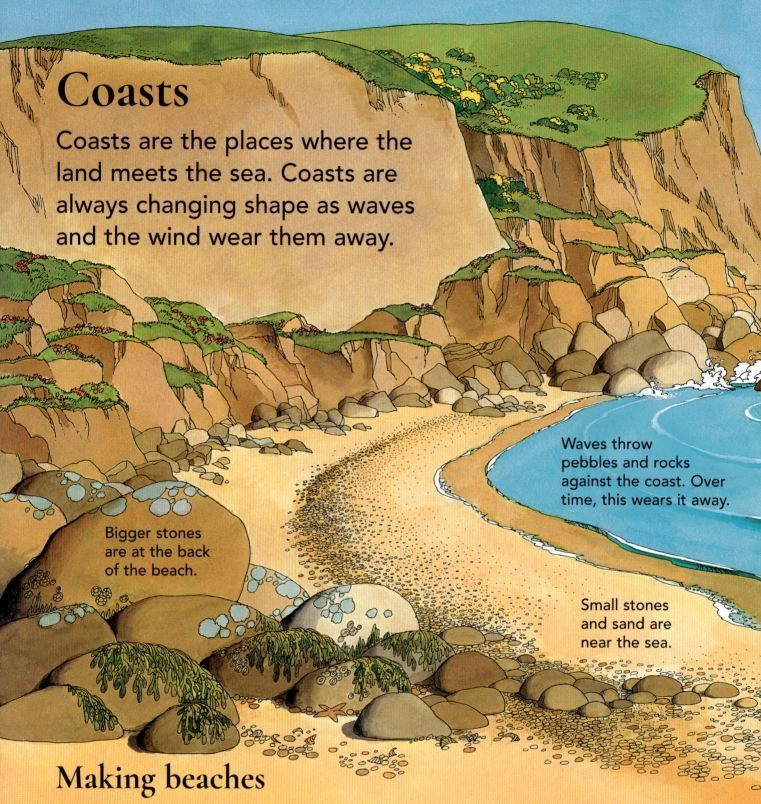

Coasts

Coasts are the places where the land meets the sea. Coasts are always changing shape as waves and the wind wear them away.

Waves throw pebbles and rocks against the coast. Over time, this wears it away.

Bigger stones are at the back of the beach.

Small stones and sand are near the sea.

Making beaches

Beaches form on low, flat parts of the coast. Waves grind down big rocks and cliffs into smaller stones and pebbles, and finally into sand. Sand often also contains tiny pieces of broken seashells.

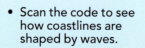

- Scan the code to see how coastlines are shaped by waves.
- For more links, go to **usborne.com/Quicklinks**

Changing coasts

Some parts of a coast are made of harder rock than others. These parts are worn away more slowly by the sea, and form a headland.

When the top of an arch collapses, a stack or stump is left.

Headland

Waves wear away softer rock in the cliffs to make caves.

An arch forms when waves wear away a hole through a headland.

Tides

The height of the sea is called sea level. The sea level in most places is constantly changing through the day as the sea moves up and down the beach. This movement is called the tide.

Tides sometimes come in very fast and trap people on beaches.

Icy world

The very cold places near the top and bottom of the Earth are called the polar regions. Huge areas of land and sea are covered in ice and snow.

The area around the North Pole is called the Arctic.

The area around the South Pole is called the Antarctic.

Polar ice

The ice in the polar regions forms flat sheets and glaciers, and covers high mountains. In the summer, some of the ice melts, but in the winter it freezes solid again.

Many penguins live in the Antarctic. They have a thick layer of feathers and fat to keep out the cold.

What is an iceberg?

Icebergs are huge chunks of ice floating in the water. The small top part, or tip, floats above the water. The rest is hidden below. The pictures on the right show how an iceberg forms.

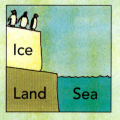

Ice

Land

Sea

A sheet of ice moves over the land to the sea.

At the sea, the ice moves out over the water.

A piece of ice breaks off. This is an iceberg.

Life near the poles

Not many people live in the Arctic, compared with most other areas of the world. No one lives in the Antarctic all the time, but scientists go there to study its animals, weather and land.

Polar animals

Animals that live in the polar regions can survive in very cold weather. They have to keep warm and find food in icy conditions.

Polar bears make long journeys over the Arctic snow and ice in search of seals, birds and fish to eat.

Antarctic icefish have special liquid in their blood to stop it from freezing.

Walruses live in the Arctic. A thick layer of fat under their skins keeps them warm.

Weddell seals hunt for food under the Antarctic ice. They make breathing holes in the ice.

- Scan the code to visit the Antarctic and spot penguins and seals.
- For more links, go to **usborne.com/Quicklinks**

Caves

A cave is an underground space with walls made of rock. Some caves are just below the surface. Others are very deep underground.

- Scan the code to explore caves and see what's inside them.
- For more links, go to **usborne.com/Quicklinks**

Making caves

Each time it rains, the rainwater seeps through cracks in the rock.

Over a long, long time, the water dissolves the rock and wears it away.

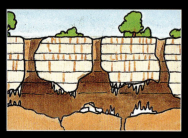

When the level of the water drops, empty caves and passages are left.

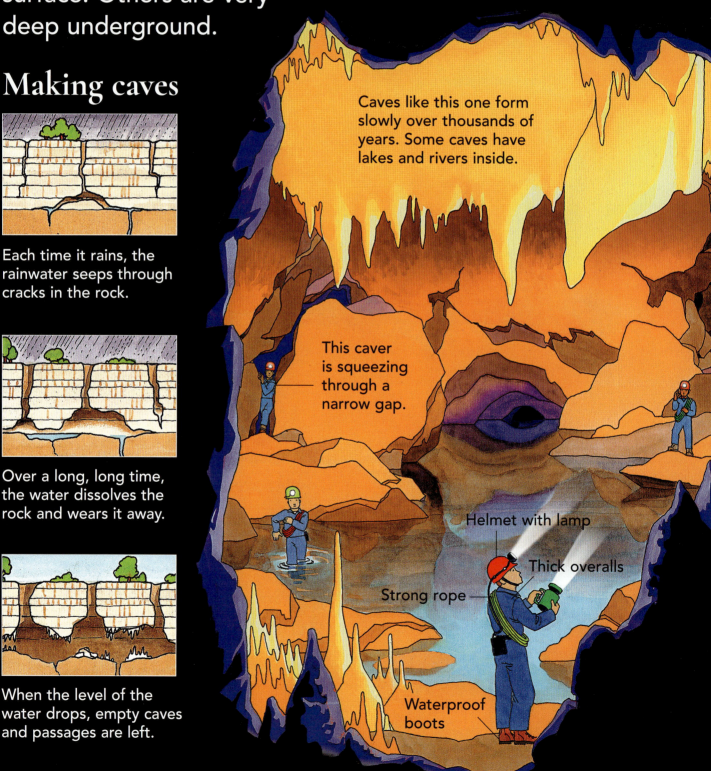

Caves like this one form slowly over thousands of years. Some caves have lakes and rivers inside.

This caver is squeezing through a narrow gap.

Helmet with lamp

Thick overalls

Strong rope

Waterproof boots

Rocky shapes

Caves are full of strange, rocky shapes which are made by water which has trickled through the rock and dissolved some of it. When the water drips, it leaves behind some dissolved rock. This builds up very slowly to make stalactites and stalagmites.

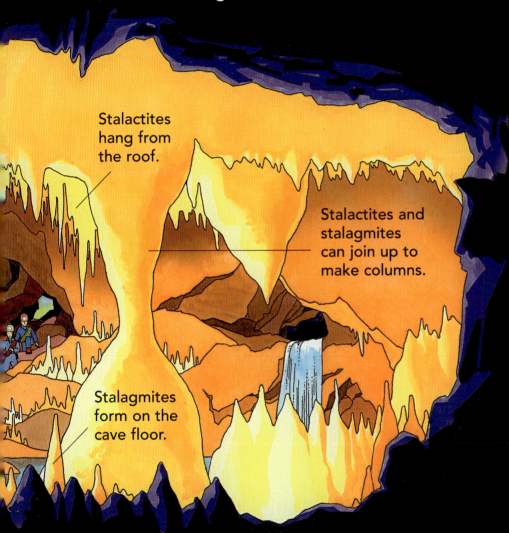

Stalactites hang from the roof.

Stalactites and stalagmites can join up to make columns.

Stalagmites form on the cave floor.

Cavers

Cavers are people who explore caves for fun, or to find out more about them. They often squeeze through narrow passages or wade through deep water. Special clothes and equipment keep cavers safe and help them explore.

Cave-dwellers

Brown bear

Brown bears and black bears sleep inside caves through the winter.

Horseshoe bat

Many kinds of bats spend the winter in caves. They fly out in the spring.

Cave painting of a bison

A long time ago, people lived in caves. They made pictures on the walls. These pictures help us learn what life was like then.

Useful Earth

We depend on the Earth to survive. It gives us food, water, air and all we need for building and making things. It also gives us the fuel we need for cooking, heating and making machines and engines go.

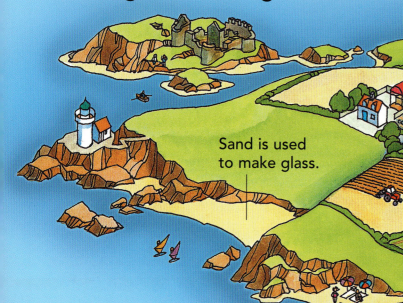

Sand is used to make glass.

We eat many kinds of plants. Some, such as cotton, are made into material for clothes. Others are made into medicines.

Fossil fuels

Coal, oil and gas are burned as fuels to generate heat and power. They come from rotted plants and animals that died millions of years ago, which is why they are called fossil fuels. One day we will run out of them.

Burning fossil fuels creates lots of a gas called carbon dioxide, which is bad for the environment. It stays in the atmosphere and causes Earth's temperature to rise, and changes weather patterns.

Oil and gas can be found under the seabed. People drill for them from rigs, like this one.

Coal and oil are taken out of the ground and used to make lots of things, such as paint, plastic and perfume.

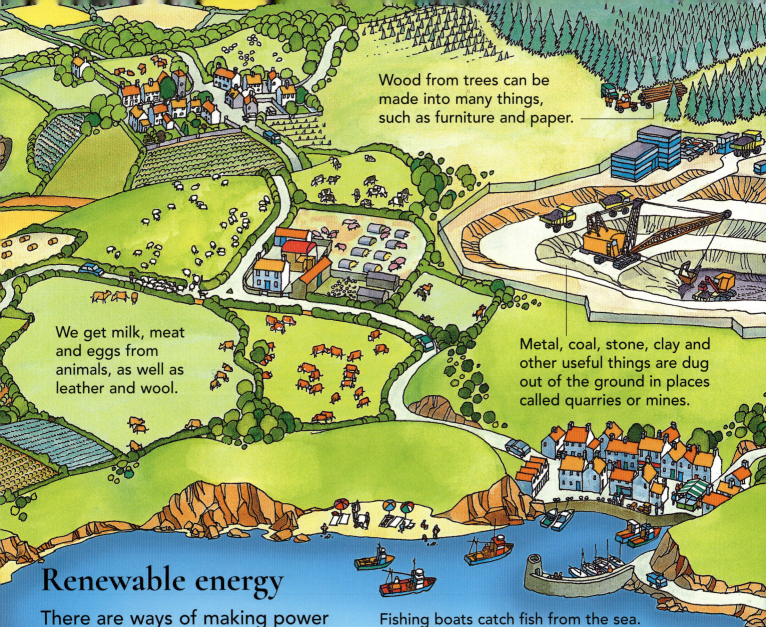

Wood from trees can be made into many things, such as furniture and paper.

We get milk, meat and eggs from animals, as well as leather and wool.

Metal, coal, stone, clay and other useful things are dug out of the ground in places called quarries or mines.

Renewable energy

There are ways of making power using the wind, water or sunshine, which won't run out. These types of power are called green energy because they are better for the environment.

Fishing boats catch fish from the sea.

- Scan the code to find out more about green energy.
- For more links, go to **usborne.com/Quicklinks**

These are wind turbines. The turning blades drive machines to make electricity.

Solar panels can absorb energy from the Sun and use it to make electricity.

Like the wind, flowing water can also drive turbines to make electricity.

World in danger

There are many things we do to our world that put animals, plants and people in danger.

Smoke and fumes from factories and cars pollute the air and heat up the Earth.

Rainforest damage

Every year, huge areas of rainforests are cut down for their wood, or burned. This is called deforestation, and it destroys the homes of the animals that live there.

These rainforest trees are being burned to make space for farming.

Pollution

Litter, sewage, fumes from factories and cars, and oil spilled from ships at sea are all kinds of pollution. Pollution harms animals and people, and the places where they live.

Oil spills from ships can spread for miles and harm many sea animals.

Chemicals from factories and farms can get into the water and soil.

- Scan the code to find out about endangered animals and how we can help protect them.
- For more links, go to **usborne.com/Quicklinks**

Animals in danger

Some animals are endangered, which means there are only a few of them left, and they could easily die out. This is because we have hunted them or destroyed their homes.

Rhinos are killed for their horns. This one has had its horns removed so hunters will leave it alone.

Golden lion tamarins became endangered due to deforestation.

Some types of leopards are endangered because people hunt them for their skins.

Fishing dangers

When people catch too many fish of the same kind, the number of those fish left in the ocean starts to go down. This is called overfishing. If this doesn't stop soon, some kinds of fish may die out completely. Fishing can also endanger ocean life in other ways.

Purse seine nets are like big bags. They are used to catch tuna fish, but dolphins often get caught in the nets by mistake.

Trawl nets drag along the seabed to catch fish. They also pull up plants, and so destroy the homes of many sea creatures.

Getting warmer

Human activity is causing the Earth's temperature to rise. As it gets warmer, the sea level rises. The ocean currents and climate also change, causing more heatwaves and floods.

Trapped heat

The Earth is surrounded by a blanket of gases called the atmosphere. Some of these, called "greenhouse" gases, trap heat around the Earth, making it warm enough for life to exist. But people do some things that make extra gases. These trap more heat, so the Earth and its oceans get warmer.

This picture shows some of the things we do that are increasing the level of (heat-trapping) gases in the Earth's atmosphere.

The atmosphere is shown here in blue.

Power stations give off greenhouse gases as they burn coal, gas and oil ("fossil" fuels) to make electricity.

Rotting waste gives off greenhouse gases, such as methane. Farmed animals produce a lot of methane too.

Gas is burned in some people's homes for cooking and heating.

The Sun's rays warm the Earth.

Some of the heat escapes back into space.

Greenhouse gases in the atmosphere stop some of the heat from escaping.

Greenhouse gases are made when forests are burned to clear land for farming and building.

Petrol and diesel cars burn fuel and produce exhaust fumes, which pollute the air and add more greenhouse gases to the atmosphere.

Rising seas

As the atmosphere warms up, ice in the Arctic and the Antarctic starts to melt into the sea. If all the world's land ice melted, the sea level everywhere would rise by more than 200ft (60m).

- Scan the code to explore why Earth and its oceans are getting warmer.
- For more links, go to **usborne.com/Quicklinks**

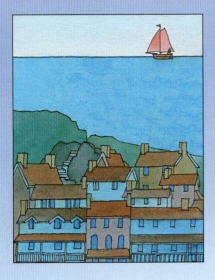

This picture shows what would happen to a town by the sea if the sea level rose by 200ft (60m).

Only a small rise in sea level would cause many islands in the sea to flood.

Stopping floods

A sea level rise of even 3ft (1m) would flood millions of people's homes. To stop this from happening, we need to stop burning fuels such as oil, coal and gas, and use renewable sources of energy instead. (See page 216.)

As land ice melts at the poles, huge chunks of it fall into the sea.

Helping our planet

Everyone can do things to help our planet. Governments can make laws, for example, that control pollution and the way that areas of open land are used. There are many ways in which you can help, too.

Look out for this recycling symbol on cans, boxes or bottles.

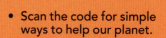

- Scan the code for simple ways to help our planet.
- For more links, go to **usborne.com/Quicklinks**

How can you help?

Remember to put cans, bottles, cartons and paper into the recycling. The metal, glass, plastic and paper can be made into new things.

Save electricity by unplugging devices and switching off lights when you go out of a room.

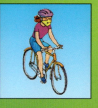

Walk or cycle short distances, and go on longer journeys by bus or train. This helps reduce pollution from cars.

If you have a garden, put up a bird table, and plant shrubs to give birds and other creatures food and shelter.

Governments around the world are protecting endangered animals, such as orangutans, by creating sancturies where they can live safe from hunters.

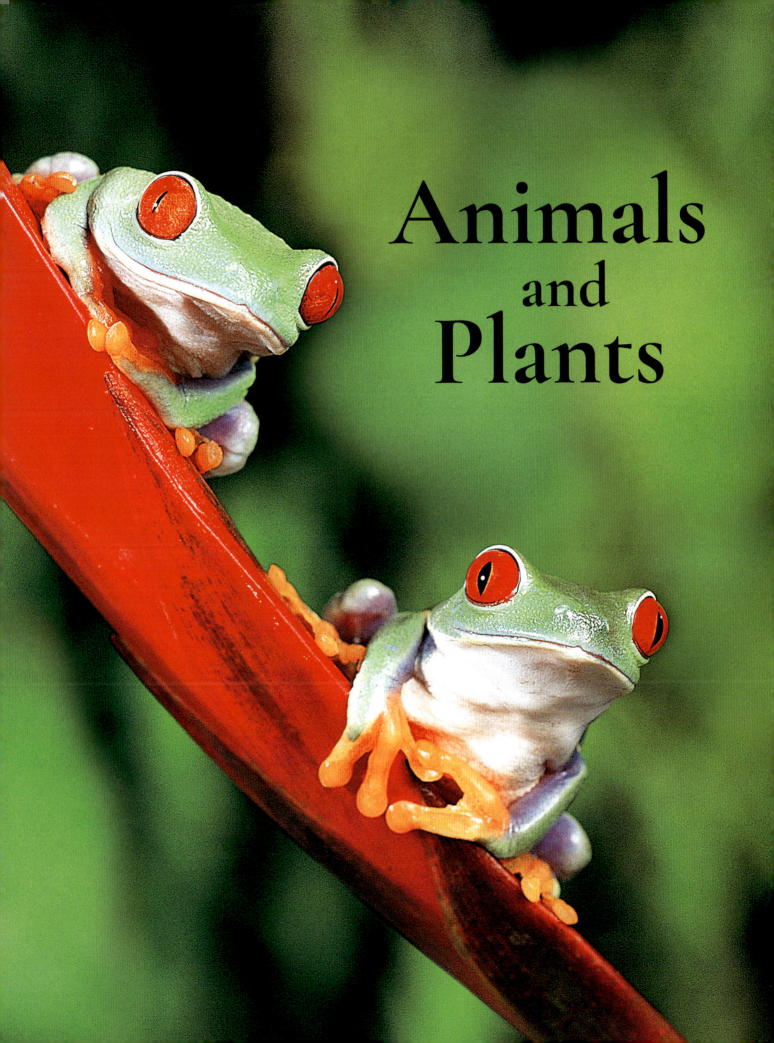

Animals
and
Plants

Living things

There are millions of living things on planet Earth, including plants, animals and people. All living things share certain features.

Living things need a gas called oxygen. A fish gets oxygen from the water it takes in through its mouth.

Air and food

As well as oxygen, most living things need food to stay alive. Plants make their own food using energy from the Sun. Animals get energy by eating plants or other animals.

A buttercup plant uses energy from sunlight to grow.

A snail gets its energy from eating the buttercup.

A thrush gets its energy from eating the snail.

- Scan the code to explore how all living things are alike.
- For more links, go to **usborne.com/Quicklinks**

New life and growth

Living things make new living things. Animals make babies, and plants produce new plants. As they get older, most living things grow and change.

Some animals give birth to live babies. Penguins, like other birds, lay eggs with the babies inside.

These baby penguins look like small versions of their parents.

Moving

All living things can move. Most animals can move from one place to another. Plants can only move parts of themselves, and they usually move too slowly for you to see.

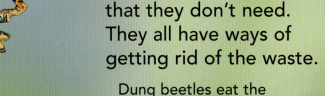

Some animals, such as this cheetah, can move at very high speeds.

Sensitivity

Living things are sensitive to changes in the world around them, such as changes of light or heat. Animals usually react to these changes more quickly than plants.

A sunflower slowly turns so the flower always faces the Sun.

Insect's wing

When an insect touches sensitive hairs on the leaves of a Venus flytrap, the leaves snap shut and trap the insect.

Waste

Plants and animals produce stuff inside them that they don't need. They all have ways of getting rid of the waste.

Dung beetles eat the dung (solid waste) of other animals.

Dung

Venus flytrap

Cells

All living things are made up of tiny units called cells. Most cells are much too small to see. Scientists have to look at them through microscopes.

- Scan the code to take a closer look at cells.
- For more links, go to **usborne.com/Quicklinks**

This picture shows human fat seen through a microscope. The pink blobs are cells.

What is a cell?

A cell is a tiny structure with its own protective skin. Inside, a cell has even smaller parts called organelles. In many living things, such as humans, millions of cells stick together to make body parts such as skin, muscle and bone.

Plant or animal?

Animal cells have a skin called a cell membrane. Inside, the parts of the cell float in a watery gel. Plant cells have a cell membrane and a tough cell wall that gives them a fixed shape.

Both plant and animal cells have a nucleus, which controls the cell.

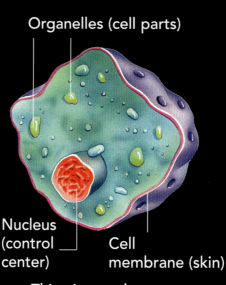

Organelles (cell parts)

Nucleus (control center)

Cell membrane (skin)

This picture shows an animal cell, cut in half so you can see inside it.

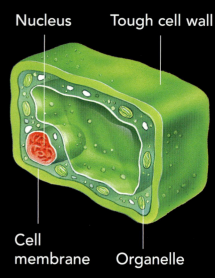

Nucleus

Tough cell wall

Cell membrane

Organelle

This picture shows a plant cell, cut in half so you can see inside it.

Single-celled life-forms

Some very small living things have only one cell. Most of them are not plants or animals, but belong to their own separate groups. Many kinds of algae are single-celled. Bacteria also have only one cell each.

Bacteria are all around us. Most are harmless, but some, like these salmonella bacteria, can make you sick.

Bacteria are extremely tiny. This photograph was taken using a very powerful microscope.

Looking at cells

Microscopes make things look bigger. When microscopes were invented, about 400 years ago, scientists could begin to look very closely at living things, and cells were discovered.

Today, powerful microscopes like this one help scientists look deep inside cells.

Animal world

There are millions of different animals, from tiny bugs to huge whales. Here are some of the different types of animals you can find out about in this book.

This arctic tern's shape helps it fly.

Mammals

Mammals feed their babies milk. Almost all have hair or fur. From polar bears to camels, mammals can be found all over the world.

Like all baby mammals, this lion cub is cared for by its mother.

Birds

Birds are the only animals that have feathers. They all have wings, but not all of them can fly. Some are powerful runners or swimmers. All birds lay eggs and take care of their babies.

Reptiles

Reptiles have dry, scaly skin and almost all lay eggs. You can find reptiles in most countries, especially in the warmer parts of the world.

This reptile is a type of African lizard called an agama. It has tough, dry skin and spikes along its back.

Amphibians

Amphibians are animals with soft, damp skin. They can breathe on land or in water. An amphibian needs to keep its body moist to stay alive, even if it lives on land.

Frogs are amphibians. They are excellent swimmers and can stay underwater for a long time.

Creepy-crawlies

The world is teeming with creepy-crawlies such as insects, spiders, centipedes and snails. The most common creepy-crawlies are insects. They all have six legs, and most have wings. There are over a million different types of insects.

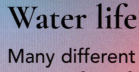

Like most insects, this wasp can fly.

Water life

Many different animals live in water – from fish to mammals such as dolphins and seals, and creatures such as jellyfish and lobsters. Some animals are even able to live in the deepest oceans.

Sea anemones and fish are both animals that live in water.

- Scan the code for facts, videos and activities about the animal world.
- For more links, go to **usborne.com/Quicklinks**

Mammals

The animals on these two pages look different, but they are all mammals. There are more than 6,000 different kinds of mammals, including you – humans are mammals, too.

Chimpanzees live in the forests of Africa.

Keeping warm

A mammal's body makes its own warmth, and it can keep its temperature the same whether the day is hot or cold. This is called being warm-blooded.

The fur on this chimp helps keep its body warm when the weather is cold.

- Scan the code to meet lots of different kinds of mammals.
- For more links, go to **usborne.com/Quicklinks**

Food for baby

All mammal mothers feed their babies milk. They make the milk in glands, called mammary glands, on their chests or bellies. Milk is a rich food that is easy for a baby to swallow.

This baby deer is sucking milk from its mother.

Flying mammal

Bats are the only mammals that can fly. Their wings are made of flaps of skin, which stretch over the bones of their arms and fingers.

Here you can see how a bat uses its arm as a wing. Long fingers support the wing skin.

Fruit bat

Swimmers

Some mammals, such as whales, live in the sea. Like all mammals, they breathe air, so they come to the surface regularly.

Humpback whale

Whales are the biggest animals in the world.

Duck-billed platypus

Egg-layers

The duck-billed platypus lays eggs rather than giving birth. It lays its eggs in a nest in a riverbank burrow. Echidnas are the only other mammals that lay eggs.

Baby mammals

Most newborn baby mammals are helpless and need a lot of care. Animals that can hide their young in a safe place, such as a nest, often have several babies. Animals that cannot do this usually have only one or two so they can guard them carefully.

Giraffe baby

Giraffes usually have only one baby at a time. A baby giraffe is an easy target for a lion. If an enemy comes near, the mother can kick it with her powerful legs.

Many babies

Mice often have eight babies at a time. The babies are born in a nest which keeps them warm. Many young are still caught by hunters such as owls and cats.

Baby mice stay with their mother for less than a month.

This giraffe mother licks her baby to clean it, so its scent does not attract predators.

Learning to hunt

Polar bear cubs spend two to three years with their mother, learning how to survive. The mother teaches them how to hunt. They leave her when they are old enough to hunt alone.

Baby polar bears stay close to their mothers.

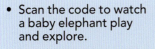

- Scan the code to watch a baby elephant play and explore.
- For more links, go to **usborne.com/Quicklinks**

Pouch home

Marsupial mammals, like this kangaroo, carry their babies around in a pouch. The baby feeds on milk from a nipple in the pouch. A baby kangaroo can travel this way until it is a year old.

The baby kangaroo also goes into the pouch if it is tired or frightened.

Long childhood

Elephants take care of their babies for longer than any other animals except humans. A young elephant stays with its mother for up to ten years.

This baby elephant is learning to use its trunk to drink and bathe.

Bird life

Birds are the only animals that have feathers. Not all birds fly, but those that can't are usually superb swimmers or runners.

Fit for flying

Many birds are excellent fliers. Most of their bones are hollow, so they are light. Strong chest muscles power birds' wings. The sleek shape of their bodies helps them move quickly through the air.

- Scan the code to find out more about why birds migrate and fly long distances.
- For more links, go to **usborne.com/Quicklinks**

A goose coming in to land lowers its feet and uses its wings to slow down.

Body shapes

Birds have different body shapes. A goose's sturdy, muscular body is ideal for making long flights to warmer countries in the winter. A kingfisher's arrow-like body lets it dart in and out of the water as it hunts.

A kingfisher uses its long, sharp beak to spear fish.

Types of feathers

Birds have three different kinds of feathers. Fluffy feathers, called down, keep them warm. Short, sturdy body feathers keep them dry. Long flight feathers help them take off, fly and land.

You can see this eagle's flight feathers on its wings.

Long flights

Birds are the greatest travelers in the animal world. Half of all types fly long distances to places where there is lots of food or where they can have babies. This is called migration.

In winter, these geese fly from Canada to Mexico in search of food.

This baby bird has a down coat to keep it warm in its cliff-top nest.

Feather growth

Baby birds are covered in down feathers. They grow body and flight feathers when they are older. All feathers get dirty and untidy. Birds clean and smooth them down with their beaks to keep them working properly.

This heron is cleaning its feathers. This is called preening.

Bodies and beaks

Different birds have different body and beak shapes to help them find and eat their food. You can see here that there are huge differences in body and beak shapes.

Sea life

Puffins live by the sea and hunt fish. Their stubby, muscular bodies and short wings help them swim well under water. They can fly, but they are much clumsier in the air than in the sea.

Wings and claws

This bald eagle's huge wings let it glide effortlessly over water as it searches for fish. Its sharp claws hold fish tightly as it returns to its nest to feed.

This is a puffin. Its webbed feet help it paddle in the sea.

This bald eagle has sharp claws for grasping fish.

Beak shapes

Birds use their beaks as tools to help them find food. This toucan's long beak lets it reach for fruit among dense forest branches.

The toucan's jagged beak helps it grip fruit firmly.

Diggers

Like many river and seabirds, the scarlet ibis has a long, thin beak. It uses it to poke around for small shrimps and worms at the muddy edges of rivers.

Spears and nets

Many birds eat other animals. Some are fierce hunters that can kill animals as big as a monkey. Here are three flesh-eating birds that use their beaks in different ways.

Scarlet ibis

A heron uses its dagger-like beak to spear fish.

A vulture's hooked beak lets it tear meat from a dead animal.

A pelican uses its sack-shaped beak like a fishing net.

- Scan the code to see how birds use their beaks in different ways.
- For more links, go to **usborne.com/Quicklinks**

Nests and chicks

Most birds build nests to protect the mother and her eggs from enemies. Nests also make a safe place for the babies when they hatch.

A warm spot

Birds sit on their eggs to keep them warm. If the eggs get too cold, the babies inside will die.

This penduline tit's nest is made of twigs, reeds, and hair.

- Scan the code to discover different kinds of nests.
- For more links, go to **usborne.com/Quicklinks**

Types of nests

Each type of bird has its own way of building a nest. Many are cup-shaped, and made of mud, hair, feathers and twigs.

A swallow's nest is made of mud, and stuck to a wall.

A tailor bird sews big leaves together with plant parts.

A long-tailed tit makes a nest of moss, lichen and cobwebs.

Breaking out

Birds sit on their eggs for two weeks or more. (Bigger birds sit for longer.) When the baby is ready to hatch, it chips its way out of the egg. Most bird babies need a lot of looking after.

A hoopoe adult brings food to its chick.

This baby moorhen is chipping its way out of its egg.

Dinner time

Baby birds are always hungry and need a constant supply of food. This adult hoopoe must make hundreds of journeys to and from its nest every day. It brings insects and grubs for its chicks.

Protecting the family

Swans build large waterside nests from plant stalks. Their babies (called cygnets) stay with them for around four months. The parents protect their young and take them to feeding places. When the cygnets leave, they live alone until they find a mate.

This mother swan and her cygnets are gathered around their nest.

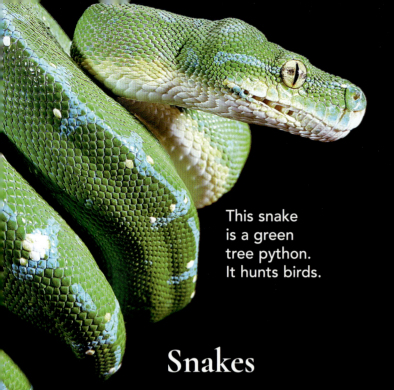

This snake is a green tree python. It hunts birds.

Reptile life

Reptiles have scaly skin and lay eggs. They are cold-blooded, which means their bodies do not make heat, so they are as warm or as cold as the air around them. Lizards, snakes, turtles and crocodiles are all reptiles.

Snakes

All snakes are meat-eaters. Some eat insects and worms. Some can eat animals as big as a crocodile. You can find snakes in almost every country in the world.

- Scan the code to watch a video about snakes and other reptiles.
- For more links, go to **usborne.com/Quicklinks**

Lizards

Most lizards are small, nimble creatures, although a few can grow to be as much as 10ft (3m) long. Like snakes, they can be found almost everywhere on Earth.

Crocodiles

Crocodiles, and their close relatives, alligators, are fierce hunters. They can be found on riverbanks in hot countries. In the right conditions, crocodiles can live for over 100 years.

Nile crocodile

This leaf-tailed gecko lives in the forests of Madagascar.

Its flat, leaf-shaped tail helps it camouflage itself among the plants and trees.

Hawksbill turtle

Turtles

Turtles live in warm, shallow seas, and only ever come onto land to lay eggs. Some swim very long distances to find a place to have babies.

Tortoises

Tortoises are similar to turtles, but they live on land instead of water. They are well protected by their hard outer shells.

Galapagos giant tortoise

Hot and cold

As reptiles are cold-blooded, heat and cold affect them more than warm-blooded animals. If they are too cold, they become sluggish. If they are too hot, they dry up and die. A reptile spends a lot of the day trying to stay at the right temperature.

This iguana's leathery skin helps prevent it from drying up.

After a cool night, the iguana sits in the Sun to warm up.

At noon, it hides in the shade for the hottest part of the day.

In the afternoon, it moves in and out of the Sun, to keep warm or cool.

Amphibians

Amphibians, such as frogs, toads and newts, look a little like reptiles but with soft, moist skin. They lay squishy eggs in water, where their young hatch and grow. Adults can live on land and in water.

Slimy skin

Many amphibians have shiny, slimy skin. They need to keep their skin moist, even when they are on land. If their skin becomes too dry, they may die.

Getting air

Amphibians are clever breathers. They can take in air through their skin on land and underwater. Some have gills, like fish (see page 79). On land, many amphibians breathe through their mouths.

This tree frog lives in rainforest trees. Moisture in the air helps keep its skin damp.

The frilly growths on this axolotl's head are gills. It uses them to breathe underwater.

Swimming

An amphibian's body has special features that let it walk or swim. Many frogs, for instance, have webbed toes. They use these like flippers to push themselves through the water.

Webbed toes

Frogs and toads

Frogs have long, strong back legs. They use them to leap around on land and swim in water. Toads have shorter back legs than frogs. They waddle rather than hop.

- Scan the code to see how a baby tadpole grows into an adult frog.
- For more links, go to **usborne.com/Quicklinks**

Many kinds of frogs have bright skin. Toads have drier, warty skin.

Toad

Frog

Salamanders

A salamander has a long tail like a lizard. Most salamanders, like this one, have foul-tasting skin which is brightly patterned. This warns predators not to try eating them because they will taste horrible.

This fire salamander has bright orange patches on its skin.

Babies

Many frogs and toads lay lots of eggs at once. When they hatch, the babies live in water. They don't look like their parents at all. When they grow up, they can move onto land.

These squishy blobs are frogs' eggs, called spawn. The babies, called tadpoles, hatch out of them.

After a few weeks, the tadpoles start to grow legs. The back legs grow first, then the front legs.

Eventually, the tail shrinks away, and the tadpole grows lungs. It can now breathe on land.

It takes about 16 weeks for a tadpole to become a frog. It still has a lot of growing to do.

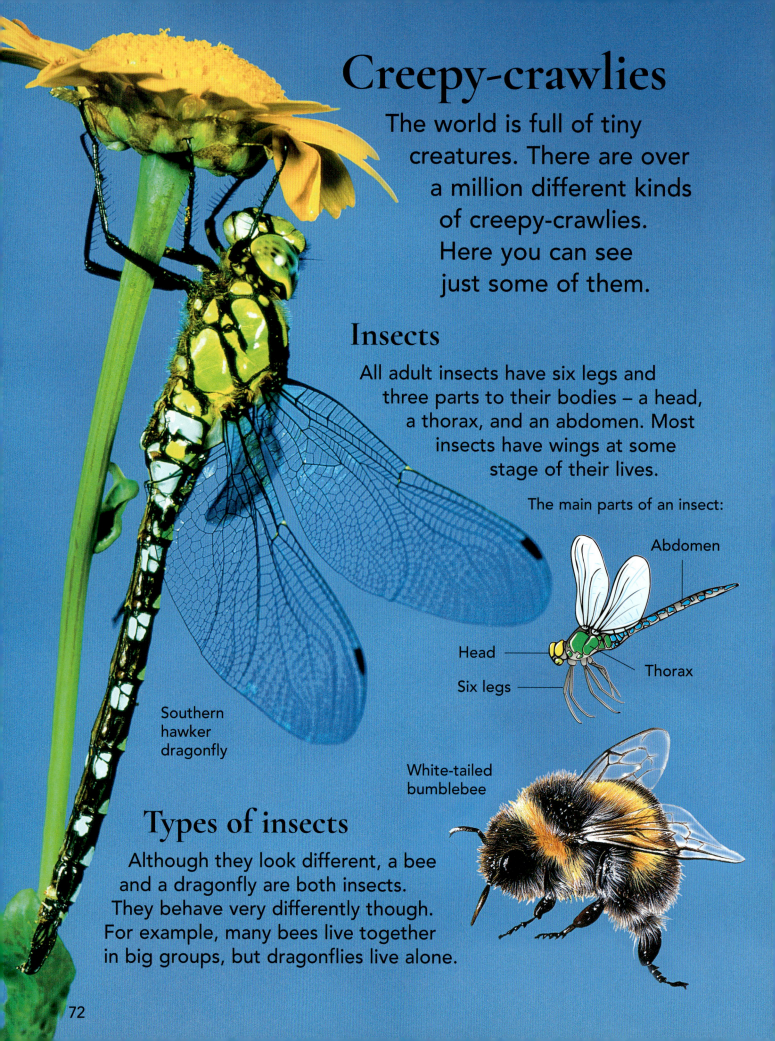

Creepy-crawlies

The world is full of tiny
creatures. There are over
a million different kinds
of creepy-crawlies.
Here you can see
just some of them.

Insects

All adult insects have six legs and
three parts to their bodies – a head,
a thorax, and an abdomen. Most
insects have wings at some
stage of their lives.

The main parts of an insect:

Abdomen

Head

Six legs

Thorax

Southern
hawker
dragonfly

White-tailed
bumblebee

Types of insects

Although they look different, a bee
and a dragonfly are both insects.
They behave very differently though.
For example, many bees live together
in big groups, but dragonflies live alone.

Spiders

Spiders are not insects. They are a type of animal known as an arachnid. Spiders have eight legs and two parts to their body. They never have wings. Many spiders spin webs to catch their food.

This golden orb weaver is one of Australia's biggest spiders.

Lots of legs

Millipedes and centipedes have the most legs of any animal. Centipedes have at least 100 pairs of legs, while some millipedes have more than 1,300. Their bodies are divided into a series of segments. Like many creepy-crawlies, they have feelers called antennae on their heads.

A pair of rainforest millipedes

- Scan the code to explore the world of creepy-crawlies.
- For more links, go to **usborne.com/Quicklinks**

The eyes are on long tentacles that can move around.

Slimy snails

Snails have a hard shell they can curl up in. This protects their bodies from enemies. Land snails lurk in damp places, such as under leaves and stones. Some snails can live underwater.

This is a kind of land snail called a grove snail. Like all snails, it slides along on its slimy belly.

Butterflies

Butterflies are among the most colorful types of insects. Most live for only a few weeks. They find a mate, lay eggs, then die.

Butterfly wings

Butterfly wings are covered in tiny colored and shiny scales. The shiny scales reflect light, which is why butterflies shimmer when they fly.

Butterflies visit plants to drink a liquid, called nectar, from flowers.

This butterfly is called a common blue. It has spread its wings to soak up the Sun's heat.

Open and shut

When a butterfly holds its wings open, it is gathering warmth from the Sun. This helps give it the energy to fly. When its wings are closed, it is resting. It faces the Sun, so its shadow is small, and enemies are less likely to spot it.

Butterfly with wings open

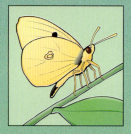

Butterfly with wings closed

- Scan the code to see how a caterpillar turns into a butterfly.
- For more links, go to **usborne.com/Quicklinks**

Wing patterns

A butterfly's beautiful, patterned wings help other butterflies spot their own kind. Their wing patterns help butterflies in other ways, too.

The circles on a peacock butterfly's wings look like eyes. This frightens enemies.

A comma's ragged wings disguise it as a dead leaf when it is on the ground.

The African monarch is poisonous. Birds learn not to eat it.

An arctic ringlet's dark wings help it soak up heat.

This mocker swallowtail is not poisonous, but birds think it is an African monarch and do not eat it.

The patterns on a tortoiseshell's wings help it attract a mate.

Making butterflies

A female butterfly lays her eggs on a plant. When an egg hatches, a caterpillar comes out and feeds on the plant. When the caterpillar is fully grown, it turns into a pupa, and then into a butterfly.

This caterpillar is ready to turn into a pupa.

The pupa forms inside the body, splitting the skin.

As the pupa hardens, changes happen inside it.

After two weeks, a butterfly comes out of the pupa.

The butterfly's body hardens and it flies off.

Seashore life

Every day when the tide goes out, it leaves pools of water trapped among the rocks on the seashore. Plants and animals make their homes in these pools.

Five-bearded rocklings use feelers around their mouths to find their way.

Butterfish have flat, slippery bodies. This helps them squeeze into gaps in the rocks, to hide from predators.

Shrimp keep the water clean, eating anything they can find.

Blennies have large front fins which they use to change direction quickly in small pools.

Seaweed grows all along the seashore.

Outside skeletons

A crab doesn't have a shell, but it has its skeleton on the outside. The skeleton is called a carapace. When the crab grows too big for its carapace, it wriggles out of it. Then its skin slowly hardens to make a new, bigger carapace.

Crab

Mussel

Upside down

Barnacles cover the rocks along the seashore. They feed by sticking their legs out of the tops of their shells.

Tiny barnacles cling to the rocks in big groups. Their tough shells protect them from danger.

Barnacles open the tops of their shells to feed. Their legs stick out to pick up bits of food in the water.

- Scan the code to explore rock pools for seashore life.
- For more links, go to **usborne.com/Quicklinks**

Air bubbles keep this seaweed floating near the surface of the water, where it is light.

Sea scorpions are fierce predators. Their huge mouths can open wide enough to swallow large prey whole.

Common starfish have five arms. If they lose an arm, another one grows in its place.

Hermit crab

Sea urchins have sharp spines on their shells to protect them.

Sea lemons scrape food off the rocks with their tongues.

Strawberry anemone

Limpets

Barnacles

Dog whelk

Underwater life

The oceans are full of living things. Some sea creatures are gentle and friendly, but others are fierce hunters.

- Scan the code to see a great white and lots of other sharks.
- For more links, go to **usborne.com/Quicklinks**

So many teeth

Most sharks have at least three rows of teeth. As they lose the ones in front, teeth from the rows behind move forward to replace them.

Most types of sharks, like this great white, are deadly hunters. They have sharp teeth for catching and eating other animals.

Rays

Most rays have their mouths on the lower side of their flat bodies. They swim along the seabed, eating things they swim over, and can crunch up shells with their teeth to get to the animals inside.

This picture shows the lower side of a ray. The position of its mouth helps it feed on the seabed.

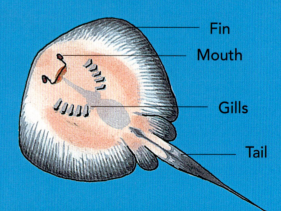

Fin

Mouth

Gills

Tail

Many rays are harmless, but stingrays can give a poisonous sting from their tails. Stingrays move along the seabed by rippling their fins.

What are fish?

Fish are a group of animals that live in water. There are thousands of different kinds. They come in different shapes and sizes, but they all have gills and fins. Gills allow them to breathe underwater, and fins help them move around.

Most fish have flat tails, which they move from side to side to swim. Their strong tail muscles make swimming easy.

Caudal fin

Fish use these top fins, called dorsal fins, to help keep their balance.

This flap, called the operculum, covers the fish's gills.

Pelvic fins help fish change direction quickly.

Fish use these fins, called pectoral fins, for turning.

This line, called the lateral line, helps fish sense movement in the water.

Slippery, slimy skin helps fish move easily through water.

Breathing

Fish breathe by taking oxygen out of the water. Here's how they do it.

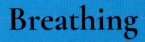
Gills under here

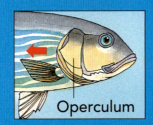
Operculum

As a fish moves forward, it takes in water through its mouth. The water passes over its gills.

The fish's gills take oxygen from the water. The water then passes out under the fish's operculum.

Fish scales

Most fish are protected by a covering of tiny plates, called scales. These scales are waterproof, and help protect the fish from pests and hunters.

Fish scales overlap each other, to make a protective cover.

The rings on a fish's scales show how old the fish is. Some fish can live for over 100 years.

Coral reefs

Corals live in warm, shallow seas. Although they look like plants, corals are really made of thousands of small animals. Large areas of coral are called coral reefs.

The coral polyps are white with a red stripe on this red horn coral. Can you spot a tiny goby fish hiding here?

- Scan the code to explore a coral reef and see what lives there.
- For more links, go to **usborne.com/Quicklinks**

Coral animals

Coral animals, called polyps, are protected by hard skeletons. When they die, the skeletons remain and new polyps grow on top of them. Over time, a coral reef slowly forms.

This is what a coral polyp looks like inside.

Poisonous tentacles for catching food

Mouth

Stomach

Stony base

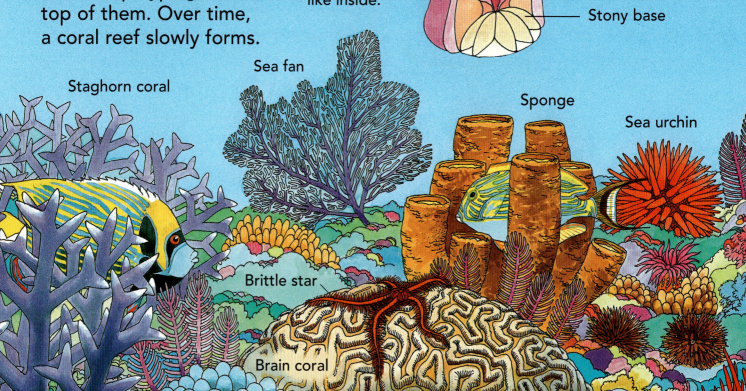

Staghorn coral

Sea fan

Sponge

Sea urchin

Brittle star

Brain coral

A coral meal

The coral polyps are well protected by their skeletons, but some fish, such as parrotfish, are able to eat them.

A parrotfish's teeth are all joined together to form a hard beak.

The parrotfish breaks off a chunk of coral, then uses its beak to crunch it up.

Reef life

Coral reefs are full of nooks and crannies where animals can hide or make their homes. This means there are always lots of fish and other animals living around them.

There are four fish and an eel hiding in this coral reef. Can you spot them all?

Giant clam

Feather star

Sea anemone

Marine mammals

Whales and dolphins look like fish, but they are actually mammals*. Unlike most mammals, they don't have hair on their bodies, but they do need air to breathe – they can't breathe underwater.

From the top

Whales come to the ocean's surface to breathe. They breathe through holes called blowholes on the top of their heads. When they breathe out, they shoot sprays of water, which is called spouting.

Sperm whales are among the deepest diving whales and can hold their breath for over an hour. They dive deep to catch giant squid to eat.

- Scan the code to see whales and find out more about them.
- For more links, go to **usborne.com/Quicklinks**

Each type of whale has a different spout shape. Here are some of them.

Humpback whale

Sperm whale

Right whale

*For more about mammals, see page 58.

A dolphin mother will care for and teach her baby, or calf, for up to six years.

Learning to breathe

When a baby dolphin is born, its mother must quickly push it to the surface of the sea and teach it to breathe. Sometimes, another dolphin helps her do this.

Using echoes

Dolphins find their way in the sea by making sounds which send back echoes. They can then tell what's around them by listening to the echoes. This is called sonar. Dolphins also use sonar to catch fish.

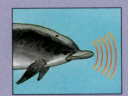

A dolphin makes a clicking sound which travels through the water.

When the sound hits some fish, it bounces back as an echo.

The dolphin can tell where the fish are by listening to the returning echo.

Deep sea

The deep sea is a very dark, cold place where some of the strangest creatures in the world live. There are no plants in the deep sea, so all the fish are hunters.

Hatchetfish have eyes on top of their heads so they can see fish which swim above them.

- Scan the code to dive into the world of deep-sea creatures.
- For more links, go to **usborne.com/Quicklinks**

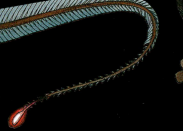

Gulper eels have enormous mouths. They can eat animals which are much larger than themselves.

Lanternfish have lights on their bodies to confuse enemies.

Vampire squid

Vampire squid live as deep as 3,000ft (900m). Their big eyes help them see in the murky depths.

Vampire squid have a clever way of escaping from enemies. They can turn themselves inside out. The undersides of their tentacles are covered in sharp spikes, to stop other animals from eating them.

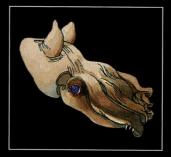

Vampire squid escape from enemies by putting their tentacles over their heads.

Their tentacles cover their bodies, making a spiky shield which protects them.

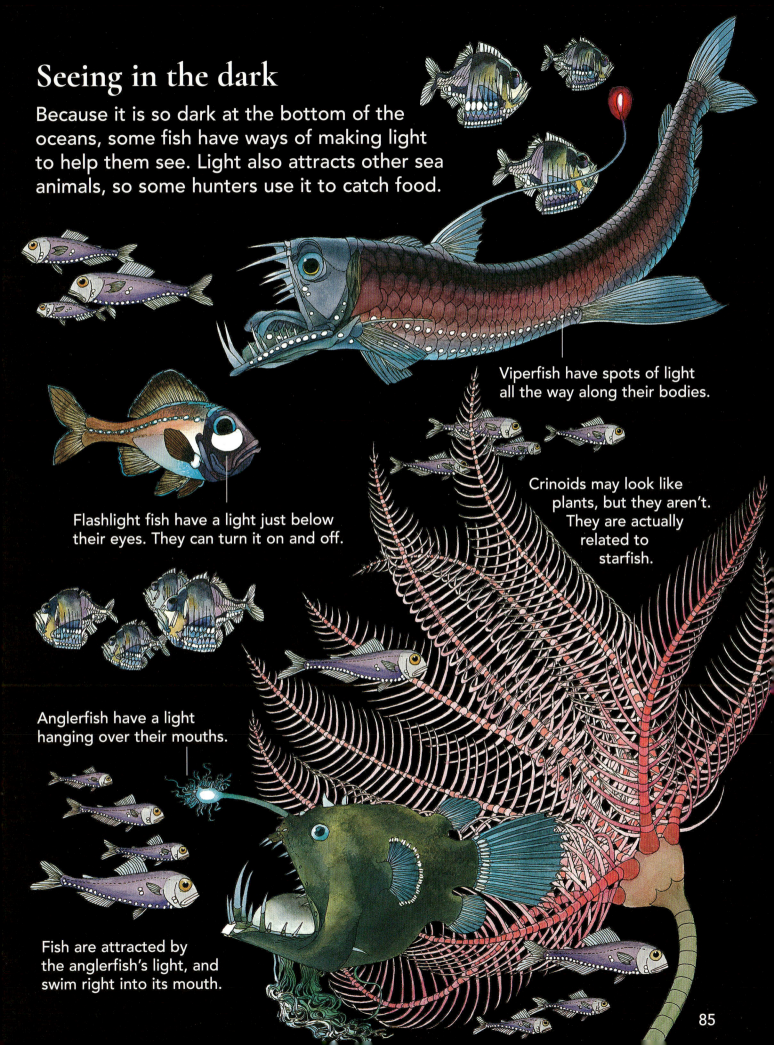

Seeing in the dark

Because it is so dark at the bottom of the oceans, some fish have ways of making light to help them see. Light also attracts other sea animals, so some hunters use it to catch food.

Viperfish have spots of light all the way along their bodies.

Flashlight fish have a light just below their eyes. They can turn it on and off.

Crinoids may look like plants, but they aren't. They are actually related to starfish.

Anglerfish have a light hanging over their mouths.

Fish are attracted by the anglerfish's light, and swim right into its mouth.

Plant world

Plants are different from animals in several ways. They can't move from place to place, and most can only react slowly to changes around them. Unlike animals, plants make their own food.

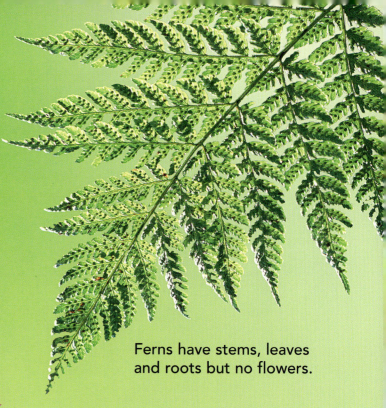

Ferns have stems, leaves and roots but no flowers.

Plant groups

There are around 400,000 different kinds of plants. They can be looked at in groups based on similar features.

Algae are simple plants with no stems, roots or leaves.

Conifers have needle-shaped leaves, and their seeds are made in cones.

Flowering plants have roots, leaves and a stem. Their seeds develop from a flower.

Mosses have thin leaves but no proper roots. They grow in damp places.

Flowering plants

The largest group of plants is flowering plants. This includes trees as well as flowers. Their main parts are the leaves, stem and roots.

Leaves have a green chemical inside which helps make food.

The stem supports the plant. Water and food travel inside it.

Roots hold a plant upright and take in water and minerals.

Making food

Plants use the Sun's energy, water and minerals from the soil, and carbon dioxide gas from the air, to make sugar in their leaves. Sugar is food for plants. This process, called photosynthesis (say "foe-toe-sin-thuh-sis"), also produces oxygen.

Carbon dioxide gas from the air

Energy from the Sun

Photosynthesis produces oxygen.

Water and minerals from the soil

Inside a flower

Flowers contain parts that can make seeds, which will grow into new plants. To make the seeds, a yellow powder called pollen has to be carried from one flower to another. The wind and small birds and insects do this job.

- Scan the code to see how bees help plants and us by collecting pollen from flowers.
- For more links, go to **usborne.com/Quicklinks**

Many flowers have bright colors and a strong smell. These attract insects to the sweet liquid, called nectar, inside.

Pollen sticks to a bee's body as it drinks nectar. This will rub off on the next flower it visits.

How plants grow

Many plants start off as seeds. Each seed has tiny parts inside that will grow into a new plant, as well as a store of food for the baby plant.

Fruits and seeds

Seeds are held in a part of the plant called a fruit. There are lots of different types. They protect seeds and help them spread to a place where they can grow. The picture shows some of the ways that fruits help seeds spread.

Sycamore fruits are wing-shaped and spin away from the tree in the wind.

Birds eat berries which have lots of tiny seeds in them.

Poppy seeds fall out of holes in pepper shaker-like fruit as the wind blows the plant.

Groundsel fruits are very light and float away in the breeze.

Many seeds eaten by an animal come out in their poop, then they grow into new plants.

Squirrels bury nuts to eat later, but often can't find them again. These grow into new plants.

Burs stick to the fur of animals that carry them away.

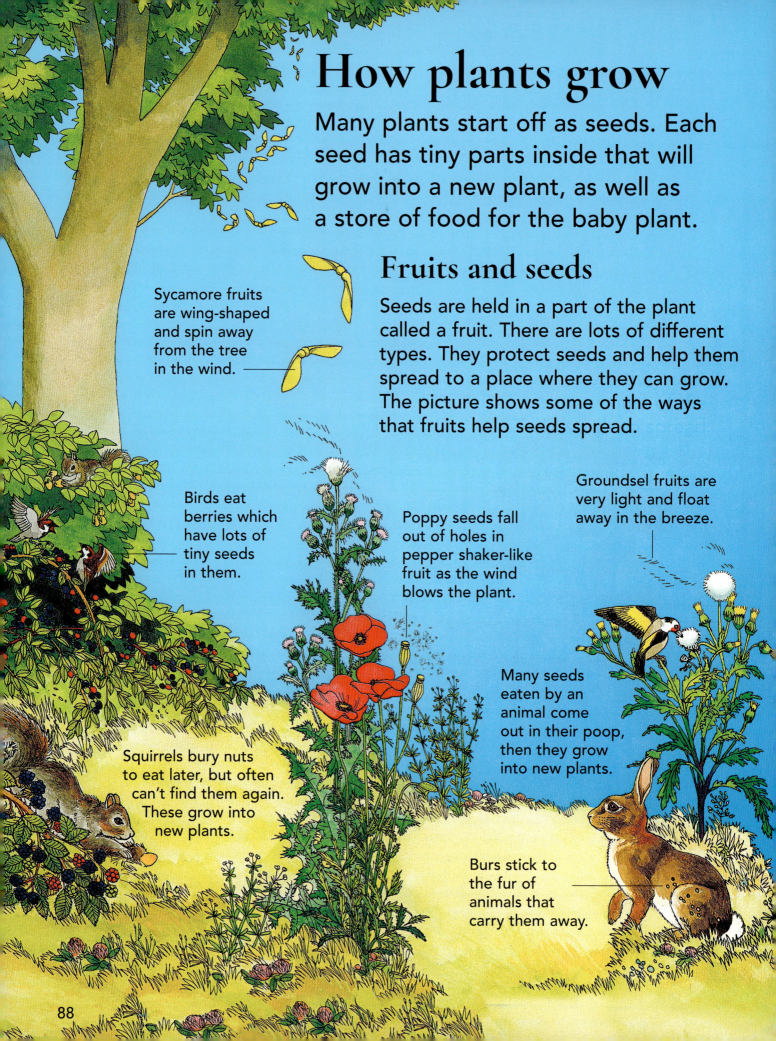

Starting to grow

To start growing, a seed needs water, warmth and oxygen. When it is warm enough, roots and a tiny shoot will push their way out. A plant at this stage is called a seedling.

Seed

A shoot pushes up.

A root pushes down.

From seedling to plant

A seedling lives off the food stored in its seed until it grows leaves to make its own food. The plant grows and has flowers and seeds of its own. The seeds grow into new plants, and so on.

These dandelion seeds are being carried away by the wind.

Life and death

The changes that happen to a living thing during its life are called its life cycle. Different types of plants have life cycles of different lengths.

Foxgloves live for many years, making seeds for new plants.

Snapdragons grow, flower, make seeds and die within one year.

- Scan the code to watch a pumpkin seed grow.
- For more links, go to **usborne.com/Quicklinks**

Trees and leaves

A tree is a plant with a thick, woody stem called a trunk. Most trees can grow for hundreds of years. Some trees are small, but many are taller than a house.

Tree bark

As a tree grows, its outer layers get harder. When they die, they form a tough layer called bark. There are many different types.

An English oak has cracked, ridged bark.

A beech tree has smooth, thin bark.

Getting bigger

Look at the rings in a tree stump. You can count these to find out how old the tree is.

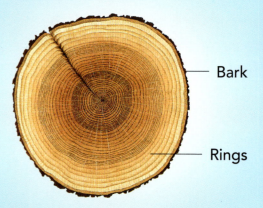

Bark

Rings

A tree grows from its middle out. One ring of new wood builds up each year, making the trunk thicker.

Tree roots

A tree uses its roots to take in water from the soil. They also act as an anchor. Tall trees, such as the cypress trees below, could not stay standing without their strong roots.

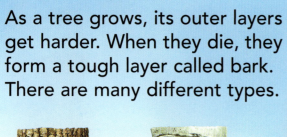

Cypress tree

Looking at leaves

Leaves contain a green chemical which absorbs sunlight to help make food (see page 87). When leaves die, the green chemical fades away and they change color.

Buckeye leaves have seven separate parts, called leaflets.

Holly has tough, spiky leaves.

Atlas cedars have bunches of thin, sharp leaves.

Oak trees have soft leaves with a wavy edge.

Losing leaves

Many types of trees start to lose all their leaves every fall. They are called deciduous trees. Trees that don't lose their leaves in this way are called evergreens.

Green leaves turn beautiful shades of red and gold before they fall from the tree.

Cypress trees are evergreen. They look similar all year round.

- Scan the code for a fun guide to trees.
- For more links, go to **usborne.com/Quicklinks**

Fungi

Fungi are not plants because they can't make their own food. Instead, they feed on living or once-living things.

- Scan the code to explore different types of fungi.
- For more links, go to **usborne.com/Quicklinks**

These clustered bonnet mushrooms are growing on a dead oak tree.

Spores

Fungi don't make seeds or pollen. Instead, they shed clouds of tiny specks called spores. These are scattered all around by the wind, and grow into new fungi.

Fungus spores seen using a microscope

Types of fungi

Fungi come in thousands of different shapes and sizes, and have lots of different uses. A fungus called yeast is used to make bread and wine. Some medicines are made from fungi, too.

Mushrooms and toadstools are fungi. Some types are safe to eat, and some are poisonous.

The green furry blobs you can sometimes see on fruit or cheese are a type of fungus known as mold. You can see some on this orange.

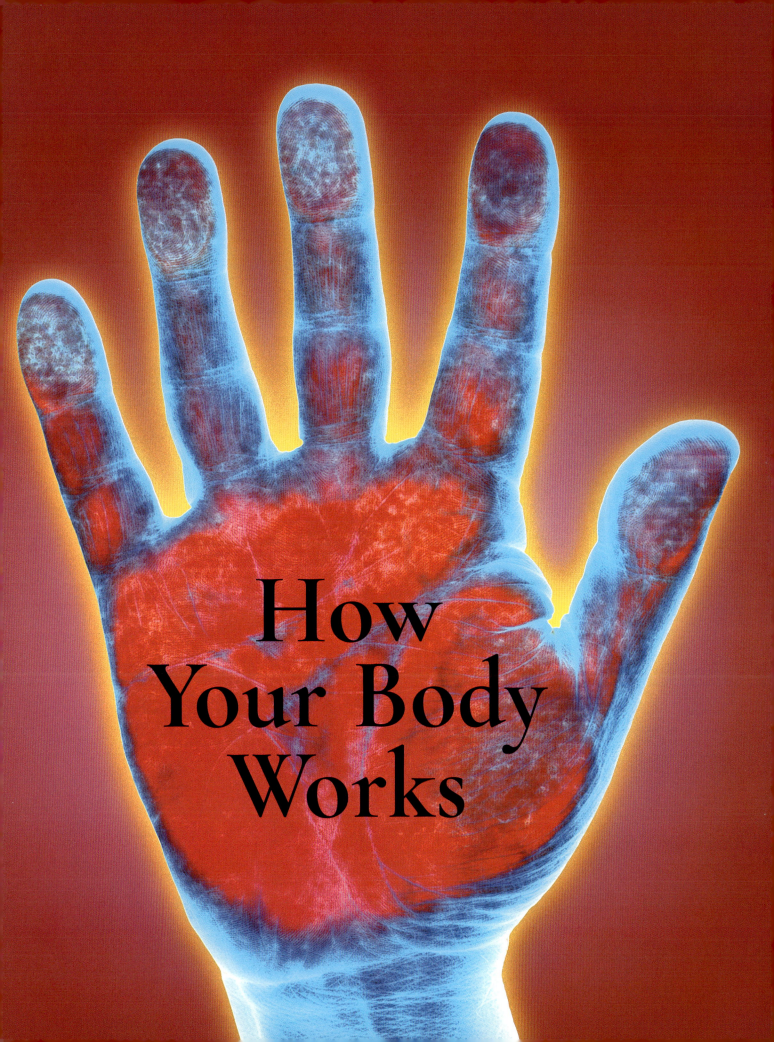

How Your Body Works

Your body

Have you ever wondered what's inside you? Your body is made up of lots of separate parts. They all do different jobs to help you stay alive.

Organs

Organs are important body parts such as the heart, lungs, stomach and brain. Most of them are in the upper body and head. You can see some of the main organs in this picture.

Each organ has a special job to do. For example, your stomach holds the food you eat, and your lungs take air into your body.

How much air can your lungs hold?

You will need: a plastic bottle with a lid; a bendy straw; a bowl of water

 1. Fill the bottle with water and put the lid on. Hold it upside down in the bowl and take off the lid.

 2. Push the straw into the neck of the bottle. Breathe in deeply, then blow gently into the straw until your lungs are empty.

All the air you breathe out will be trapped at the top of the bottle. This is how much air your lungs can hold.

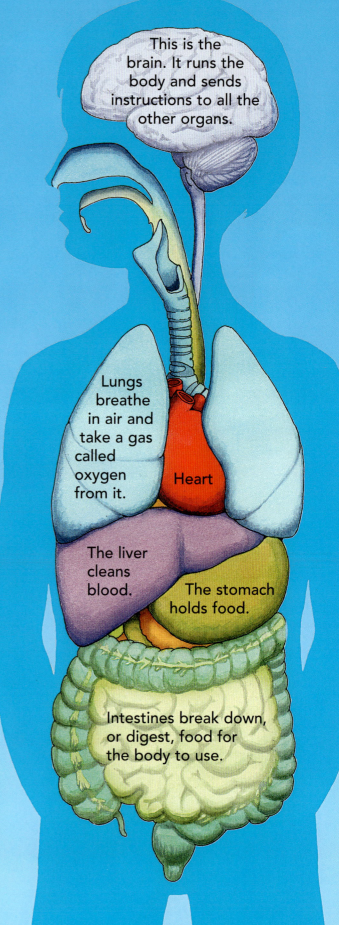

This is the brain. It runs the body and sends instructions to all the other organs.

Lungs breathe in air and take a gas called oxygen from it.

Heart

The liver cleans blood.

The stomach holds food.

Intestines break down, or digest, food for the body to use.

Blood

As well as organs, a human body contains up to 21 cups (five liters) of blood. The heart pumps blood around the body along thousands of tubes called blood vessels. As it flows along, blood delivers oxygen and food to every part of the body.

Blood is made of cells (see page 54) floating in a liquid called plasma. This picture shows different types of blood cells.

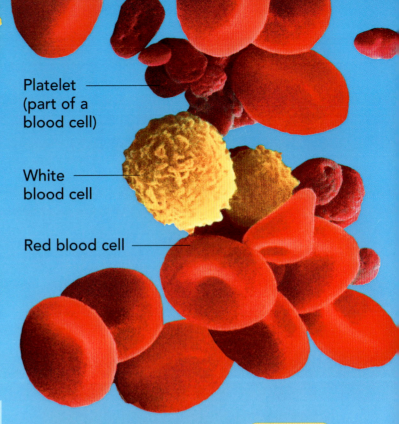

Platelet (part of a blood cell)

White blood cell

Red blood cell

Feel your pulse

To feel your blood being pumped around your body, press two fingers on the inside of your wrist. The beating you feel is called your pulse.

- Scan the code to find out more about what's inside you.
- For more links, go to **usborne.com/Quicklinks**

Safe in your skin

Your skin gives your whole body a waterproof covering and protects your insides from dirt and germs.

Skin is made up of two main layers. The top layer of skin is called the epidermis.

Underneath, is a thicker layer called the dermis.

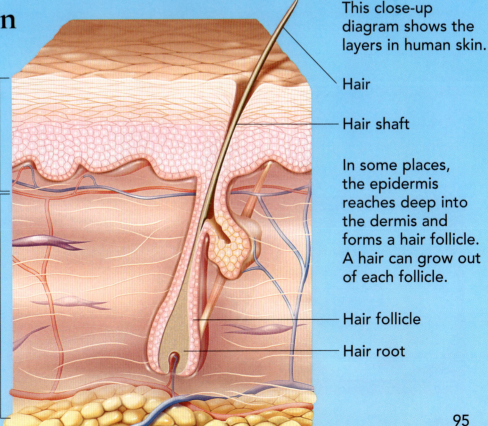

This close-up diagram shows the layers in human skin.

Hair

Hair shaft

In some places, the epidermis reaches deep into the dermis and forms a hair follicle. A hair can grow out of each follicle.

Hair follicle

Hair root

Bones and muscles

Bones and muscles are your body's support system. They hold you up and let you move around. Without them, you'd be nothing but a helpless blob.

Your skeleton

Together, your bones make up your skeleton, which acts as a framework for your whole body. Bendy joints where bones meet let you move into different positions.

Bones protect your insides too. For example, rib bones in your chest stop the organs inside from getting squashed.

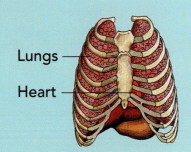

Lungs

Heart

Soft skeletons

A baby's bones are partly made of a bendy material called cartilage. As the baby grows, most of the cartilage slowly changes into hard bone.

This is an X-ray picture of a newborn baby's skull. As the baby grows older, the gaps in its skull will slowly close up, and the skull will get harder.

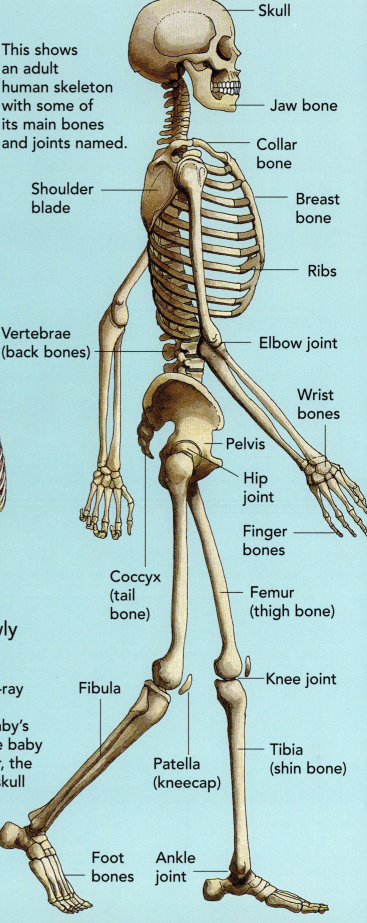

This shows an adult human skeleton with some of its main bones and joints named.

Skull

Jaw bone

Collar bone

Shoulder blade

Breast bone

Ribs

Vertebrae (back bones)

Elbow joint

Wrist bones

Pelvis

Hip joint

Finger bones

Coccyx (tail bone)

Femur (thigh bone)

Knee joint

Fibula

Tibia (shin bone)

Patella (kneecap)

Foot bones

Ankle joint

There are over 600 muscles in the human body. This picture shows some of the main ones.

Muscles

The bones of your skeleton are moved by muscles. These help you move in all kinds of ways, from walking or swimming to playing an instrument or using a computer.

You also have other muscles (in your heart, for example) that work without you even thinking about them.

This is the Achilles tendon. Tendons attach the muscles to the bones.

Trapezius

Triceps

Deltoid

Biceps

Gluteus maximus

Rectus abdominis

Quadriceps

Gastrocnemius

Gracilis

Moving muscles

Muscles work by contracting (getting shorter). As a muscle contracts, it pulls on the bones it's joined to, and they move. These little pictures show how muscles contract to bend and straighten your arm.

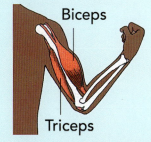

Biceps

Triceps

To bend your arm, the biceps muscle contracts, pulling up the lower arm.

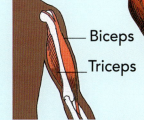

Biceps

Triceps

To straighten your arm, the triceps muscle contracts, pulling the lower arm down.

What happens to food?

The food you eat gives you the energy you need to live. But to get this energy, you have to turn food into chemicals in your body. This is called digestion.

Your food's journey

As food travels into and through your body, it gets turned into smaller and smaller bits. Follow the steps on the big picture to find out how this happens.

1 When you chew food, your teeth cut and mash it up.

2 Saliva (spit) mixes with the food, making it soft, mushy and easy to swallow.

3 When you swallow, food is forced down your throat into a tube called the gullet.

4 Muscles in your gullet squeeze the food down into your stomach.

Mouth

Throat

Gullet

Salivary glands (where saliva is made)

Did you know?

• An adult's salivary glands make about 6.5 cups (1.5 liters) of saliva each day.

• Your stomach can hold up to 17 cups (4 liters) of food and stretch to the size of a melon.

• Your small intestine is coiled up. If it were stretched out, it would be around 23ft (7m) long.

• Food takes between 24 and 72 hours to make its complete journey through your body.

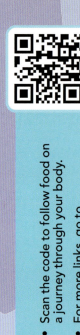

• Scan the code to follow food on a journey through your body.

• For more links, go to **usborne.com/Quicklinks**

Food for your cells

After food has been broken down into chemicals, it is carried all around your body in your blood. Some food is used to give your cells the energy they need to work – for example, to make muscles move. Some food is used to build new cells and repair injuries. If you eat more food than you need, your body stores it as fat.

Waste

Most food contains bits that can't be fully digested, such as some vegetable skins. Undigested food goes into your large intestine and collects into lumps, which end up in the toilet.

Millions of tiny bacteria, like these E. coli bacteria, live inside your intestines. They help themselves to your food, but are usually harmless.

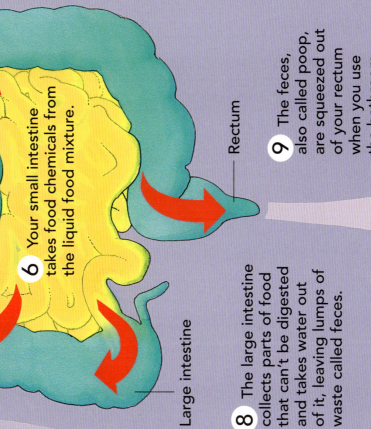

5 Your stomach squeezes the food and mixes it with acid, making a thick liquid.

6 Your small intestine takes food chemicals from the liquid food mixture.

7 The food chemicals are taken to your liver, ready to be sent around your body.

8 The large intestine collects parts of food that can't be digested and takes water out of it, leaving lumps of waste called feces.

9 The feces, also called poop, are squeezed out of your rectum when you use the bathroom.

Rectum

Large intestine

Water in your body

All your body's cells need water to work properly. Without water, you would only stay alive for a few days.

Water balance

To stay healthy, you need to keep the same amount of water in your body all the time. You lose water when you sweat and when you go to the bathroom. You have to drink to put back the water you've lost.

To stay healthy, you should drink plenty of water every day.

You take in water in drinks and in food. Some foods are more than nine-tenths water.

When you feel thirsty, your body is telling you it needs more water.

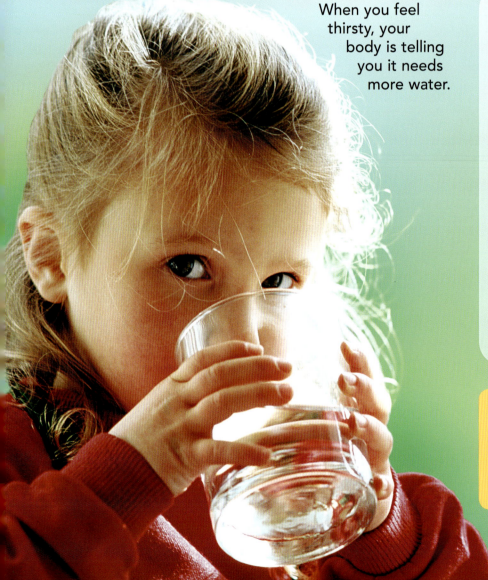

See your breath

You lose a little water every time you breathe out. Try this to see for yourself.

Breathe gently onto a mirror. See how your breath makes a mist on the glass.

The mist is made up of tiny droplets of water that you've breathed out.

- Scan the code for tips on how to make sure you drink enough water.
- For more links, go to **usborne.com/Quicklinks**

Waste water

Your kidneys control how much water is in your body. They get rid of any extra water that you don't need. They also clean your blood by taking out harmful chemicals produced by your body's cells.

Your kidneys turn the extra water and chemicals into a liquid called urine (pee). Follow the numbers to see where the urine goes.

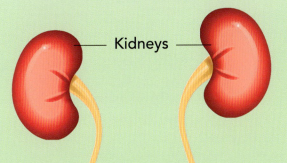

1 Your kidneys take out waste water and chemicals from your blood. They turn this into urine.

Kidneys

2 The urine trickles down two tubes, called ureters.

Ureters

3 Urine collects in a stretchy bag called your bladder.

Bladder

4 When you go to the bathroom, your bladder opens. The urine comes out of a tube called your urethra.

Urethra

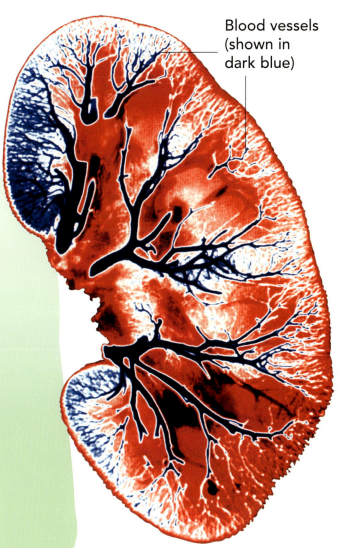

Blood vessels (shown in dark blue)

Your kidneys clean all the blood in your body every four minutes. This X-ray photo shows inside a kidney.

Babies and toddlers can't control when they get rid of urine. That's why they have to wear diapers.

Your brain and senses

Your brain controls your body. Your five senses – sight, hearing, touch, taste and smell – tell your brain what's going on around you, so it can make decisions.

Brain bundle

Your brain is made of a big bundle of cells called neurons. When you think, your neurons are passing signals to each other. Some types of neurons, called nerves, link your brain to your sense organs and to other parts of your body.

This picture shows a signal (in green) jumping between two neurons in your brain.

This scan of a person's head shows the brain inside the skull.

The skull protects your brain.

The brain is this blue and yellow area. The yellow lines are folds in the brain's surface.

The brain stem links your brain to your spinal cord and so to the rest of your body.

Seeing things

When light shines on something, it reflects, or bounces off. Your eyes collect the reflected light and turn the patterns into signals your brain can understand.

4 The optic nerve (made of neurons) carries signals to your brain.

1 Light bounces off an object.

2 The light enters your pupil, which is the black dot in the middle of your eye.

3 Patterns of light hit your retina, an area of light-sensitive cells on the inside of your eye.

- Scan the code to explore your five senses.
- For more links, go to **usborne.com/Quicklinks**

How you hear

Sound is the vibration (back and forth movement) of tiny particles in the air. When vibrations reach your ears, they are turned into signals that are sent to your brain.

1 Sounds make vibrations that travel through the air.

2 The vibrating air hits a patch of skin called the eardrum.

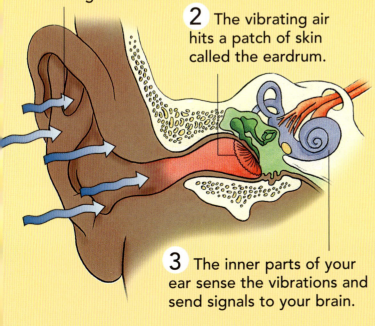

3 The inner parts of your ear sense the vibrations and send signals to your brain.

Taste and smell

Sensitive spots on your tongue, called taste buds, can detect a few simple tastes, such as sweet and sour. More sensitive cells in your nose detect different smells, and also help you tell the difference between flavors.

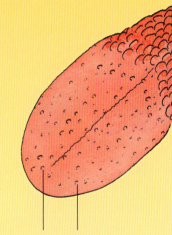

Tiny pink bumps on your tongue have taste buds in them.

Touch

There are millions of sensitive nerve endings in your skin. They can feel heat, cold, pressure and pain.

Some blind people use their fingers to read Braille writing, which is made up of tiny bumps.

Babies

Babies come from inside their birth mothers. After growing there for about nine months, they are big enough to live in the outside world.

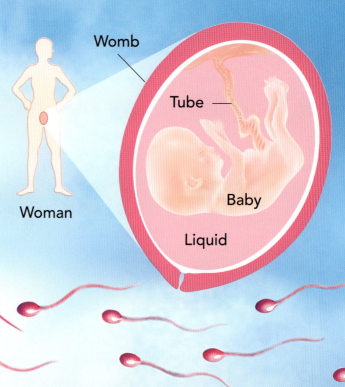

This unborn baby has been growing inside its birth mother for eight weeks.

Making a baby

To make a baby, you need a man and a woman. The woman has little eggs inside her body. The man makes tiny swimming cells called sperm inside his body.

The sperm swim into the woman's body. When one sperm joins up with an egg, a baby starts to grow.

One sperm is joining with this egg to make a baby start to grow.

Inside the womb

The baby grows inside the woman's womb. This is filled with a watery liquid which helps keep the baby safe. A tube carries oxygen and food from the woman's body to the baby.

Womb

Tube

Baby

Liquid

Woman

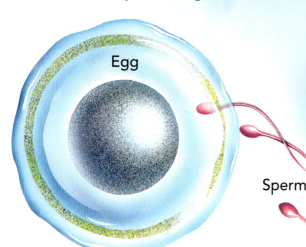

Egg

Sperm

Growing and moving

After about four months, the baby has grown so much that it makes a bump in the woman's tummy. Sometimes, she can feel the baby kicking and wriggling inside her.

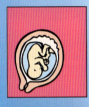
Unborn baby at four months

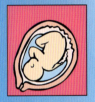
Unborn baby at six months

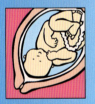
At nine months, the baby is ready to be born.

- Scan the code to find out more about babies.
- For more links, go to usborne.com/Quicklinks

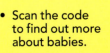

This baby boy is four days old.

Being born

When the baby is ready to be born, the woman's womb starts to squeeze. The baby comes out her vagina, or doctors might need to help get the baby out with an operation. The birth can take many hours.

Like Mom or Dad?

The baby may look like its birth mother or father, or a mixture of both. Who it looks like depends on its genes. These are instructions in the baby's cells that tell the body how to grow. A baby's genes come from the father's sperm and the mother's egg.

Each sperm has half the genes needed to make a baby. The rest of the genes come from the mother's egg.

Sperm

Staying healthy

When your body isn't working properly, you might feel sick. There are lots of ways to look after yourself and help your body stay healthy.

Eating well

You need to eat different types of food to stay healthy. The picture below is a guide to how much of each type of food you should eat every day.

Eat only small amounts of fatty or sugary foods, such as butter, cake, candy and sugary drinks.

Eat two servings of foods from the milk group, such as milk, yogurt and cheese.

Eat three servings of vegetables, such as carrots, peas and broccoli.

Keeping clean

Keeping clean helps stop harmful germs from building up on and in your body and making you sick. Washing your hands after going to the bathroom and before eating helps stop germs from spreading. Brushing your teeth helps get rid of the germs that make holes in your teeth.

Eat two servings of foods from the protein group. This includes fish, eggs, nuts and beans as well as meat.

Eat two servings of fresh, dried, canned or frozen fruit.

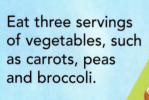

Eat six servings from the grain group each day. This group includes bread, pasta, rice and cereals.

Staying in shape

Exercising is an important way of looking after your body, and can be lots of fun too. Different types of exercises can help your body in different ways.

Swimming is a good way to exercise and keep your body healthy.

Jogging and skipping strengthen your heart and lungs, so you can be active for longer.

Canoeing and rowing make your muscles stronger so they work better without straining.

Gymnastics and dancing help you bend and stretch more easily, and stop you from getting stiff.

Sleeping

It is very important to get enough sleep. While you are asleep, your body tissues have the chance to grow and repair themselves. Children need more sleep than adults because they have more growing to do.

- Scan the code to find lots of ways to exercise and stay in shape.
- For more links, go to **usborne.com/Quicklinks**

Germs

Germs are everywhere. Usually, they don't do any harm. But some kinds can make you sick if they get inside you.

- Scan the code to watch an experiment that shows how soap fights germs.

- For more links, go to **usborne.com/Quicklinks**

What are germs?

Germs are tiny living things that can carry illnesses. Some travel through the air and some live in food or water. Others get passed on when people cough or sneeze. There are two main kinds of germs – bacteria and viruses.

These bacteria make your throat sore. They're shown 50,000 times bigger than they really are.

These bacteria give you a stomach ache and make you feel sick.

These viruses can give you a cold.

Washing your hands with hot, soapy water helps stop germs from spreading.

Cooking food properly kills any germs that are living inside it.

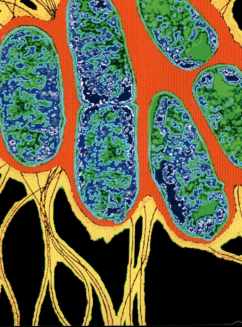

Fighting germs

Your body can fight off some germs by itself. Special white cells in your blood hunt down germs and kill them. Some white blood cells make chemicals that kill germs. Others gobble the germs up.

Here you can see a white blood cell swallowing a germ.

Germ

White blood cell

This girl is having an injection, called an immunization. Immunizations protect you from dangerous germs that could make you very ill.

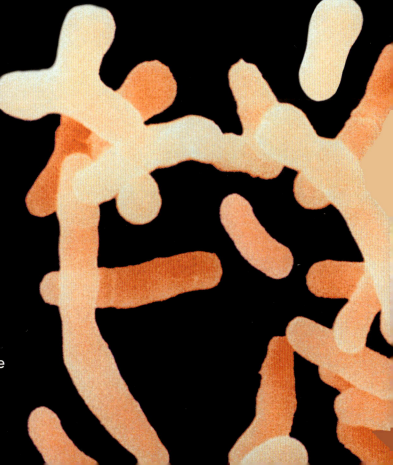

Friendly bacteria

Not all bacteria are bad. Inside your stomach, you have millions and millions of bacteria that are actually good for you. They help break down your food. They even make some of the vitamins you need.

This is what some of the bacteria that live inside your tummy look like.

Teeth

Imagine trying to eat an apple if you had no teeth. You use your teeth to cut up your food and crush it into small pieces that you can swallow.

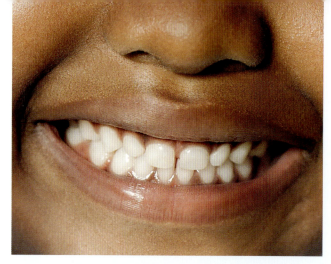

Your teeth have a tough, white covering called enamel. Enamel is the hardest thing in your body.

Types of teeth

When you're little, you have 20 small teeth. They are called milk teeth or baby teeth. When you're about six years old, your milk teeth start to fall out. New, bigger teeth grow in their place. You will have these new teeth for the rest of your life.

Most grown-ups have 32 teeth. Different shapes of teeth do different jobs.

Sharp incisors are for biting off pieces of food.

Pointy canines can tear food.

Molars have a big, bumpy surface for chewing food.

This boy has lost some of his milk teeth. They were pushed out by bigger teeth growing underneath.

Premolars are smaller than molars, but they're good at chewing too.

Inside a tooth

The part of a tooth you can see is called the crown. Underneath, your teeth have long roots that fit into holes in your jawbone. Your teeth are very hard on the outside. But inside, they're soft – and they're alive.

This is what a tooth looks like inside.

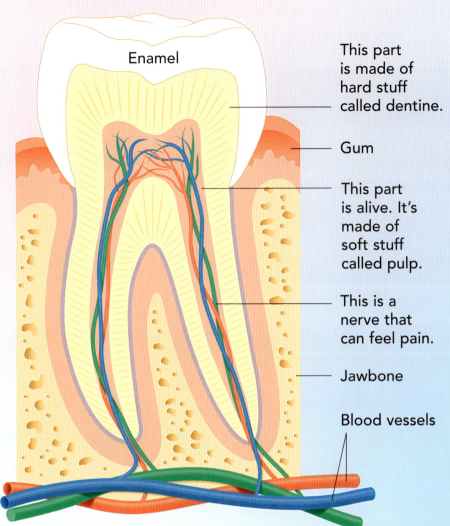

Enamel

This part is made of hard stuff called dentine.

Gum

This part is alive. It's made of soft stuff called pulp.

This is a nerve that can feel pain.

Jawbone

Blood vessels

- Scan the code to meet your teeth and find out more about them.
- For more links, go to **usborne.com/Quicklinks**

Tooth care

Did you know you have lots of germs living inside your mouth? Some feed on any sugary food stuck to your teeth. They can eat away at your teeth and make holes in them. Here's how you can keep your teeth healthy.

Try not to eat or drink too many sugary things.

Brush your teeth at least twice a day to clean away any leftover food.

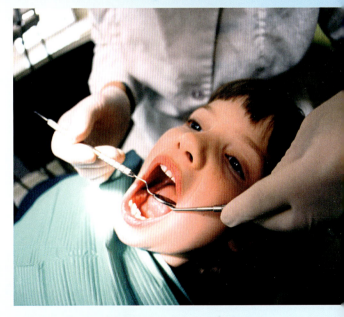

It's a good idea to visit a dentist regularly. Your dentist can check if your teeth are healthy and can show you how to clean them properly.

Growing and changing

Your body is getting bigger all the time. It keeps on growing from the time you are born until you're about 20 years old.

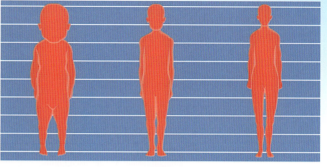

Babies have big heads compared with their bodies.

By seven, your body and legs have grown much longer.

Grown-ups have long legs. Their heads look small compared with their bodies.

Changing shape

Each year, you grow about 2½in (6cm) taller. Some of your bones grow faster than others. This means that your body changes shape as you grow up.

As you grow, your bones get longer. Look at the bones in these two X-ray pictures.

This is the hand of a three-year-old.

This is the hand of a grown-up.

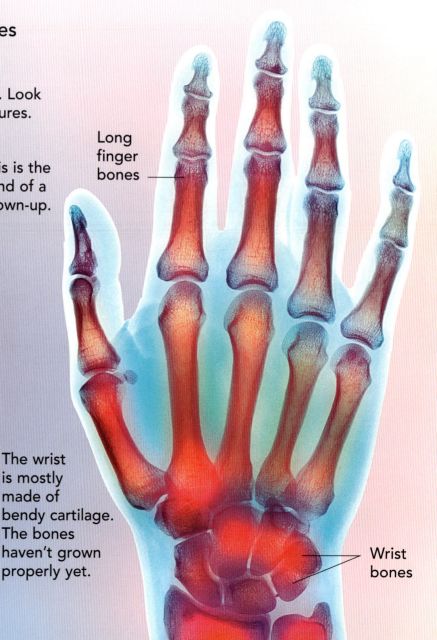

Long finger bones

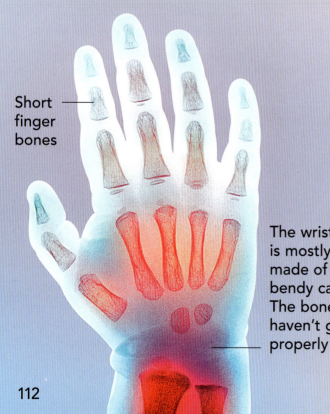

Short finger bones

The wrist is mostly made of bendy cartilage. The bones haven't grown properly yet.

Wrist bones

Learning and doing

Tiny babies can't do anything for themselves. Slowly, they learn to use their muscles, so they can sit up and crawl around. By the time they're two, most can walk and talk.

As you get older, you may learn to do more complicated things, such as balance on your hands.

- Scan the code for more facts about growing and changing.
- For more links, go to **usborne.com/Quicklinks**

Getting old

As people grow old, their bodies change again. Their bones and muscles shrink and they can get tired more easily.

By the time people are in their sixties, their hair may have turned gray and their skin looks different.

Becoming an adult

Between the ages of about 10 and 18, lots of changes happen to your body. This time is called puberty. It's when you change from a child into an adult.

Girls' and boys' bodies change in different ways:

Boys' voices get deeper, and their shoulders and chests get broader.

Boys grow hair on their faces.

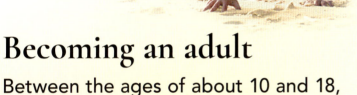

Girls grow breasts.

Their hips get wider.

Doctors and medicine

When you are sick, you might visit a doctor. A doctor's job is to find out what is wrong and tell you what to do to feel better. Doctors also give people advice on how to stay healthy.

Making it better

The pictures below show several ways the doctor might help you get better. Sometimes they may just tell you to rest a lot or change what you eat.

You may have to take medicine, either by drinking it in a liquid or by taking some pills.

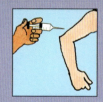

A doctor may put a needle into your body to give you medicine. This is an injection.

A broken bone may need a plaster cast. This holds the broken ends together so that the bone mends straight, not crooked.

Finding out

The doctor asks how you are feeling and checks your body for signs of illness. You may need to have some tests done to find out what is wrong.

X-rays are used to take pictures of the bones inside your body. This picture shows a broken arm.

- Scan the code to see what happens when you visit the doctor.
- For more links, go to **usborne.com/Quicklinks**

History

The first people

The first people lived by hunting animals, catching fish and gathering plants to eat. As the seasons changed, they moved around from place to place looking for food.

In the summer, people lived in tents that they made from branches and animal skins.

In the winter, when it was cold, they sometimes sheltered in caves.

Finding food

People spent a lot of time looking for food. They hunted deer, horses, bison and wild pigs for meat. They also ate plants and small animals.

These are some of the things that the first people ate.

Berries

Fish

Snails

Mushrooms

Dandelion leaves

Nuts

Crabs

Birds' eggs

Lizards

Shellfish

These animals were painted on the wall of a cave at Lascaux, in France.

Cave paintings

Inside the deepest, darkest caves, people painted pictures of the animals they hunted. They may have thought that the pictures were magical and would help them with their hunting.

- Scan the code to see cave paintings of animals up close.
- For more links, go to **usborne.com/Quicklinks**

Stone tools

The first people used tools made from a kind of stone called flint. They made spears with a sharpened flint tip for hunting. They also made flint axes and knives for cutting up meat.

This is a flint tip from an arrow.

The first farmers

Farming began when people learned how to plant seeds to grow food. They also tamed animals, such as sheep and cows. This meant that people could stay in one place, instead of moving around to find food.

This clay pot was made by early farmers in Turkey.

Growing food

The plants farmers grow are called crops. Around 12,000 years ago, people in West Asia began growing wheat and barley crops. They ground the grain into flour for making bread.

Making things

Farmers didn't need to spend all day looking for food, so they had time to learn new things. They made clay pots for storing and cooking food. They also learned how to make cloth by spinning and weaving wool.

This is part of a farming village in West Asia. It has a wall around it to keep out wild animals.

These are wheat plants. You can see the grains at the top of each stalk.

This man is offering gifts to a statue of the village goddess.

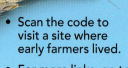

- Scan the code to visit a site where early farmers lived.
- For more links, go to **usborne.com/Quicklinks**

New tools

The first farmers made tools from stone, bone and wood. Later, people learned how to make things from metal, such as copper.

This is a sickle. It was a tool used for cutting crops.

Stone blade

Wooden handle

People carry water from the stream.

People use sickles to cut the crops.

People make mud bricks to mend the wall.

Roofs are covered with straw to keep homes warm and dry.

Cows are kept for their meat, milk and skins.

121

Ancient Egypt

The Ancient Egyptians were farmers who lived along the banks of the river Nile. They were ruled by a powerful king or queen called a pharaoh (say "fair-ro").

- Scan the code to watch a video of how mummies were made.
- For more links, go to **usborne.com/Quicklinks**

A gold mask from the tomb of the pharaoh Tutankhamun

Pharaohs and pyramids

Some pharaohs were buried inside huge, stone pyramids on the edge of the desert. The pharaoh's body was placed in a secret room in the middle of the pyramid. There are still over 100 pyramids in Egypt, and each one took at least 20 years to build.

These are the pyramids at Giza. Three pharaohs and their wives were buried here.

A pharaoh named Menkaure was buried inside this pyramid.

This is the Great Pyramid. It is made up of over two million stone blocks.

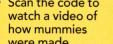

Menkaure's three wives were buried in these smaller pyramids in front.

Mummies and coffins

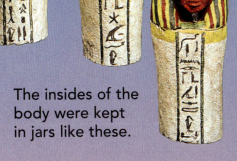

The Egyptians tried to stop dead people's bodies from rotting away. They thought this would allow them to have another life after they died. They took out the person's insides, dried the body out and wrapped it in bandages. Bodies kept like this are called mummies.

The insides of the body were kept in jars like these.

Mummies were put inside a painted wooden coffin called a sarcophagus.

Picture writing

Egyptian writing was made up of lots of pictures, or symbols, called hieroglyphs (say "hi-ro-gliffs"). There were over 700 different symbols. Here are just a few of them.

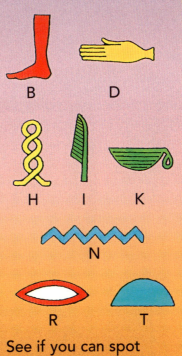

B

D

H

I

K

N

R

T

See if you can spot the symbols for "I," "N," "R" and "T" in this Egyptian painting.

Ancient Greece

In ancient times, Greece wasn't all one country like it is today. Instead, each city had its own rulers. The greatest of these cities was Athens, which is now the capital city of modern Greece.

The Parthenon temple was the finest building in Athens.

Big buildings

In every city in Greece, people built huge, stone temples for their gods and goddesses. Greek temples usually had a triangular-shaped roof held up by rows of tall pillars.

Spot the pillar

The Ancient Greeks used three types of pillars in their buildings. Can you spot which type they used for the Parthenon?

Doric pillar

Corinthian pillar

Ionic pillar

This is the ruin of the Parthenon temple. It stands on a hill high above the city.

The walls and pillars are made from a stone called marble.

The first plays

The first great plays were written by the Ancient Greeks. They believed that performing the plays would please their gods. People put them on at long festivals, where there were prizes for the best plays.

- Scan the code for more about the ancient Olympic Games.
- For more links, go to **usborne.com/Quicklinks**

Actors playing gods can fly through the air on this crane.

Musicians

Scenery

Stage

Actors wear masks and costumes to show which parts they are playing.

The Olympic Games

The Ancient Greeks loved athletics. Their famous athletics competition was the Olympic Games, which took place every four years at a place called Olympia.

These actors are called the chorus. They perform songs and dances to explain what is happening on the stage.

This Ancient Greek painting shows an athlete training for the long jump.

Ancient Rome

About 2,000 years ago, Rome was one of the biggest cities in the world. At that time, the Romans ruled all the lands around the Mediterranean Sea. These lands were called the Roman Empire.

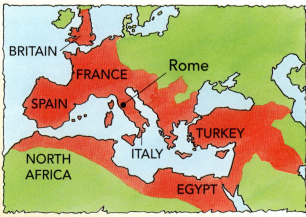

On this map, all the lands shown in red were once part of the Roman Empire.

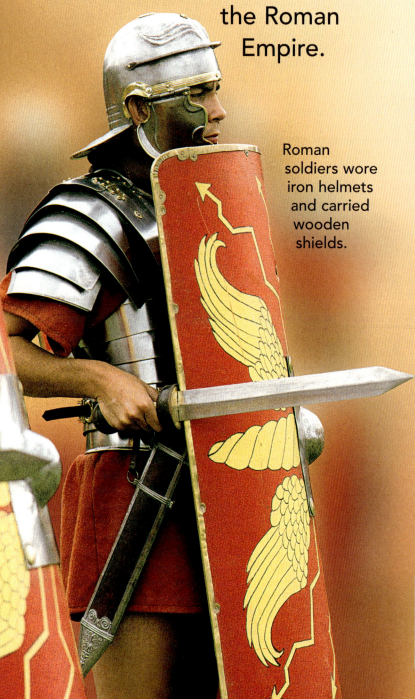

Roman soldiers wore iron helmets and carried wooden shields.

The Roman army

The Romans had a huge army of well-trained soldiers. They used their army to fight for new lands and to protect the Empire from enemies. Most soldiers fought on foot using a spear, a sword and a dagger.

Roman soldiers built long, straight roads linking towns all over the Empire.

- Scan the code to discover what it was like to be a Roman soldier.
- For more links, go to **usborne.com/Quicklinks**

Home comforts

In Rome, rich people lived in comfortable houses with large gardens. Some houses even had toilets, running water and a kind of central heating.

This is a Roman house. Parts of it have been cut away so you can see inside.

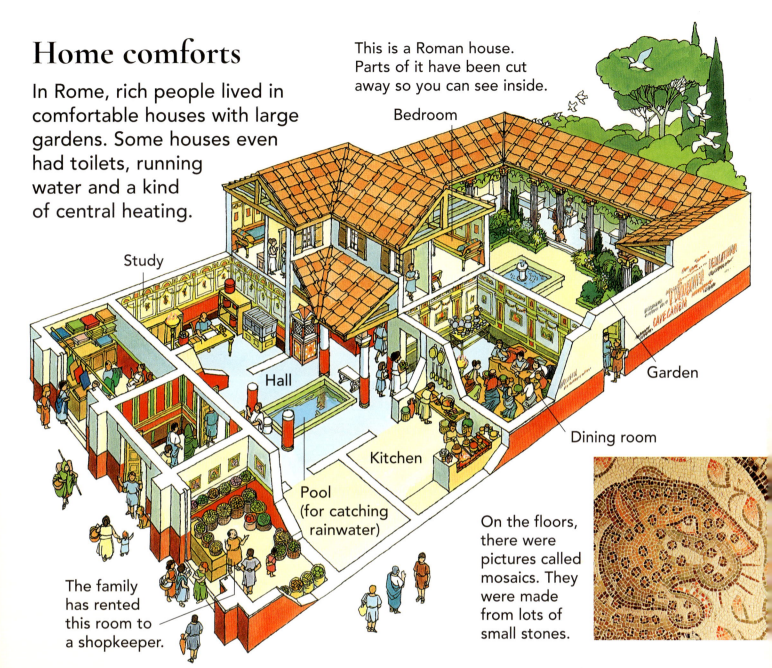

Bedroom

Study

Hall

Garden

Kitchen

Dining room

Pool (for catching rainwater)

The family has rented this room to a shopkeeper.

On the floors, there were pictures called mosaics. They were made from lots of small stones.

Roman pastimes

The Romans loved watching chariot races. These took place at a huge racetrack called a circus.

People also enjoyed watching gladiators fight each other. Gladiators often died in these brutal fights.

Most Romans went to the public baths every day to relax, exercise, meet friends – and to get themselves clean.

The Vikings

The Vikings came from Norway, Sweden and Denmark. They were great sailors and traders, but they were also fierce warriors. They attacked and robbed villages all around the coasts of Europe.

This man is dressed as a Viking warrior.

Greenland

Iceland

North America

British Isles

France

Spain

Italy

The Vikings lived here.

The Vikings sailed to all these places.

A Viking longship

Viking ships

The Vikings made their attacks in fast boats, called longships. The ships were strong enough to sail across rough seas. They weren't very deep, so they could also travel up shallow rivers.

This carved dragon's head is meant to scare enemies.

The Vikings in this ship are on their way to launch a raid.

This big oar at the back is for steering the ship.

Viking homes

Viking chiefs lived in large homes called longhouses. Each longhouse had only one big room, where everyone ate, worked and slept. There weren't any windows, so it must have been very dark inside.

Part of this longhouse has been cut away so you can see inside.

The roof is covered with straw and the walls are made of logs.

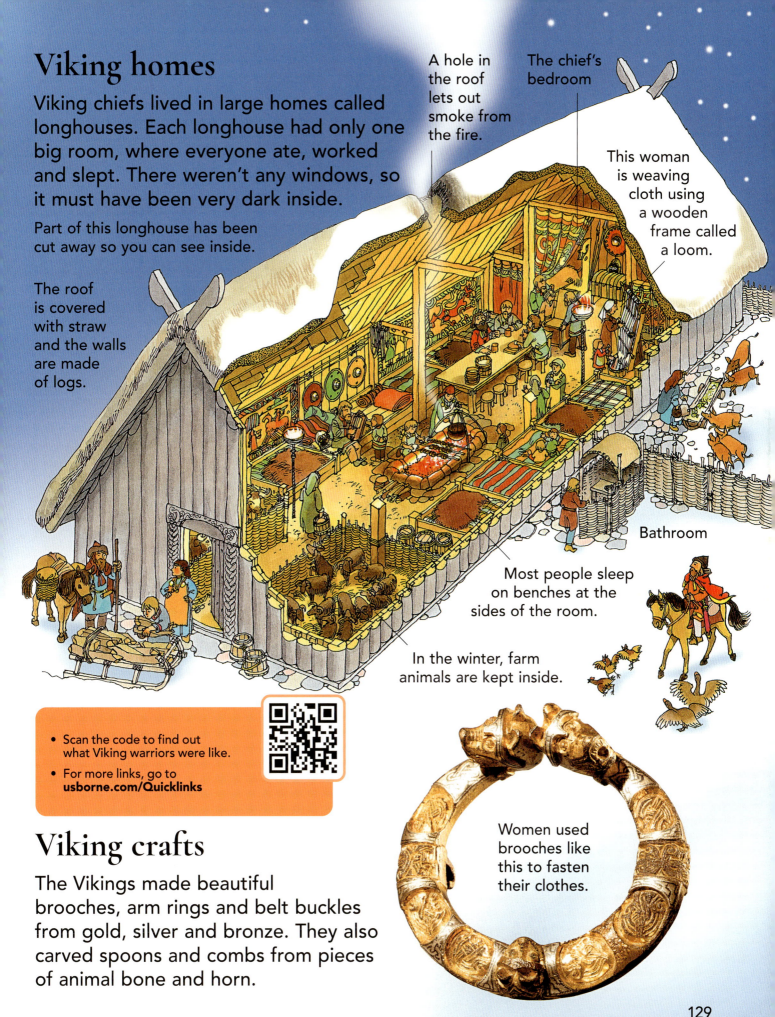

A hole in the roof lets out smoke from the fire.

The chief's bedroom

This woman is weaving cloth using a wooden frame called a loom.

Bathroom

Most people sleep on benches at the sides of the room.

In the winter, farm animals are kept inside.

- Scan the code to find out what Viking warriors were like.
- For more links, go to **usborne.com/Quicklinks**

Viking crafts

The Vikings made beautiful brooches, arm rings and belt buckles from gold, silver and bronze. They also carved spoons and combs from pieces of animal bone and horn.

Women used brooches like this to fasten their clothes.

African kingdoms

Africa is an enormous continent. Before modern African countries were created, different areas had their own way of life. In some places, rich kingdoms grew up.

An artist in Benin, in West Africa, made this beautiful bronze statue.

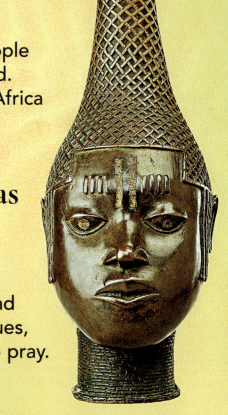

Traders from North Africa used camels to get across the Sahara Desert to Mali.

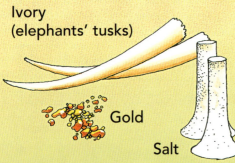

Ivory (elephants' tusks)

Gold

Salt

These are some of the things the traders bought and sold.

Kingdom of gold

In Mali, in West Africa, people dug gold out of the ground. Traders came from North Africa to buy the gold, and Mali became very rich.

The spread of ideas

The North African traders were Muslims, and many people in Mali became Muslims too. Their cities had big buildings, called mosques, where Muslims could go to pray.

This is the Grand Mosque in Djenne, in Mali. The walls are made of mud.

Stone city

In the grasslands of southern Africa was the city of Great Zimbabwe. Its people grew rich by trading gold and copper. The king lived inside a walled fortress in the middle of the city.

- Scan the code to explore ancient buildings from African kingdoms.
- For more links, go to **usborne.com/Quicklinks**

This is the fortress at Great Zimbabwe.

This tower is made of stones. It is solid all the way through.

The houses are made of clay and gravel.

Grass roof

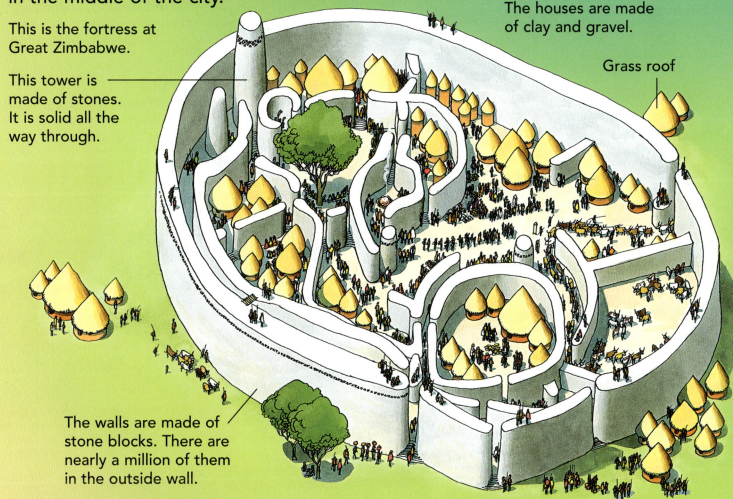

The walls are made of stone blocks. There are nearly a million of them in the outside wall.

Rock churches

Ethiopia was a Christian kingdom. King Lalibela of Ethiopia believed that God had told him to carve churches out of solid rock. He built 11 churches like this. Some of them were linked together by tunnels under the ground.

This is one of King Lalibela's churches. All of them were carved in the shape of a cross.

Living in a castle

In the Middle Ages (between 500 and 1,000 years ago), kings and lords in Europe often fought each other for land. They built castles with strong, stone walls to protect themselves from their enemies.

Inside a castle

A lord lived in a castle with his family and all his soldiers and servants. It must have been very cold inside, because the first castles had no glass in the windows.

This picture shows part of a castle. Some of the walls have been cut away to let you see inside.

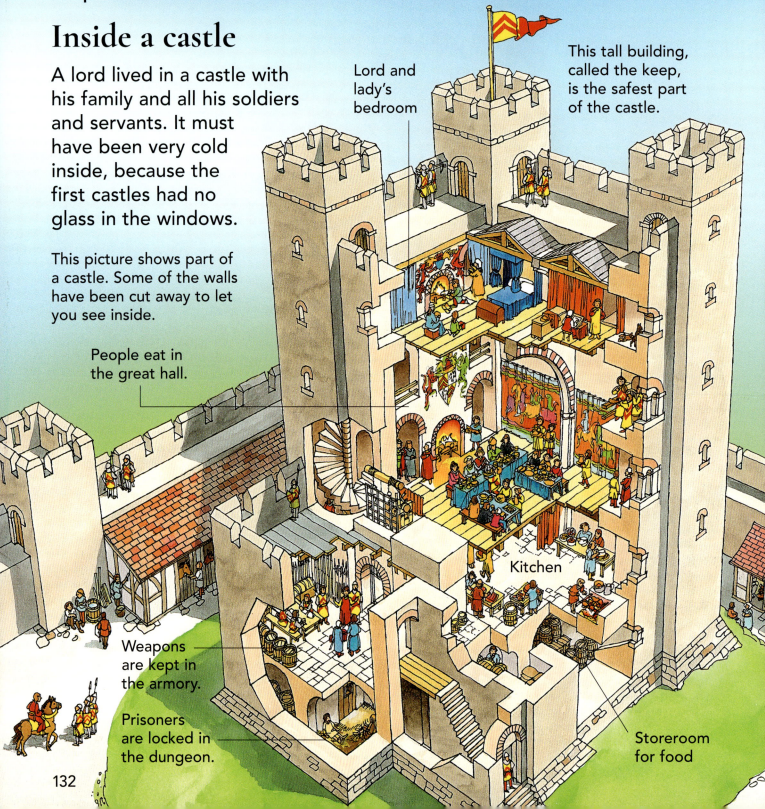

Lord and lady's bedroom

This tall building, called the keep, is the safest part of the castle.

People eat in the great hall.

Kitchen

Weapons are kept in the armory.

Prisoners are locked in the dungeon.

Storeroom for food

Noble knights

Knights were soldiers who fought on horseback. Only boys from noble families could train to be knights. A good knight had to be strong and brave. He also had to promise to fight only for his lord.

This picture from the Middle Ages shows two knights taking part in a contest called a joust.

Painted shield

Chainmail shirt made from lots of metal rings

This knight is being knocked off his horse.

This long spear is called a lance.

- Scan the code to see inside a castle from the Middle Ages.
- For more links, go to **usborne.com/Quicklinks**

High walls keep enemies out.

Guards look out for enemies.

Fun feasts

Feasts took place in the great hall of the castle. The guests ate lots of rich food, such as roast swan, spiced beef, squirrel stew and sugared mackerel. For dessert, there might be apple pie or honey cakes.

A jester told jokes to make the guests laugh.

Musicians, called minstrels, played their instruments and sang.

Inca cities

The Incas lived in the Andes mountains of South America. Most of them were farmers, but they were also great builders. They were ruled by an emperor called the Inca.

These people are acting out an old Inca festival at the city of Cuzco, in Peru.

Cities of stone

The Incas built huge cities from massive blocks of stone. They used stone hammers to shape the blocks so they would fit together perfectly. Each city had temples, palaces, and observatories for watching the stars.

These are the ruins of the Inca city of Machu Picchu, high up in the Andes mountains.

- Scan the code to visit the Inca city of Machu Picchu.
- For more links, go to **usborne.com/Quicklinks**

Aztec life

The Aztecs lived in what is now Mexico. They were fierce warriors and were often at war with nearby groups. Winning wars gave the Aztecs new land, and they became very powerful.

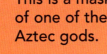

This is a mask of one of the Aztec gods.

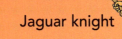

The best Aztec warriors were the Eagle knights and Jaguar knights.

Eagle knight

Jaguar knight

- Scan the code to find out more about the Aztecs.
- For more links, go to **usborne.com/Quicklinks**

Island city

The Aztecs' capital city was called Tenochtitlán. It was built on islands near the edge of Lake Texcoco, which were joined to the mainland by raised roads. In the middle of the city was a huge square filled with temples built on top of tall pyramids.

Part of Tenochtitlán city

Floating fields

In the lake all around Tenochtitlán, farmers grew food in huge, floating fields. The fields were like giant baskets filled with mud and soil. People grew corn, beans, tomatoes and peppers. They used the corn to bake thin pancakes called tortillas.

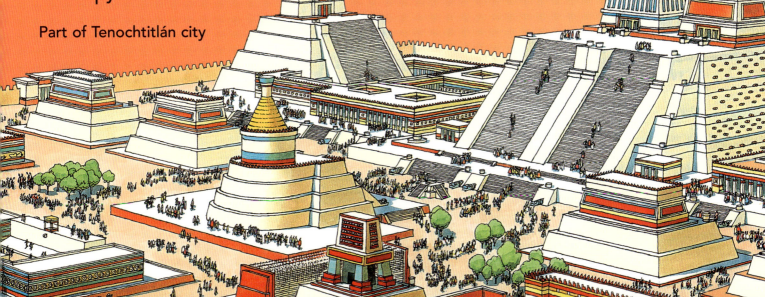

The Chinese invented gunpowder. They used it for making fireworks, as well as weapons.

Ming China

Around 500 years ago, China was ruled by a family of emperors called the Ming. The Ming emperors made Beijing their capital city. They lived there in a huge palace, called the Forbidden City.

The Forbidden City

The Forbidden City was made up of great halls, temples, courtyards and gardens. It was surrounded by a wall and a moat (a big ditch filled with water). Only the emperor's family and servants were allowed inside.

The palace has 9,999 rooms and is as big as 74 soccer fields. It took a million workers 14 years to build. In this picture, you can see a royal procession in front of the Hall of Supreme Harmony.

Officials and soldiers

Made in China

Porcelain jar

In Ming times, the Chinese made many beautiful things. They are especially famous for making a kind of fine pottery called porcelain. They also made a very expensive kind of cloth called silk.

This wooden box is covered with a shiny varnish called lacquer.

Time for tea

The Chinese started growing tea about 1,700 years ago. At first, they used the leaves to make medicines. Later, tea became a very popular drink. The Chinese made their tea in teapots and drank it out of little bowls.

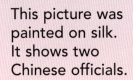

These Chinese workers pick the leaves from tea plants by hand.

This picture was painted on silk. It shows two Chinese officials.

- Scan the code to explore the Forbidden City.
- For more links, go to **usborne.com/Quicklinks**

The emperor's coach is pulled by elephants.

Tudor England

The Tudors were a family of kings and queens. They ruled England for over a hundred years and made the country rich and powerful.

This is a painting of a Tudor king, Henry VIII.

These coins came from the wreck of a Tudor warship.

Explorers and pirates

In Tudor times, explorers sailed to North and South America to conquer new lands. They brought back new foods, such as potatoes. Some English explorers were pirates, too. They stole treasure from Spanish ships on the coast of America.

- Scan the code to find out about Henry VIII and Tudor times.

- For more links, go to **usborne.com/Quicklinks**

Henry VIII

Henry VIII became king when he was 17 years old. He argued with the head of the Church in Europe (the Pope), who wouldn't let Henry divorce his wife. So, Henry set up his own English Church, which allowed divorce. He married six times. He divorced two of his wives and had two others beheaded.

Elizabeth I

Queen Elizabeth was the last and greatest of the Tudors. She ruled England for 45 years. During her reign, England fought off an attack by a group of Spanish ships called the Spanish Armada.

This is a portrait of Elizabeth I. She was the third, and last, of Henry VIII's children to rule England.

Plays and playhouses

In Elizabeth's time, people loved going to see plays. In London, actors performed in playhouses such as the Globe. The most popular plays were written by William Shakespeare.

Here you can see actors performing a play at the Globe theater.

A flag is flown during the play.

The roof is covered with straw.

This roof keeps the actors dry if it rains.

The walls have been cut away to let you see inside.

Stage

Oak beams

Rich people watch from seats around the sides.

Poorer people stand in the yard around the stage.

Moving to America

In 1620, a group of religious English people called the Pilgrims, or the Pilgrim Fathers, went to colonize* and settle in North America. They landed on the east coast, at a place they named Plymouth.

The Pilgrims sailed to America on a ship called *The Mayflower*. This is a painting of their ship.

Learning to survive

The Pilgrims' first winter was hard. Many died from cold and hunger, and they were feared by the Indigenous American tribe that already lived there. Eventually they made peace, and the Indigenous Americans taught the Pilgrims how to grow corn, beans and pumpkins.

The first Thanksgiving

Relieved by their first successful harvest, the Pilgrims invited the Indigenous Americans to a feast. Every November, many Americans celebrate this event with a Thanksgiving meal.

The roofs are covered with reeds.

The houses are made of wooden planks called clapboards.

Fish hanging up to dry

This picture shows the Pilgrims' village at Plymouth. You can see the Pilgrims preparing for their Thanksgiving meal.

*For more about colonization, see page 144.

- Scan the code for more about the Pilgrims who settled in America.
- For more links, go to **usborne.com/Quicklinks**

This fence keeps wild animals out of the village.

The gardens are planted with beans, onions, turnips and squash.

Women are plucking wild turkeys.

A boy is grinding corn to make bread.

These Indigenous Americans are bringing a deer for the feast.

Fighting for land

More and more Europeans came to settle in America, moving farther west in search of large areas of land to farm. These people were known as pioneers, and they built mines and cattle ranches. Pioneers took their land from Indigenous Americans, who fought hard against them. Eventually, the settlers claimed the country as their own, and created the United States of America.

This woman is stewing pumpkins to put in a pie.

This is Sitting Bull, a famous Indigenous American chief.

Mughal India

At one time, most of India was ruled by Mughal emperors. The Mughals were Muslims who invaded India from Central Asia. They were great warriors, but they also loved art, music and poetry.

Mughal buildings

The Mughal emperors were incredibly rich. They used a lot of their money to build beautiful palaces, forts, tombs and mosques (places where Muslims go to worship). Some emperors even built completely new cities.

The finest craftsmen worked to decorate the inside of each building.

The most famous Mughal building is the Taj Mahal. It was built by the emperor Shah Jahan as a tomb for his beloved wife, Mumtaz Mahal.

These tall towers are called minarets.

The emperor and his wife are buried in a small underground room beneath the dome.

French finery

Around 380 years ago, the most powerful ruler in Europe was King Louis XIV of France. Louis became king when he was just five years old, and he reigned for 72 years. He was fabulously rich and lived a life of luxury.

This is the Hall of Mirrors in King Louis' palace at Versailles. The palace has 700 rooms and took 47 years to build.

French fashions

In the 1700s, rich nobles at Versailles wore the most fashionable clothes in Europe. Their clothes were made of the finest silk and were decorated with beautiful embroidery, jewels, lace and ribbons.

- Scan the code to explore the magnificent Palace of Versailles.
- For more links, go to **usborne.com/Quicklinks**

Here you can see what rich French nobles were wearing in the 1770s.

Lace cravat

Silk breeches

Silk stockings

Some skirts were so wide that women had to go through doors sideways.

Women had very tall hairstyles, up to 3ft (1m) high.

Rich men wore wigs made of human, horse or goat hair.

Rich and poor

In 1789, the poorer people of France rebelled against the rich. They killed the king, the queen and hundreds of nobles, and began ruling the country themselves. This was called the French Revolution.

143

Colonization and enslavement

By 1500, European explorers had traveled to and claimed many new lands, which were known as colonies. They often enslaved the people who lived there, which meant they had to work for the invaders for no pay and were treated like property.

Wealthy empires

A number of countries ruled by one person was known as an empire. At this time, Spain had a large empire, with many colonies in South America. Britain was also growing its empire, with colonies in North America and the Caribbean.

The colonies provided European nations with new foods and materials to trade with each other. The empires made some countries very rich.

Goods such as silk, tobacco and tea were transported over long distances by merchant ships like these. People from the colonies were traded as payment.

- Scan the code to find out more about the trade triangle.
- For more links, go to **usborne.com/Quicklinks**

Finding a workforce

European colonizers often thought people who looked different to them had strange customs and were less intelligent and less important. They tried to enslave Indigenous American people, but many were able to escape in a familiar land. So, Europeans settlers decided to find workers from Africa instead.

Crops such as cotton, sugar and cocoa were harvested on large farms called plantations.

Seeds from a cotton plant

Far from home

Africans didn't have powerful enough weapons to fight back against the Europeans. Millions were enslaved and taken to North and South America, and the Caribbean. They worked on plantations, and down mines collecting precious metals.

This map shows the large distances traveled by the slave ships and the merchant ships. Millions of enslaved people died on the journey, from disease and lack of food.

While traders and their nations grew rich, enslaved people suffered at the hands of cruel slave owners for hundreds of years.

Changing attitudes

In 1807, Britain passed the Abolition of Slavery Act. It was the work of years of protest led by ordinary women and men, politicians and formerly enslaved people. This ended trade in enslaved people. In 1833, owning enslaved people in the colonies was finally banned. Gradually, slavery was outlawed by all other European countries, and finally abolished in the USA in 1865.

Trade triangle

→ Enslaved people are taken to work in the Americas and Caribbean.

→ Sugar, cotton, rum, tobacco and coffee head to Europe.

→ Guns, wine and textiles are taken to white settlers in Africa.

Property not people

Enslaved people had no rights – they owned nothing, couldn't marry, and even their children could be sold off to other slavers.

Sometimes enslaved people found ways around the rules set by their masters. These people are attending a secret "broomstick wedding."

Industrial Britain

The invention of the steam engine greatly changed the way people in Britain lived and worked. These changes quickly spread through Europe, then the world. This is known as the Industrial Revolution.

Steam trains carried goods and passengers cheaply from town to town.

Making changes

Before the Industrial Revolution, most goods, such as fabric, pottery and glass, were handmade. With the invention of new, steam-powered machines, goods could be made much faster and more cheaply than ever before. Many new factories sprung up all over the country.

The first steam-powered factories were for making fabric. Machines like these looms could do the work of hundreds of people.

Full steam ahead

The sudden demand for steam power for both factories and transportation meant a need for coal. Coal-mining in Britain boomed. A vast railway network was built across the country to carry all the new goods, coal and passengers.

- Scan the code to discover what life was like for Victorian children who had to work.
- For more links, go to **usborne.com/Quicklinks**

The Victorians

After the Industrial Revolution came the Victorian Era, when Queen Victoria ruled Britain. Some people were enjoying the wealth that the Industrial Revolution had brought, but for most Victorians, life was defined by hard work and poor living conditions.

Growing up as a Victorian

Boys from rich families went to school. Girls were usually taught at home.

Children from poor families had to work in coal mines and factories.

Homeless children were sent to live in a harsh place called a workhouse.

Living in a town

Rich people owned grand houses at the edges of towns. Many ordinary people moved to towns and cities to work in factories. They lived in rows of tiny houses, with no running water or inside toilets. The air was full of smoke from the factories, and the streets were filthy. People often got sick and died.

The houses are overcrowded in this Victorian town. People burn coal to keep warm and chimneys let out the smoke. The streets are lit by gas lamps.

People work long hours in cloth factories like this one.

World War I

World War I began in 1914. On one side were Britain, France, Belgium, Russia (and their colonies), who were called the Allies. On the other side were Germany and Austria. Later in the war, other countries joined in too.

- Scan the code to explore life in the trenches for World War I soldiers.
- For more links, go to **usborne.com/Quicklinks**

In the trenches

A lot of the fighting happened in northern France. Soldiers on both sides dug rows of deep ditches, called trenches, to protect themselves from enemy bullets.

The soldiers lived in the trenches for weeks at a time. During a battle, they climbed out and charged at the enemy. Millions of men died in these terrible battles.

Trenches were often very wet. They had walkways made of wooden planks called "duckboards" to stop the soldiers from sinking into the mud. Here you can see some British soldiers in a trench.

The men rest in holes dug into the sides of the trench.

The men's feet are always wet, and often get sore.

Duckboards

Officers live in underground shelters, called dugouts.

The trenches are full of rats, fleas and lice.

New weapons

Both sides tried new ways of fighting to win the war. The Germans were the first to use poison gas, while the British invented tanks.

German fighter plane

Both sides used planes to spy on enemy trenches and to shoot down enemy aircraft.

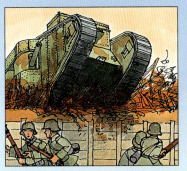

Tanks could run over barbed wire and machine guns, but they often broke down.

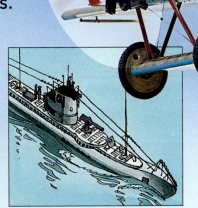

German submarines, called U-boats, attacked ships on their way to Britain and France.

Soldiers wore masks to protect them from poison gas.

German trench

A soldier called a sentry keeps watch.

Sandbags

Machine gun

Barbed wire

The war ends

In 1917, the United States of America joined the war on the side of the Allies and helped them win. The war finally ended at 11 o'clock on November 11, 1918. It had killed over 16 million people.

On November 11 every year, many people around the world remember those who have died in wars.

149

DIG FOR VICTORY

World War II

World War II started when Germany invaded Poland in 1939. Later, Japan attacked America. Lots of countries and colonies joined together to fight against Germany and Japan.

There wasn't much to eat during the war. This British poster is telling people to grow their own food.

The Blitz

In just a few months, the Germans took over most of western Europe. Then they began bombing cities in Britain. This was called the Blitz. The bombs wrecked buildings and killed thousands of people.

The British dropped bombs too. Below you can see the ruins of the city of Cologne in Germany.

- Scan the code to find out about city children who had to leave their homes during the war.
- For more links, go to **usborne.com/Quicklinks**

In Britain, children from big cities were sent away to the countryside to keep them safe from the bombs.

The Holocaust

The German leader, Adolf Hitler, and his supporters were known as "Nazis." The Nazis wanted to kill anyone who didn't match their idea of white-skinned perfection, including those who were Jewish, disabled or gay. During the war, they tried to kill all the Jews in Europe. They murdered six million Jewish people. This terrible crime is called the Holocaust.

Pearl Harbor

In 1941, Japanese planes launched a surprise attack against American battleships in Pearl Harbor, in Hawaii. The United States joined the war, and the fighting spread to islands in the Pacific Ocean and Japan itself.

Landing craft

American soldiers used special boats to land on the islands in the Pacific Ocean. The ramps at the front meant they could run straight onto the shore.

The war ends

Germany and Japan didn't have enough soldiers or weapons to win the war. The Germans were forced to stop fighting in May 1945. In August, the Americans dropped huge bombs on two cities in Japan, Hiroshima and Nagasaki. The Japanese finally gave up in September. The war was over, but it had killed more than 70 million people.

The bombs dropped on Japan were a new kind of bomb, called an atomic bomb. They are also known as nuclear bombs.

The Civil Rights Movement

In 1863, American President Abraham Lincoln declared all enslaved people in the USA to be free. However, Black Americans still faced another century of hatred and injustice, particularly in the South.

Sojourner Truth (a former enslaved woman) meeting with President Abraham Lincoln to talk about civil rights.

A country divided

During 1863, the Northern and Southern states were fighting the American Civil War. The war began in 1861 because the states disagreed about the use of enslaved labor. Some in the North wanted to end slavery, but the Southern states relied on enslaved people to work on the plantations. Eventually, the South was defeated and slavery was ended in 1865.

Black and white football fans in the 1950s had to sit in different areas to watch a game.

Still not equal

Despite freeing enslaved workers, the South struggled to accept Black Americans into society and limited their work, pay and freedom. By 1896, Black people were segregated, meaning they were unable to use the same public spaces as white people. They had to use separate bathrooms, schools and seating areas. This division continued for many years.

- Scan the code to find out more about Rosa Parks and her protest for civil rights.
- For more links, go to **usborne.com/Quicklinks**

This statue of Rosa Parks, sitting on a bus seat, can be seen in Alabama, USA.

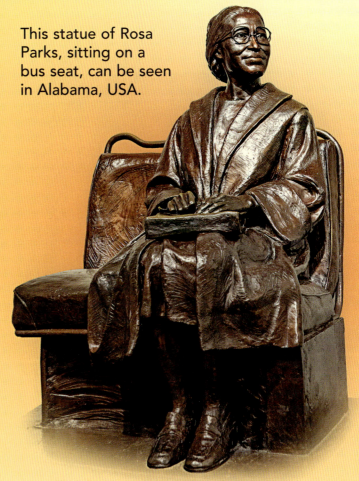

Taking a stand

In 1955, a Black woman named Rosa Parks was arrested for refusing to give up her seat on the bus to a white man. Alongside Dr. Martin Luther King Jr., she was one of many ordinary African Americans who became part of the Civil Rights Movement, protesting against racial discrimination and demanding equal rights.

Making change

The Civil Rights Movement organized peaceful protests all across the country. Laws were also slowly being passed to end segregation. In 1964, 100 years after slavery was ended, the Civil Rights Act finally gave more rights to Black Americans.

Dr. Martin Luther King Jr., speaking in 1963.

Acts of violence

Trouble between Black and white people continued, particularly in the South. In 1965 in the state of Alabama, peaceful protesters were violently attacked by the police. TV cameras filmed it all, and it became known as "Bloody Sunday." Then, in 1968, Dr. King was shot dead.

Black Americans achieved an equal right to vote in the 1960s, bringing an end to the Civil Rights Movement. However, the fight for racial justice and freedom from discrimination in the USA and other countries still continues to this day.

The modern world

These are some of the discoveries and inventions that have changed people's lives since the end of World War II.

1952 The first passenger jet began flying.

1953 The first climbers reached the top of Mount Everest, the highest place on Earth.

1967 A doctor named Christiaan Barnard carried out the first heart transplant.

1969 Neil Armstrong was the first person to walk on the Moon.

1972 A game called Pong was the first computer game.

1977 The first MRI scan was performed on a patient.

1979 The first cell phones went on sale in Japan.

1981 The first PC, or personal computer, was made.

1985 DNA fingerprinting was first used.

1989 The World Wide Web was invented.

1997 A sheep named Dolly was the first large animal to be cloned. A cloned animal is an exact copy of another animal.

This is a picture of the space rocket that took Neil Armstrong to the Moon.

1998 Google was founded.

1998 The first part of the International Space Station was launched into space.

2002 The Euro was adopted as the main currency by the European Union.

2002 The African Union was founded.

2003 The Human Genome Project was completed.

2007 The iPhone was launched.

2014 The first self-driving car was sold to the public.

2015 Liquid water was discovered on Mars.

2020 The first COVID vaccine was delivered.

2021 The first malaria vaccine was approved.

- Scan the code to find out how to become an inventor.
- For more links, go to **usborne.com/Quicklinks**

How People Live

People around the world

There are around eight billion people living in the world today. No two of us are the same, as nobody looks, thinks or feels exactly the same as anybody else.

- Scan the code to learn how to say "hello" to people around the world.
- For more links, go to **usborne.com/Quicklinks**

What is a person?

Humans are probably the most intelligent creatures on Earth. We can make things, solve problems and create beautiful works of art. Most scientists believe that it took an extremely long time for us to develop into the amazing people we are today.

These Aboriginal boys from Australia are taking part in a ceremony to mark their change into adults. The patterns painted on their skin are believed to help them grow.

The way we look

Everyone looks different from everyone else in the world. For example, some people are taller or shorter than others, with darker or lighter skin or eyes of a particular shape. Even identical twins don't look exactly alike.

These children have different skin and hair color and different shaped eyes, noses and mouths.

What we say

There are up to seven thousand languages. Some are used by only a few people. Others, such as Mandarin Chinese, are spoken by many millions.

Six-month-old babies could learn to speak any language.

What we do

In different parts of the world, people have their own ways of doing things. These are called traditions and customs. Along with beliefs, they can affect how people behave, what they wear, what they eat and how they celebrate important times in their lives. For example, the way we greet other people varies from place to place.

In countries such as Germany, people usually shake hands when they meet.

French people often greet each other with several kisses on the cheeks.

In India, people put their hands together and bow their heads to greet each other.

What we think

People have many different beliefs about the world around them. These beliefs are often called a religion. You can find out more about the religions of the world on pages 182–183.

Homes

Homes have many uses – they are places where we eat, sleep and keep our things. Any type of dwelling, such as a house, a hut, a caravan or a tent, can be a home.

Building homes

In some countries, builders make houses, often using wood, stone or bricks. In other places, people build their own homes. They use materials that are easy to find, such as wood, mud or grass.

These round homes in the Kalahari Desert in Botswana are built from woven sticks covered with mud. The roofs are made from grasses.

What's in a house?

A house has areas where you can sleep, prepare food, eat and relax. In some homes, everything is done in one room, but many houses have a different room for each activity.

Roof tiles and wooden boards keep out the wind and rain.

Rain collects in a roof gutter and flows down a pipe into the drain.

Shutters can be closed to keep out the hot Sun.

Weather and environment

Houses have to be built in a style that works with the local weather and environment.

This beach house in California, USA has been built on stilts so it stays dry when the tide comes in.

Some Japanese homes have walls of washi paper to control humidity (water in the air), temperature and light.

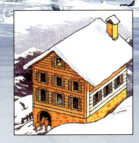

Snow settles on the sloping roof of this Swiss chalet and helps keep the heat inside the house.

In hot countries, many houses are painted white to reflect the Sun, so the house stays cool inside.

On the move

Some people, known as nomads, don't live in one place all the time. They move from place to place, taking their homes with them. Other people, known as refugees, have to leave home. They may be fleeing danger, or looking for work.

This family from Central Asia travels from one place to another, living in a tent called a yurt.

- Scan the code to see how a yurt is assembled.
- For more links, go to **usborne.com/Quicklinks**

159

Cities and towns

A city is a big, busy town where many people live and work. Over half of all the people in the world live in a town or city. In cities there are often a lot of people living in a small area.

City living

People living in towns and cities need houses, hospitals and schools. They also need places where they can enjoy themselves, such as parks and museums. There must be work for people to do, too, so they can afford to live there.

In the middle of a city, there are often large and well-known stores as well as many smaller ones.

Cities have restaurants and shopping malls where people can enjoy themselves.

Tall apartment buildings are one way that cities can have lots of people living on a small amount of land.

City problems

Many people like living in a city. There is plenty to do, and everything you need is nearby. But city life is not always easy. For example, it can sometimes be hard to find a job or a home that you can afford to live in. Cities can also be crowded and noisy, and living spaces can be cramped.

- Scan the code to find out what it's like to live in a city.
- For more links, go to **usborne.com/Quicklinks**

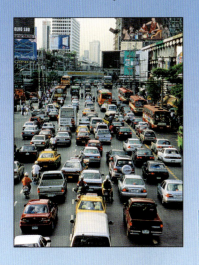

Often in cities, roads are jammed with too many cars.

Getting around

Driving around a city in a car can be slow and may not be good for the environment. Taking buses, trains and trams or riding bikes and scooters is better for the environment and can help reduce traffic. Some towns and cities are adding in cycle lanes and making larger areas where no vehicles are allowed at all, so people can safely cycle or walk instead.

Most cities have parks for people to enjoy. This is Central Park in New York City, USA.

161

How a country is run

The way a country is run and the people who lead it are very important for the people who live there. The leaders decide what laws are made and how much money can be spent, for example, on schools and roads.

Who's in charge?

The people who run a country are called the government. A government that people choose, or vote for, is called a democracy.

If one person or a group of people rules a country without giving anyone a choice, it is called an autocracy.

Barack Obama was President of the USA from 2009–2017. The President is the head of the government.

In 1994, for the first time, all South African people were allowed to vote for their government. People lined up for hours waiting to vote.

- Scan the code for more about voting and democracy.
- For more links, go to **usborne.com/Quicklinks**

Making a choice

In a democracy, people choose their government in an election.

On election day, adults cast a vote, by putting a mark or a number on a paper next to the name of the person they want to support.

Without showing anyone who they voted for, they put their paper into a locked ballot box.

After an election, all the votes on the ballot papers are counted. The person with the most support wins.

Money and power

A democratic government makes laws based on how it thinks society should work. It collects taxes (a set amount of money) from working people, to spend on things that benefit everyone, such as hospitals and public transportation.

This is the White House in Washington, D.C., where the US President makes decisions.

At the top

In the past, many countries were ruled by kings, queens or emperors. When a ruler died, the power to rule was usually passed on to a son or daughter. Today, there are not many really powerful royal families.

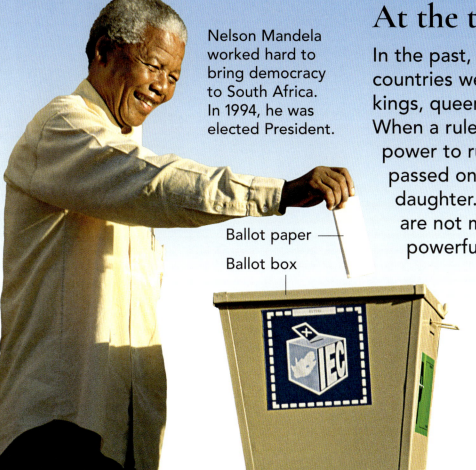

Nelson Mandela worked hard to bring democracy to South Africa. In 1994, he was elected President.

Ballot paper

Ballot box

This scepter belongs to the British king or queen. It is a symbol of his or her power.

163

Food and cooking

The food people eat and the way they cook is very different around the world. Everyone needs food, but over 700 million people in the world do not have enough.

A healthy diet can include brown bread, nuts and eggs, and plenty of fruit and vegetables.

Growing and buying

The main food of a country is called its staple food. Rice is the staple food of about half the world. Other staples include maize, wheat and potatoes. Some people grow their own fruit and vegetables, but most staple foods are grown on farms, then sold in stores and at markets.

A vegetable market in Hong Kong, China

How people cook

Cooking food can make it taste better and keep longer. It helps kill germs that might make you sick, too. Cooked food is also easier to digest (see page 98). There are many different ways of cooking.

This Indian woman is cooking meat in a clay oven called a tandoor.

In China, food is often cooked in bowl-shaped metal pans called woks.

- Scan the code to see different kinds of bread around the world.
- For more links, go to **usborne.com/Quicklinks**

This famous Spanish dish is called paella. It is cooked in a shallow pan, sometimes over a wood fire.

Feasts and festivals

When people celebrate, food is often a big part of the festival. It is important in several religions too. For example, during the holy month of Ramadan, Muslims eat nothing during the day until sunset. When Ramadan ends, they hold a feast to celebrate.

Mealtime customs

There are many different ways of eating across the world. Some people kneel on the floor to eat, and some sit at high tables. Many people eat with their hands, while others use tools, such as a knife and fork.

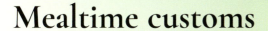

In China, people use long sticks called chopsticks.

Clothes

People may have first worn clothes to protect themselves from the weather. Clothes became a way of showing where you came from, your job, how rich you were, and your personality.

Sadhu holy men wearing traditional clothes in Nepal

Clothes for climates

People usually wear clothes that suit their way of life. This often means dressing for the climate where they live. In cold climates people wear layered clothes to trap air, which keeps them warm.

Loose robes shield people from the scorching Sun in hot, dry, desert climates.

- Scan the code to see Maasai clothing and beads.
- For more links, go to usborne.com/Quicklinks

Traditional clothes

In some places, people still wear the style of clothes they have worn for centuries. They follow tradition rather than fashion. A country's traditional dress is called its national costume.

This Maasai woman wears many traditional beaded necklaces.

This Japanese woman wears a gown called a kimono.

This Moroccan water carrier is wearing a traditional hat.

This Indian woman wears a sari over a small top.

Learning

Children go to school, or are taught at home, in order to learn the things they need to know when they grow up. Around the world, schools and ways of learning can be very different.

- Scan the code to find out about going to school in different parts of the world.
- For more links, go to **usborne.com/Quicklinks**

Science is an exciting subject you can learn at school.

Children in this village in Nepal sit outside on the ground to learn.

This boy in a remote part of Australia learns from his home.

Taking tests

In most schools, you have to take tests sometimes. These are important, and show how well you understand the things you have learned. You need to pass these tests if you want to go to college or university, or do certain jobs.

Survival skills

Not all the children in the world go to a school. In poorer countries, some children have to work to help their families. They do not learn to read or write, but are taught life skills, such as hunting and farming.

A young girl from a tribal family in Liberia, Africa is helping prepare palm fruit for her family to eat.

Jobs people do

People work to earn money for themselves and their families. Many people enjoy their work. Some jobs require training, particular skills, or studying to a high level.

This boy has a part-time job before school each day. He delivers newspapers to people's homes.

Changing times

In many parts of the world, the way people work has changed through the ages. For centuries, most people farmed their own land. Then, about 200 years ago, factories started being built and many people started working in those. Nowadays, lots of people also work using a computer, often in an office or at home.

Surgeons

Motorcycle courier

Work clothing

For some jobs, people have to wear special clothes. This may be a uniform that makes them easy to spot. It may be things such as hard hats and goggles that help protect them while they work.

Welder

Chefs' hats stop hairs from dropping into the food while they are cooking. Aprons protect their other clothes.

Builder

Can you guess why all these people wear special clothes?

Police officers

Teamwork

Many people work as part of a team. Each person in the team has a different job to do. This team of workers is building a brick house.

- Scan the code to find out about lots of different jobs.
- For more links, go to **usborne.com/Quicklinks**

In this picture, parts of the walls and roof of the house have been cut away so you can see inside.

A roofer fixes the tiles to the roof.

Bricklayers stick the bricks together with a mixture called mortar.

A carpenter builds the wooden parts of the house and fits the doors and windows.

This worker is getting ready to lay waste water pipes.

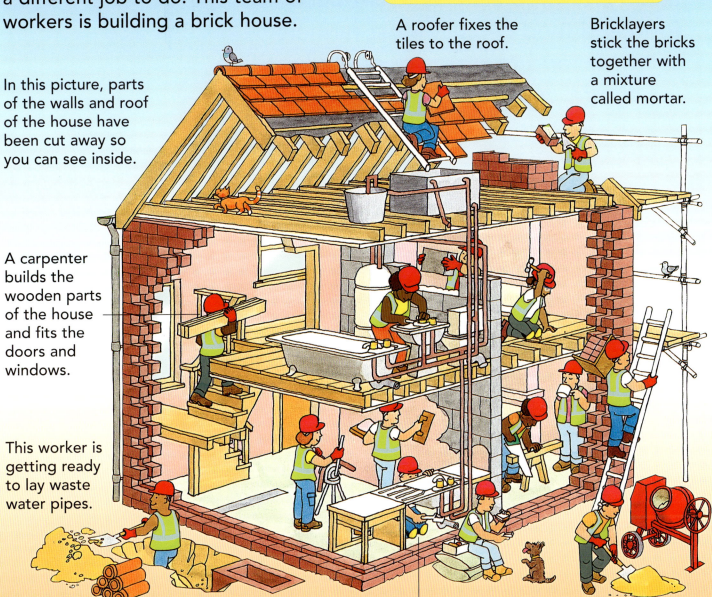

A plumber puts in the water pipes.

This worker is mixing the mortar for the bricklayers.

Children at work

In many countries, teenagers can have a part-time job, such as working in a store at the weekend. Some young people start full-time work at 16 or 18, after they have left school.

In other countries, children start work much younger, usually with their families. These children often attend school only part-time, or not at all. Over 150 million of the world's children do some kind of work.

Farming

Farmers grow plants called crops, and many keep animals to produce food and feed people. Most farmers sell their food to stores or at markets for other people to buy.

These farmers in Thailand are planting rice shoots by hand.

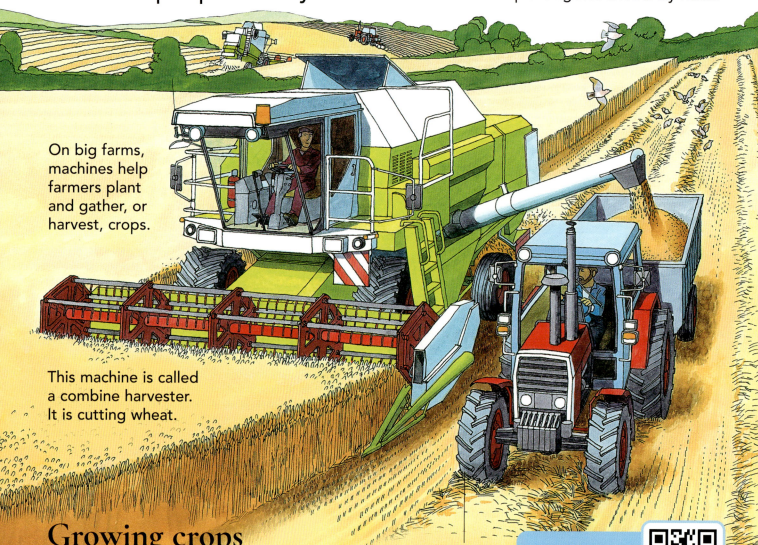

On big farms, machines help farmers plant and gather, or harvest, crops.

This machine is called a combine harvester. It is cutting wheat.

This tractor is pulling a trailer to collect the wheat grains.

- Scan the code to watch a combine harvester at work.
- For more links, go to **usborne.com/Quicklinks**

Growing crops

The type of crop a farmer can grow depends on the soil, the type of land and the weather. Rice needs hot, wet weather, while wheat grows best in cooler, drier places.

Keeping animals

Keeping animals is called livestock farming. Animals give us milk, wool, eggs and leather, as well as meat. Some farmers keep just one kind of animal.

Farmers keep sheep for meat, wool and milk.

Hens are kept for their eggs as well as their meat.

Goats are kept for their milk, meat and skin.

Milk, meat and leather come from cows. One cow can make over 3,000 gallons of milk each year.

Using chemicals

Some farmers need to produce as much food as they can in a short time. They use machines to spray crops with chemicals to help them grow and to kill pests and diseases.

These sunflowers are being sprayed with fertilizer to help them grow. Lots of countries have strict rules about chemical farming.

Organic farming

Farming without chemicals is called organic farming. It is harder to produce lots of food this way, but many people think organic foods are healthier than other kinds.

Lots of different vegetables can be farmed organically.

Sports and games

People play sports and games for fun, to stay in shape, because they want to win, or as part of a festival. There are hundreds of sports. Many need fitness and skill.

- Scan the code to meet athletes and find out about Olympic sports.
- For more links, go to **usborne.com/Quicklinks**

Playing together

Some games and sports, such as darts, are played by just one person. Others, such as baseball and rowing, involve teams. In a team sport, everyone has to work together to succeed.

In a team game, such as ice hockey, each player has their own job to do. These players move a puck toward the other team's net, or goal. The goalie tries to stop them.

How to play

Different sports have different rules. In some sports, such as basketball or netball, you score points from shooting the ball into the basket or goal. In others, like swimming and track, the winner is the fastest person or team.

In games such as soccer, the team that scores the most goals wins.

The Olympic Games

The world's main sporting event is the Olympic Games (see page 125). Athletes show off their skills at many sports, such as running and archery. The Games are held every four years, in different cities around the world. They are followed by the Paralympic Games, where atheletes with disabilities compete.

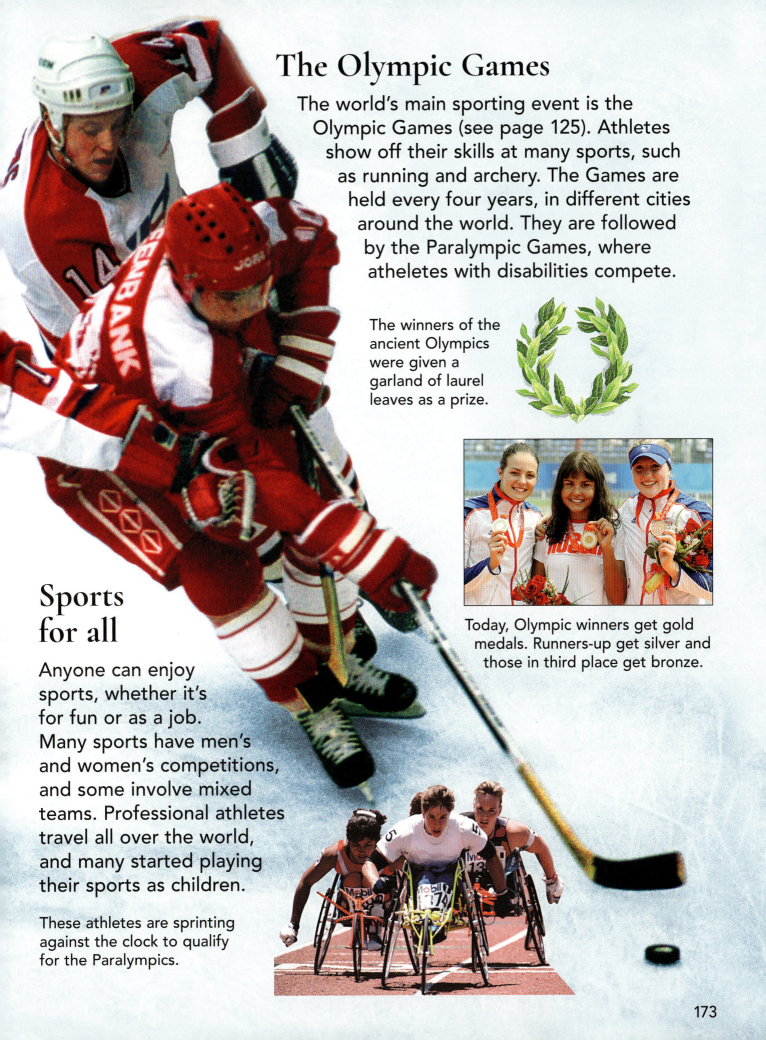

The winners of the ancient Olympics were given a garland of laurel leaves as a prize.

Today, Olympic winners get gold medals. Runners-up get silver and those in third place get bronze.

Sports for all

Anyone can enjoy sports, whether it's for fun or as a job. Many sports have men's and women's competitions, and some involve mixed teams. Professional athletes travel all over the world, and many started playing their sports as children.

These athletes are sprinting against the clock to qualify for the Paralympics.

173

Storytelling

The first stories were passed down through generations of families and communities by word of mouth – people would remember and retell them, instead of writing them down.

Tales are still told in groups around campfires, often based on local legends.

Myths and legends

Traditional stories can evolve as they are retold, and fact and fiction can become difficult to tell apart. Stories about historical people and events are known as legends.

Myths are stories often linked to spirituality and nature. They are tales of good and evil, filled with amazing events and powerful non-human creatures.

The Romans believed that tidal waves and earthquakes happened when the sea god, Neptune, was angry.

- Scan the code to discover more about myths and storytelling.
- For more links, go to **usborne.com/Quicklinks**

This 19th century picture shows some of the different ways scribes (writers) worked.

Carving into wax with a metal stylus (a type of pen)

Chiseling into stone

Quill and ink on parchment

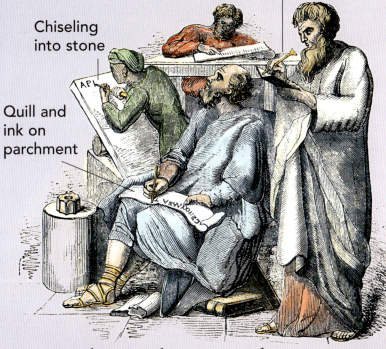

Writing it down

To record what they said, early people made marks that stood for words. The first types of writing were rows of pictures, or symbols. These then became letters, which stood for sounds.

The Ancient Egyptians made the first paper, called papyrus. People also wrote on parchment made from dried animal skins. They used pens made from feathers (quills) or reeds, dipped in ink.

Spreading the word

Printing newspapers and books allowed facts, news, ideas and stories to be shared with many people. Books were first printed in China over 1,000 years ago, using carved blocks of wood dipped in ink and printed onto fabric. In Europe, the invention of the first printing press meant many copies of a book could be printed quickly.

In Europe, the printing press was first used in about 1450.

Libraries hold books that people can borrow to read and then return. These children in Brazil are borrowing books from a mobile library that travels from village to village.

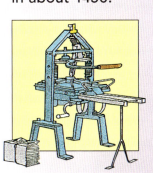

Art and design

Every work of art is different. Artists may try to create something which is beautiful, or shocking, or shows people how they feel. Whoever sees their work usually feels something, too – they may like it, or they may hate it.

This painting from 1892 is by famous French artist Paul Gauguin. It is called *When will you marry?* and shows a mother and daughter in Tahiti.

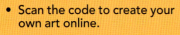

- Scan the code to create your own art online.
- For more links, go to **usborne.com/Quicklinks**

What is art?

People can disagree about what is a work of art and what is not. There are different styles. Some traditional artists work from real life and copy what they see. Others use colors, lines and shapes to express thoughts and feelings. This style is often called modern art.

Artwork can be made out of many different materials, such as stone, clay, wood, metal, fabric, paper or cardboard.

3D pieces of art are often called sculptures. This is a famous sculpture by Rodin called *The Thinker*. It is made of a metal called bronze. You can see the original in Paris.

Traditional art

Some types of art are traditional, which means they are part of a certain culture or community. Traditional art-making methods and skills are passed down through generations of people.

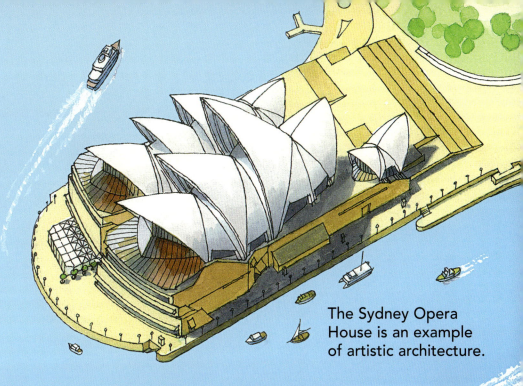

The Sydney Opera House is an example of artistic architecture.

Experimenting

Artists often like to try out new ways of making art, which can include film-making, digital illustrations or photography. Some artists make large artworks out of unusual materials such as clothing, lights or even vehicles. This is called installation art.

A group of artists half-buried ten cars in a field in Texas, USA in 1974. They called their sculpture *Cadillac Ranch*. You can still see it there.

Artistic design

Artistic design is about making everyday useful objects look attractive. Some examples include buildings (architecture), bridges, furniture and clothing. If an art and design style becomes fashionable, it gets used over and over again, such as in the "Art Deco" period in the 1930s.

Acting and dancing

All over the world, people act and dance to entertain each other. They might use acting and dancing to celebrate an event, tell a story, communicate a message or to show feelings.

These people are making a commercial. The camera operators are filming the actors. Everyone may have to repeat a scene many times before it is right.

Recording the action

Movies, TV shows and some commercials tell stories that are acted out and recorded, so we can watch the performance over and over again. People can watch movies and TV shows together at home, or on a big screen in a movie theater.

On the stage

A story which is acted out is called a play, and is written by a playwright. Some plays are based on true stories, while others are made up. Plays are performed "live" to audiences, so each performance is a little different. Plays with singing and dancing are known as musicals.

Plays are often performed on stage in a theater. Clothes, make-up, masks, scenery, lights and music may be used to create the world of the story.

These actors are performing in a famous comedy called *A Midsummer Night's Dream* by William Shakespeare (see page 139).

Dance for joy

Most kinds of dancing are done to music. Some dances are fast, while others are slow and graceful. You can learn the steps and movements of a dance or make up your own. People may dance to show how they feel, to stay in shape, or at celebrations and festivals.

Ballet dancing uses many carefully-planned movements. Some take years of training and incredible strength to do well.

Dance styles

Many cultures have their own traditional, or classical, dances, with special shoes or costumes. Contemporary is a style of dance that is often performed barefoot and focuses on storytelling and emotions rather than particular movements.

Dancers in Bali use every part of their body in their dance, including their eyes, face, neck and hands.

- Scan the code to watch ballet dancers in a performance of *The Nutcracker*.

- For more links, go to **usborne.com/Quicklinks**

Music

Music is a pattern of sounds put together to make a tune or rhythm. You can make music with just your body by singing, clapping, whistling or humming. Musical instruments can help you make other musical sounds.

- Scan the code for games and activities about music.
- For more links, go to usborne.com/Quicklinks

Here are some different groups of musical instruments.

These are string instruments. You pluck their strings or rub them with a bow.

These are both woodwind instruments. You blow into them to make a sound.

Percussion instruments make sounds when you hit, shake or scrape them.

These are brass instruments. You play them by buzzing your lips on the mouthpiece.

These boys are making music with cymbals, drums, horns, clapping and singing, during Bohag Bihu, an Indian spring festival.

Why make music?

Music can make us want to dance, sing, or even cry. People often create or listen to it to show how they feel. It may be used to celebrate big events such as weddings, and in religious ceremonies.

In West African music, rhythms are usually more important than tunes. These Gambian women are dancing to the rhythm of a drum.

Performing together

Performances of music are called concerts, either by a single musician or singer, or a group. A group of musicians playing or singing together is known as a band. A large organized group of singers is called a choir.

A large group of musicians playing different instruments is called an orchestra.

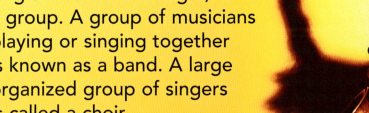

Types of music

There are different types of music. "Classical" music often doesn't involve any words, though opera is a type of classical music that tells a story. Lots of music originates from a certain time period, country or culture, such as rock, pop, reggae, soul, hip-hop, dance, folk and so on.

Jazz is a style of popular music. It began early in the last century in New Orleans, USA. This jazz musician is playing a saxophone.

Religions

A religion is a belief in something greater than any person. It may be a belief in one God, or in several gods. For some people, their religion influences how they live their life. Here are some of the many religions of the world.

Like many boys in Buddhist countries, this boy is spending time as a monk, learning about his religion.

Buddhism

Buddhism teaches people to think deeply about life and what is really important. This thinking is called meditation. Buddhism is based on the ideas of a South Asian prince who became known as the Buddha.

Christianity

People who follow Christianity are called Christians. They believe God watches over them and wants them to be good. Christians believe that a man named Jesus was the Son of God. Christians have a holy book called the *Bible*.

The birth of Jesus is called the Nativity. Christians celebrate this at Christmas.

- Scan the code to watch a video about Buddhist monks.
- For more links, go to **usborne.com/Quicklinks**

Hinduism

Hinduism has many gods and beliefs. The main god is Brahman. Hindus believe in reincarnation, when people live many lives one after the other, which only ends when the believer becomes close to Brahman.

The Hindu god Krishna is usually shown with blue skin. Here he is playing his flute.

Islam

Followers of the religion of Islam are called Muslims. They obey the laws of God, who is called Allah. A man named Muhammad taught Allah's laws. These were written down in the Muslim holy book, the *Qur'an*.

This Muslim girl is praying to Allah.

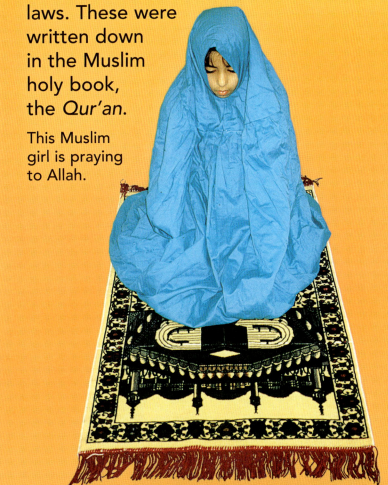

Judaism

Followers of Judaism are called Jews. They worship God in a building called a synagogue. The Jewish holy day, or Shabbat, is from sunset on Friday to sunset on Saturday.

This boy is in a synagogue, reading from the Jewish holy writings. He is wearing a cap and shawl to show that he respects God.

Sikhism

A person who follows Sikhism is called a Sikh, which means "learner." Sikhs believe in one God, whom they worship in a building called a gurdwara. There, they listen to readings from the Sikh holy book, the *Guru Granth Sahib*.

This is a symbol of Sikhism. It is called the khanda.

What is science?

Science is what we know about the world around us. What is gravity? Is there life on other planets? How do our brains work? Science tries to answer all these questions and many more.

Scientists have found out why leaves turn red or brown in the fall.

Being a scientist

People who do science are called scientists. They study things by looking at them closely, asking questions, and doing experiments to find out how they work.

Scientists who study animals, such as this macaw, are called zoologists. Studies of macaws have shown that their bright feathers may help them find a mate.

- Scan the code to see how science can explain why flamingos are pink.
- For more links, go to **usborne.com/Quicklinks**

Branches of science

There are hundreds of different kinds, or branches, of science, and many different kinds of scientists. Here are just a few of them.

Botanists study plants.

Biologists study living things.

Chemists study chemicals.

Technology

Scientists can use their understanding of the world to design or invent new things. Without science, we wouldn't have many of the machines and medicines we have today. Using science in this way is called technology.

Scientists can use their scientific knowledge to help them invent things, such as this cell phone and charger.

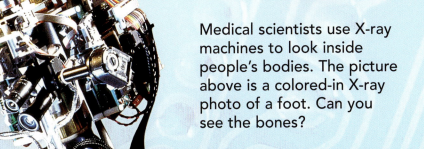

This is a machine called a robot. It can move around and make its own simple decisions. Some robots can be used to do dangerous jobs instead of humans.

Medical scientists use X-ray machines to look inside people's bodies. The picture above is a colored-in X-ray photo of a foot. Can you see the bones?

What scientists do

To find out about things, scientists do experiments. These are tests that show how living things, objects or substances behave.

Asking questions

Scientists use experiments to help them answer questions. For example, a scientist might ask, "What kind of fish do penguins like to eat?"

As an experiment, they could offer a penguin two different types of fish and see which one the penguin chooses to eat.

This penguin is part of an experiment to answer the question "Where do penguins go?"

Scientists have fitted this penguin with a special jacket containing a radio transmitter. (It doesn't hurt the penguin at all.)

The transmitter sends signals for the scientists to collect. From this, they can track the penguin's movements.

Theories

Scientists think up theories that might answer their questions, or explain how things work. For example, they might have a theory that penguins travel to a certain area because there is more food there. Then they do experiments to test their theories.

Scientists write down their results and repeat their experiments to make sure they work.

- Scan the code to discover some of the exciting jobs scientists do.
- For more links, go to **usborne.com/Quicklinks**

Observing

Observing means watching and measuring things very carefully. It's an important part of being a scientist.

Scientists often use tools to help them observe things. For example, astronomers (space scientists) use powerful telescopes to study planets, stars and galaxies.

This is a comet. Comets are balls of ice and dust that zoom through space. By observing the path of a comet, astronomers can work out where it will go next.

Do your own experiment

Find out if adding salt to water will make a difference to how things float in it. You will need:

2 half-full glasses of water; 2 fresh eggs; 10 heaped teaspoons of salt

1. Stir the salt into one glass of water until it has dissolved and is invisible.

2. Put an egg in each glass. Do both eggs float? Do they both behave the same way?

You can find out more about floating on pages 204–205.

Telescopes make far away things look closer. There is a huge telescope in this observatory that a team of astronomers uses to watch the night sky.

Atoms and molecules

Everything is made out of tiny particles called atoms. Atoms can join together in groups called molecules.

- Scan the code to find out what atoms have to do with you.
- For more links, go to **usborne.com/Quicklinks**

What is an atom?

An atom is like a tiny ball. It has a center, or nucleus, and outer layers called shells. There are over 100 types of atoms.

Atoms are so tiny that you can't see them. A piece of paper, such as this page, is about a million atoms thick.

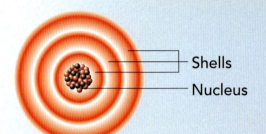

Shells

Nucleus

In atom diagrams, different colors are used to show different types of atoms.

Atoms are made up of even smaller particles. You can see some of them in the nucleus of the atom above.

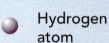 Hydrogen atom

 Iron atom

 Gold atom

 Oxygen atom

Making molecules

Atoms sometimes join together to make bigger units called molecules. This joining together is called bonding.

These pictures show two types of atoms bonding to make water molecules.

Did you know?

- Most of an atom is empty space.

- Some types of atoms, such as francium, do not exist naturally. They can only be made by scientists in a lab.

- Atoms constantly move around, even in solids. They jiggle, vibrate and bump into each other.

Hydrogen atoms

+

Oxygen atoms

=

Water molecules

=

Water

Water is made up of lots of water molecules.

Materials

All the things around us – rocks, air, water, sand, glass, wood, plastic, and even our bodies – are made of atoms and molecules. Scientists call all these different types of stuff "materials."

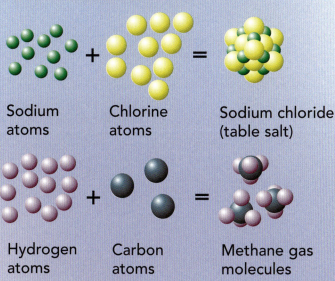

Sodium atoms + Chlorine atoms = Sodium chloride (table salt)

Hydrogen atoms + Carbon atoms = Methane gas molecules

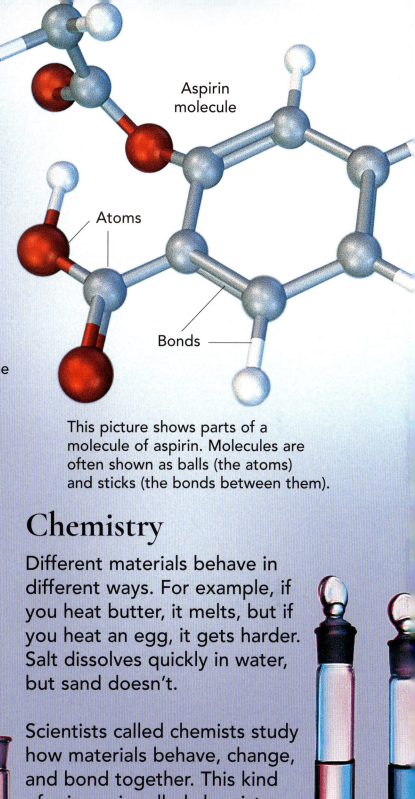

Aspirin molecule

Atoms

Bonds

This picture shows parts of a molecule of aspirin. Molecules are often shown as balls (the atoms) and sticks (the bonds between them).

Chemistry

Different materials behave in different ways. For example, if you heat butter, it melts, but if you heat an egg, it gets harder. Salt dissolves quickly in water, but sand doesn't.

Scientists called chemists study how materials behave, change, and bond together. This kind of science is called chemistry.

Materials hunt

Can you find things made of these materials in your home or classroom?

 Paper

 Ceramic

 Plastic

 Wood

 Glass

 Metal

Chemists mix materials together in glass beakers and flasks like these.

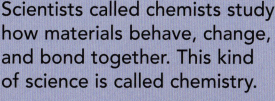

Solids, liquids and gases

Most materials can exist in three different forms: solid, liquid and gas. In solids, molecules are packed closely together. In liquids and gases, they're more spread out.

- Scan the code to explore more about solids, liquids and gases.
- For more links, go to **usborne.com/Quicklinks**

Solids

Gold is a solid.

The molecules in solids are firmly attached to each other and don't move around much. Because of this, most solids stay the same shape.

Molecules in solids are packed tightly together.

Liquids

Liquids, like water, flow into every part of a container.

The molecules in liquids are not so squashed together. They can move around more and are not as firmly fixed to each other. This is why liquids can flow, splash and be poured.

Molecules in liquids are not packed together.

Gases

The molecules in gases are not attached to each other at all and move around all the time at high speed. This means that gases quickly spread out to fill the space they are in. They have no shape of their own.

Many gases are invisible. These flames aren't gas, but they show the shape a gas makes as it burns.

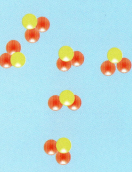

Gas molecules don't stick to each other at all.

Make a gas

You can make carbon dioxide gas and blow up a balloon with it. You will need:

an empty jam jar; some baking soda; some vinegar; a balloon; a spoon

1. Fill a quarter of the jar with vinegar. Put the baking soda into the balloon, using the spoon.

2. Stretch the neck of the balloon over the top of the jar. Don't let any baking soda spill into the jar.

3. Quickly lift the balloon up to tip all the baking soda into the jar. The vinegar will react with the soda, making bubbles.

When the vinegar and baking soda react (see page 195), they make carbon dioxide gas which fills the balloon, blowing it up a little.

Three forms

The same material can exist as a solid, a liquid or a gas. For example, water exists as a liquid, as solid ice, and as a gas called water vapor.

There is water vapor in the air. As it cools, it forms clouds and may turn into rain.

Ice is frozen water. It is a solid.

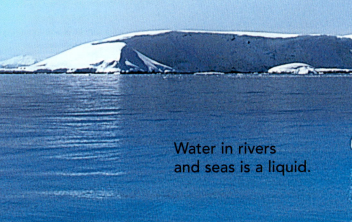

Water in rivers and seas is a liquid.

How materials change

Materials can change all the time. They can grow, shrink and change between a solid, a liquid and a gas. They can also combine to make new materials.

Changing state

Materials can change between solid and liquid, or between liquid and gas. These changes are called changes of state. They often happen when materials heat up or cool down.

 When juice gets very cold, it turns from a liquid to a solid. This is called freezing.

 Wax turns from a solid into a liquid as a candle burns. This is called melting.

 When you heat water, it turns from a liquid into a gas. This is called boiling.

 When water vapor cools, it turns into a liquid – rain. This is called condensing.

Inside a freezer, it's cold enough for water to freeze into ice.

Getting bigger

Water expands (gets bigger) when it freezes. Most materials, however, shrink as they get colder and expand as they get hotter. For example, some thermometers* contain a liquid that expands as the temperature rises.

A non-digital thermometer contains liquid in a narrow tube. (In this photo, the liquid is black.) As the liquid warms up, it gets bigger and fills more of the tube.

Make water get bigger

Here's what you will need:

a plastic bottle (don't use a glass bottle); a piece of foil; a freezer

1. Fill the bottle to the top with water. Cover the top with the foil.

2. Stand the bottle upright in the freezer. Leave it there overnight.

3. The water pushes the foil upward as it freezes and gets bigger.

*For more about thermometers, see page 201.

Mixing materials

Materials can be mixed together to make new materials. If you mix sand, cement, broken stones and water, you get concrete. Concrete is useful for building, because it is stronger than any of the ingredients by themselves.

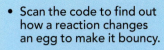

- Scan the code to find out how a reaction changes an egg to make it bouncy.

- For more links, go to **usborne.com/Quicklinks**

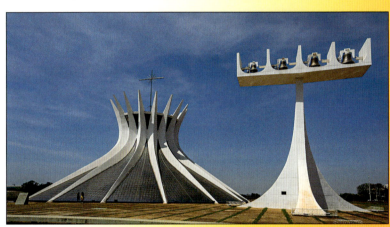

The Catedral Metropolitana in Brazil is made of 16 curved concrete columns.

Reactions

In a mixture, materials are combined but their molecules do not change. Sometimes, however, materials react with each other. This means that when they are in contact, their molecules change, and they turn into different materials.

Rusting happens to iron when it is left out in the rain or in damp air.

Iron reacts with oxygen molecules and water molecules.

The reaction makes a new type of molecule called iron oxide, or rust.

These rocks formed in Mono Lake in California, USA because of a reaction between two different chemicals in the lake.

Energy

Energy is the power that makes things happen. You can't see it, but it's all around you, making all kinds of objects move and work.

Plants change light energy from the Sun into food energy.

All kinds of energy

Energy comes in many types, or forms. For example, heat, light, electricity and sound are all forms of energy. You can't destroy or make energy. This means the amount of energy in the Universe is always the same. But one form of energy can change into another form.

Electrical energy flows into lights and changes into heat and light energy.

Movement energy

Whenever something moves, it has energy. The form of energy involved in movement is called kinetic energy.

People shouting and machines moving release a lot of sound energy.

Stored energy

Potential energy is energy that is stored, ready to use. When it's used, it turns into another form of energy, such as kinetic energy or heat.

To fly, these birds change energy stored in their bodies into kinetic energy.

- Scan the code to explore how energy makes rollercoasters so much fun.
- For more links, go to **usborne.com/Quicklinks**

At the top of this rollercoaster, the car contains potential energy.

As the car goes down the hill, its potential energy changes into kinetic energy.

These flags have kinetic energy as they flutter in the breeze.

These children have a lot of kinetic energy because they are running fast.

This man is using the stored energy in his body to lift the hammer. Now the hammer has potential energy.

Food turns into stored energy in our bodies. A caramel apple will give these boys enough energy to walk for 20 minutes.

Forces

A force is a push or a pull that makes an object do something. For example, if you kick a ball, the force of your kick makes the ball move. Forces can also make things change their direction, speed and shape.

Direct forces

Some forces work by touching the object they are pushing or pulling on. These are called direct forces. Kicking a ball, lifting a pen or pulling your sock off are all examples of direct forces.

From a distance

Some forces don't have to touch the things they work on. For example, gravity* pulls you down when you jump off a wall. A magnet pulls paperclips toward it.

Pushing a sled is a direct force.

Pulling a sled uphill on a rope is a direct force.

Gravity is a distant force. It is pulling the sleds downhill, but not touching them.

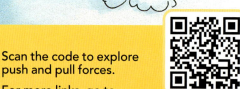

- Scan the code to explore push and pull forces.
- For more links, go to **usborne.com/Quicklinks**

*For more about gravity, see page 202.

Balanced forces

When something isn't moving, you might think that there are no forces working on it. In fact, there are, but they are balanced against each other, and cancel each other out.

These two tug-of-war teams are not moving, because the forces they have are balanced. To win, one of the teams must use more force.

Using forces

We use forces all the time to move things, lift things and travel around. Machines help us use forces to do things we can't do on our own. They use energy to create the right kinds of force to do different jobs.

Scissors are simple machines. Their sharp blades use pushing and pulling forces from your fingers to cut things.

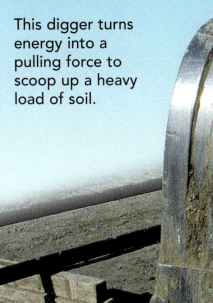

This digger turns energy into a pulling force to scoop up a heavy load of soil.

Hot and cold

Heat is a form of energy. If you heat something up, you are giving it more energy. Cold is simply a lack of heat energy.

Heating up

When most materials heat up, their molecules spread out. This makes them expand, or get bigger. When they cool down, they contract, or get smaller, again. As air heats up, it expands a lot. Hot air rises above cold air. This is why hot air balloons float.

The hot air inside these balloons is less dense than the cold air they float in. For more about density, see page 204.

Moving around

Heat moves from hotter to colder places. For example, hot food gets cold because its heat moves into the cooler air around it. You can't usually see heat, but it can be photographed with an infrared camera.

This picture was taken using an infrared camera. The red areas show where the buildings are giving off the most heat.

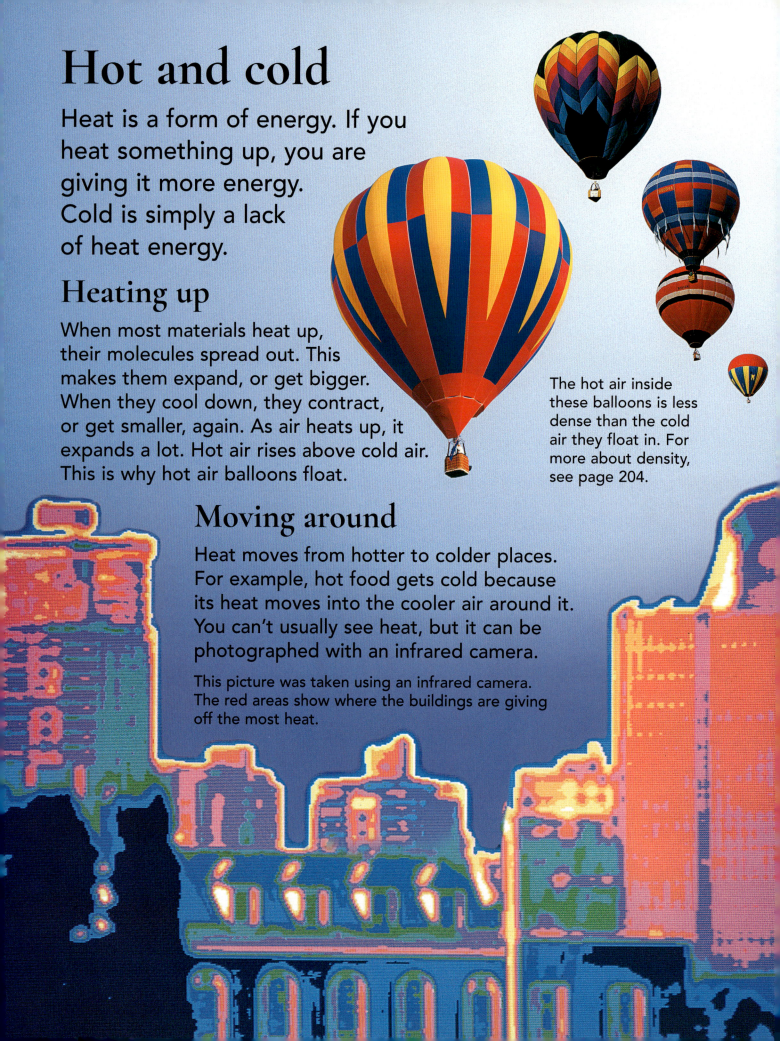

The Golden Gate Bridge in San Francisco, USA

Bridge gaps

Bridges often get slightly longer as they heat up in the Sun. Large bridges have special joints with gaps in them, so that there's room for them to expand.

Expansion joints like these allow bridges to expand and contract. Without them, bridges could break and collapse.

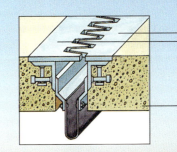

When a bridge expands in hot weather, these plates are pushed together.

Bridge

Expansion and contraction

You can do an experiment to see how air expands when it is heated and contracts when it cools down. You will need:

a bowl; a plastic bottle; a balloon

1. Ask an adult to hold the empty bottle under hot water for a minute. Stretch the balloon over its neck.

2. Half-fill the bowl with cold water and stand the bottle in it. The air cools and shrinks, pulling the balloon inside.

3. Empty the bowl and ask an adult to add hot water to it. The expanding warm air pushes the balloon out again.

- Scan the code to see pictures of animals taken by an infrared camera.
- For more links, go to **usborne.com/Quicklinks**

Measuring hotness

Temperature means how hot something is. It is measured in degrees Fahrenheit (°F) or Celsius (°C). Normal room temperature is about 68°F (20°C).

Temperature is measured using a thermometer. Can you see what the temperature is on this digital thermometer?

Gravity

When you jump up in the air, you drop back down again. This is because there's an invisible force pulling you down to the ground. This force is called gravity.

Size matters

Everything has gravity. The bigger an object is, the stronger its gravity is. Very big planets, like Jupiter, have much stronger gravity than Earth. Small planets and moons have weaker gravity than Earth.

Mars

Mercury

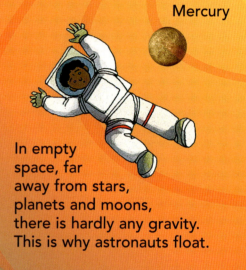

In empty space, far away from stars, planets and moons, there is hardly any gravity. This is why astronauts float.

Jupiter's gravity is more than twice as strong as Earth's. If you could visit Jupiter, you wouldn't be able to move because its gravity is so strong.

Jupiter's moon Io is small, and its gravity is much weaker than the Earth's. You could jump many times higher on Io than you can on Earth.

Jupiter

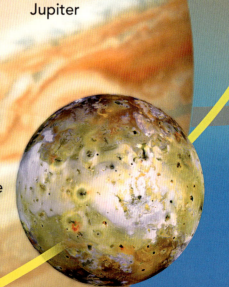

This is Io, one of Jupiter's many moons.

The Sun

Venus

The Earth is in orbit
around the Sun.

Our Moon
is in orbit
around
the Earth.

In orbit

In space, large objects orbit, or travel around, each other. Planets orbit the Sun. Moons orbit planets. This happens because of gravity. Gravity doesn't pull planets and moons right together, because they're moving too fast. This diagram shows how orbits work.

Moon

Planet

Moons move very fast. A moon is always trying to fly away from its planet in a straight line.

Meanwhile, the planet's gravity pulls the moon toward it. The two forces balance out and the moon circles around the planet.

- Scan the code to investigate the invisible force of gravity.
- For more links, go to **usborne.com/Quicklinks**

Testing gravity

Gravity pulls objects at the same speed, even if they have different weights. Try testing this yourself.

You will need:

tissue paper; a coin; two identical boxes (such as small food containers with lids)

1. Carefully tear or cut a piece of tissue paper the same size as the coin. It will be lighter than the coin.

2. Drop the paper and the coin from the same height. The paper falls more slowly because air gets in its way.

3. Now put the coin in one box and the paper in the other. Put the lids on and drop both boxes together.

4. The boxes have the same air resistance and land at the same time, even though they are different weights.

Floating

If you drop a stone into water, it will sink to the bottom. But if you drop a balloon into water, it will float. Why do some things float and others sink? Floating is all about density – how heavy something is for its size.

Weight and density

Two objects that are the same size yet different weights must have different densities. A cork and an iron bolt are similar in size, but the bolt is denser. The denser object will be heavier than the lighter one.

Upthrust

Things float in water because water pushes up on them more than they push down. This upward force is called upthrust. If an object is denser than water, the water cannot provide enough upthrust, so the object sinks.

Objects that are denser than water sink. Anything less dense than water floats.

Does it float?

Guess which things will float in water and then see if you were right. You will need:

a bowl of water; solid things, such as a cork, a candle, a coin, an apple, a raisin, a plastic toy, an eraser.

1. Make a chart to compare your guesses with what actually happens.

2. Try floating different objects and write down which of them really float.

Will it float?	Guess	Actual
Cork	✔	☐
Coin	✔	☐
Candle	✘	☐
Apple	✘	☐

- Scan the code to see experiments about floating and density.
- For more links, go to **usborne.com/Quicklinks**

How do ships float?

Some ships are so huge, it seems amazing that they float – but they do. Even if a ship is made of heavy iron, it has a lot of air inside it. This makes the ship less dense than water, so it floats.

Hot air balloons float because hot air is less dense than cold air.

People are almost the same density as water, and only just float. Air-filled life rings can help people to float better.

This ring of buoys keeps swimmers safe from boats.

Floating in air

Floating in air is just like floating in water. Anything that is less dense than air will float in it. But because air is very light itself, not many other things are light enough to float in it.

These balloons are filled with helium gas that's less dense than air. It makes them float.

Salty sea

Salty water is denser than pure water. This makes it easier for people to float in it. A lake between Israel and Jordan called the Dead Sea has water that's so salty, it's very easy to float in.

This woman is floating in the very salty water of the Dead Sea.

Friction

Whenever an object tries to slide across a surface, it is slowed down by the two surfaces gripping each other. This force is called friction.

- Scan the code to investigate how friction works.
- For more links, go to usborne.com/Quicklinks

The rough...

The rougher the surface, the more friction there is, and the more the object slows down.

This woman's snowboard has a smooth surface, which reduces friction between it and the snow.

...and the smooth

Very smooth surfaces don't have much friction, and often feel slippery. If you are on a smooth surface, you can move fast without being slowed down very much.

Getting a grip

Friction also helps things stay in one place. When you walk, friction is what helps your feet grip the ground. Without friction, your feet would slip out from under you.

The soles of hiking boots are molded into rough ridges. This makes lots of extra friction to stop the walker from slipping.

Hot friction

Wherever there is friction, there is heat. This is because as objects rub together, friction turns kinetic, or movement, energy into heat energy. There's more about energy on pages 196–197.

These people are using the heat from friction to start a fire. This method of starting fires has been used by humans throughout history.

Coin warmer

You could try this experiment to see how friction can heat things up. See if you can warm up a metal coin using friction.

You will need:

a coin; a pad of paper

1. Hold the coin flat on the paper with one finger on top of it, like this:

2. Press down and rub the coin very fast from side to side about 50 times.

The coin warms up because there is lots of friction between it and the paper. The friction turns the energy of the coin's movement into heat energy.

Streamlining

Even air and water cause friction when things move through them. Cars, planes and boats are built so that water or air can move past them in smooth lines to reduce friction. This is called streamlining.

Dolphins have streamlined bodies which help them move fast in water.

Magnets

Magnetism is a type of pulling force. It happens because of the way atoms are arranged in some kinds of metals. A magnet is a piece of metal that can pull some metals toward itself.

Iron filings (tiny bits of iron) stick to the parts of this horseshoe-shaped magnet where its magnetic force is strongest.

Pushing and pulling

Magnetic forces are strongest at the two ends of a magnet. These ends are called the north pole and the south pole. If you try to put two magnets' poles together, they will either stick to each other or push each other away.

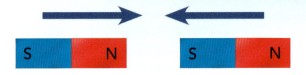

A north pole and a south pole always pull toward each other. This is called magnetic attraction.

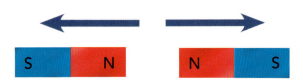

Two poles of the same type always push each other away. This is called magnetic repulsion.

Magnetic fields

The area of force around a magnet is called its magnetic field. Our planet has a magnetic core, which gives it a magnetic field.

A compass has a magnetic needle inside. The needle's north pole always pulls toward the north (top) of the Earth. As opposite poles attract, this means the top of the Earth is actually the south pole of Earth's magnetic field.

Magnets at work

You might use magnets at home to stick notes on your refrigerator, but they have lots of other uses. For example, because magnets only attract some metals, such as iron, they can be used to separate different metals from each other in a recycling factory.

What's magnetic?

Try testing different objects around your house with a magnet. You will need:

a magnet; objects such as pins, bottles, cans, coins, books, scissors

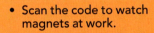

Will it stick?

	Guess	Actual
Tin can	☑	☐
Coin	☑	☐
Bottle	☒	☐
Ball	☒	☐

1. Guess which objects the magnet will attract.

2. Now test them by seeing if the magnet sticks to them.

The objects the magnet sticks to are metal, and probably contain some iron, steel or nickel.

This huge magnet is being used to separate iron from other types of metal so that it can be reused.

"Maglev" trains use magnetic repulsion to make them float just above a rail. This allows them to move very smoothly.

- Scan the code to watch magnets at work.
- For more links, go to **usborne.com/Quicklinks**

The Sun

Light and color

Light is a form of energy. Most of the light on our planet comes from the Sun. Light comes from other places too – electric lights, candle flames and even some types of animals.

Lines and shadows

Light always travels in straight lines. If light hits an object that's not see-through, it can only shine past it, not around it. This makes a shadow where the light can't reach.

Light can turn a corner if it reflects (bounces) off a surface, such as a mirror.

Shadows happen because rays of light cannot bend around objects.

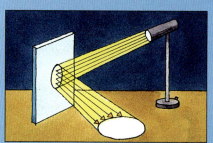
If you shine a lamp or flashlight at a mirror, the light will bounce off it.

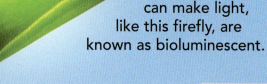

Animals that can make light, like this firefly, are known as bioluminescent.

The speed of light

When you flick a light switch, light seems to fill the room instantly. This is because light travels very fast. It moves at 186,000 miles (300,000km) per second.

It takes eight minutes for light to travel from the Sun to the Earth.

- Scan the code to see animals that are bioluminescent.
- For more links, go to **usborne.com/Quicklinks**

Seeing light

We see things because our eyes are designed to collect and sense light (there's more about eyes on page 103). When we see an object, we're really seeing light reflecting off it.

We see the Moon because light from the Sun reflects off it.

Did you know?

• Most people can detect at least 1 million different shades of color.

• Some people are colorblind. They may see some colors but find it hard to tell the difference between certain colors.

• Many animals see only in shades of gray, not in color.

• Scientists think it's impossible for anything in the Universe to travel faster than light.

Colors

Bright white light is made up of different colors of light mixed together.

We see colors because some objects only reflect one color of light. For example, a green leaf only reflects green light, so it looks green.

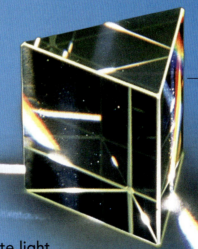

A piece of shaped glass called a prism can split white light into all its colors.

White light shining into the prism

Separate colors of light shining out of the prism

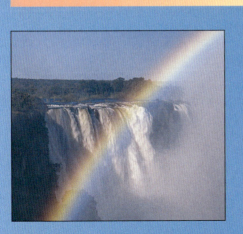

Sometimes raindrops act like mini-prisms. They split sunlight into lots of colors, making a rainbow.

Sound

Sound is a form of energy. It is made of vibrations (back-and-forth movements) that can move through air, solid things and liquids. Sounds can't travel in space.

Sound vibrations

When you speak, hit a drum or clap your hands, molecules in the air vibrate. We hear the sounds when those vibrations hit our ears. (Read more about ears on page 103.)

The loudest sounds, such as a rocket lift-off (180 decibels), will damage your ears.

A rattlesnake can make a rattling sound with its tail to scare enemies. The movement of rings on its tail makes molecules in the air vibrate.

How loud?

The volume (loudness) of a sound depends on how big the vibrations are. Volume is measured in units called decibels (dB). This chart shows how loud different sounds are.

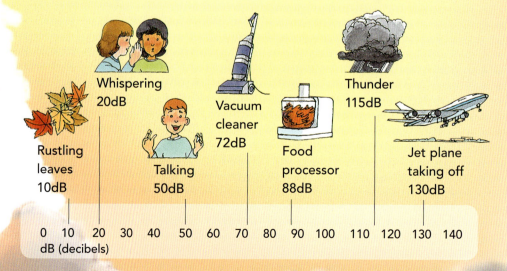

Rustling leaves 10dB

Whispering 20dB

Talking 50dB

Vacuum cleaner 72dB

Food processor 88dB

Thunder 115dB

Jet plane taking off 130dB

0 10 20 30 40 50 60 70 80 90 100 110 120 130 140
dB (decibels)

212

High and low

Pitch is the highness or lowness of a sound. Fast sound vibrations make higher pitched sounds. Slower sound vibrations make lower sounds. Some animals can hear pitches we can't hear.

- Scan the code to watch an experiment about sound vibrations.
- For more links, go to **usborne.com/Quicklinks**

This farmer's whistle makes a very high sound. Dogs can hear it, but people can't.

Elephants can make sounds so low that people can't hear them.

Scientists know that blue whales make the lowest, loudest sound of any animal.

Making music

Musical instruments have parts that vibrate to make sounds. When someone plays an instrument, they make different notes by changing the speed of the vibrations.

On a violin, shorter strings vibrate faster and make higher-pitched notes. Violin players make the strings shorter or longer with their fingers.

Feel sound vibrations

You can't normally feel sound vibrations in the air, but you can in this experiment. You will need:

a speaker; a blown-up balloon

Turn the speaker on and hold the balloon next to it. The vibrations travel through the balloon and into your fingers.

Electricity

Electricity is a very useful form of energy. It can be easily changed into other forms of energy, such as light and heat. It makes things like toasters, televisions and computers work. Much of the electricity we use comes from power stations.

In this power station, machines called generators turn heat energy from burning fuel, such as coal or gas, into electricity.

Lightning is a kind of static electricity that's made when water molecules inside clouds rub together during storms.

Lightning

Cables and transmission towers carry electricity to transformers.

Getting electricity

Electricity travels from power stations to homes along underground cables, or wires attached to high towers. They are kept out of reach, because if electricity touches you, it can give you a dangerous shock.

Transformers make electricity safe for us to use.

Here, the cables go underground.

Static electricity

Static electricity is a form of electricity that builds up in some substances when they are rubbed together. It can make objects stick to each other. Do you ever feel a small shock when you touch metal? This is caused by a small build-up of static in your body as you move around.

- Scan the code for static electricity experiments to try.
- For more links, go to **usborne.com/Quicklinks**

Make some static electricity

For this experiment, you will need:
a balloon; a sweater

1. Blow up a balloon and rub it up and down on a sweater a few times.

2. Gently put the balloon on the wall. Static electricity makes it stick there.

Using electricity

When an appliance, such as a toaster, is plugged in, it is connected to the electricity supply. Electricity flows into it and gives it the energy to work. Plastic does not conduct (carry) electricity well, so it is used to cover electrical appliances. This stops you from getting a shock.

Can you guess which of these uses the most electricity in one minute?

Answer: hairdryer

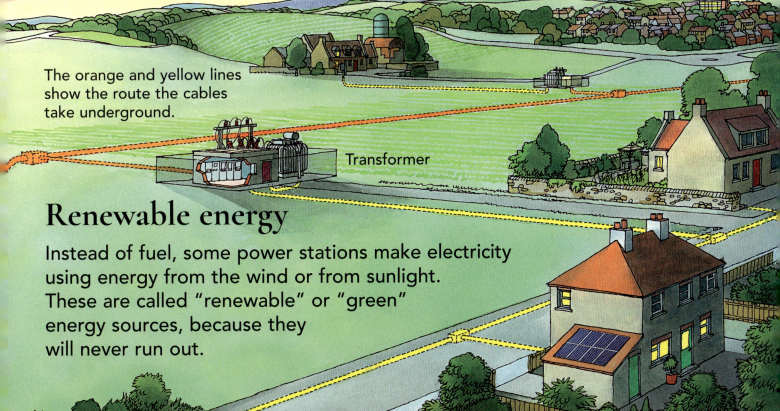

The orange and yellow lines show the route the cables take underground.

Transformer

Renewable energy

Instead of fuel, some power stations make electricity using energy from the wind or from sunlight. These are called "renewable" or "green" energy sources, because they will never run out.

Renewable power

Some power stations burn fossil fuels, and others use renewable sources of energy*. Whatever the energy source, most power stations use a turbine and a generator to create electricity.

- Scan the code to visit a wind turbine and see how it works.
- For more links, go to **usborne.com/Quicklinks**

Using wind and water

Kinetic energy (see pages 196–197) from fast-flowing water and wind can be used to make a turbine spin, which powers a generator to make electricity. Follow the numbers to see how this works.

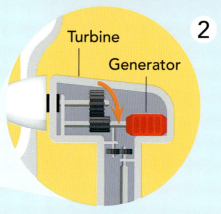

Turbine

Generator

2 The spinning turbine powers the generator, which makes electricity.

Wind

1 Wind turns the blades of the turbine.

Transmission tower

Transformer substation

Sea

Wind turbine

3 Transformers make the electricity efficient for us to use.

4 Electricity joins the main power supply via transmission towers.

Heat and steam

Thermal power stations heat water to create steam, which turns the blades of a turbine. Many burn biomass (natural waste such as dead plants and manure) for heat.

Some power stations use renewable heat sources, including geothermal (heat from the Earth) and solar thermal (heat from sunlight).

Hydro dams use water to make power.

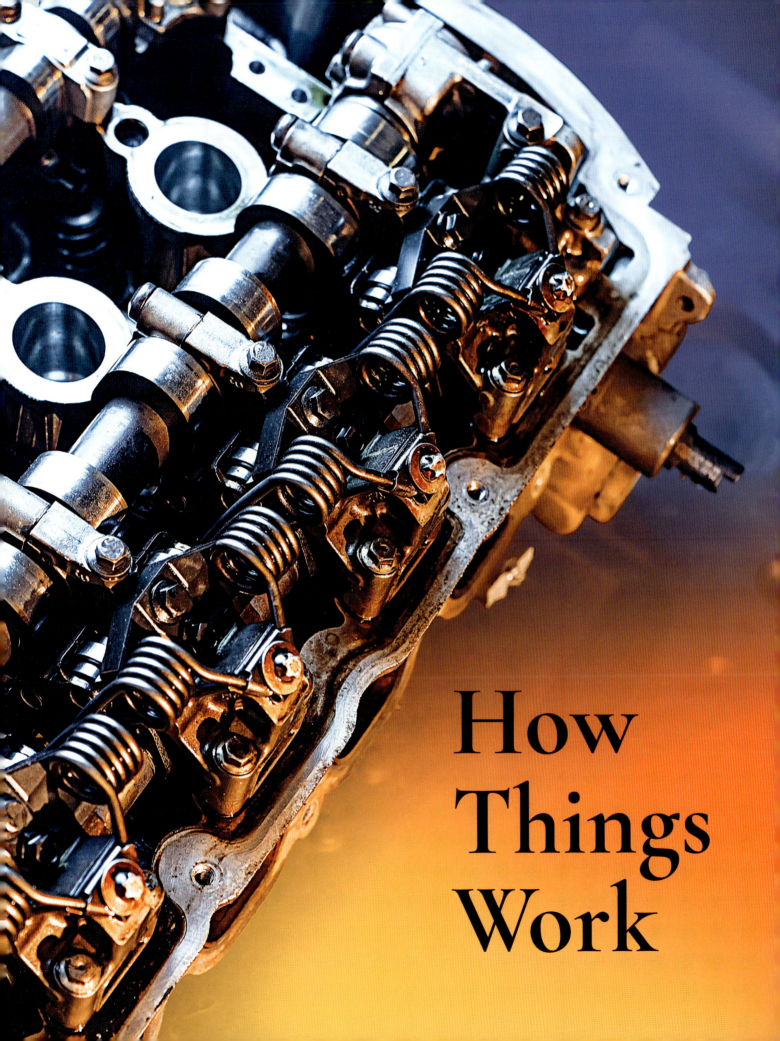

How Things Work

Cameras

Cameras capture photos and videos. Light reflecting off an object is what allows your eyes to see it. A camera also uses reflected light to take a picture.

- Scan the code for more about how digital cameras make photos.
- For more links, go to **usborne.com/Quicklinks**

Parts of this camera have been cut away so you can see inside.

You push this button to take a photo.

This glass lens lets light into the camera.

A digital single-lens reflex (DSLR) camera uses mirrors to help you take a photo. They reflect the image from the lens to the viewfinder.

This is the viewfinder. You look through it to see your subject (what you're taking a picture of).

This image sensor is made up of light-sensitive cells. It detects the light reflected by an object.

Batteries power the camera. Often they are rechargeable.

Saving a photograph

In a digital camera, a processor stores the photo on a memory card as a digital image file. A traditional film camera stores the photo on a reel of photographic film.

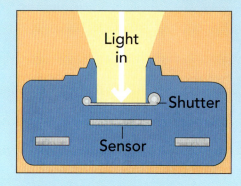

Inside the camera, a flap called the shutter covers the sensor, which stops any light from touching it.

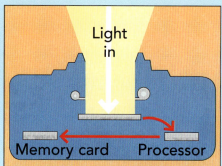

When you press the button, the shutter opens. Light enters the lens and hits the sensor, which captures the photo.

Digital images

Every digital image is made up of tiny squares called pixels. The number of them along the height and width of an image is called its resolution. The larger the number of pixels in an image (the resolution), the clearer it looks.

An image that is 820 pixels wide and 680 pixels high has a resolution of 820x680.

When the resolution is too low, the pixels are visible.

Televisions

Many TV screens use OLED (Organic Light Emitting Diode) technology, which enables lots of tiny cells to emit colored light when an electrical current is passed through them.

The OLEDs make up the pixels in the screen. The larger the number of pixels per square inch (PPI) the screen can display, the clearer the image will be.

How TV screens work

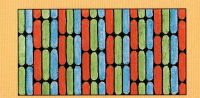

Red, green and blue OLEDs make up each pixel, arranged in a grid pattern on the screen.

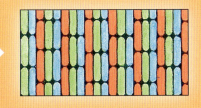

When the TV is on, electricity flows through the OLEDs, making them glow.

The OLEDs are so tiny that the colors mix to create the image you see on the screen.

Movies

A movie is made from a sequence of images, called frames, shown very quickly one after another.

The first movies were a sequence of photos on long strips of photographic film. The pictures below are frames of a galloping horse. As the strip of film quickly moves along, it looks like the horse is moving.

Moving pictures

Movies used to be shown using film projectors. A film projector has two big wheels, called reels. The reels turn, winding the film off the top reel and onto the bottom one.

Each frame of the film passes in front of a bulb, which shines a bright light through it.

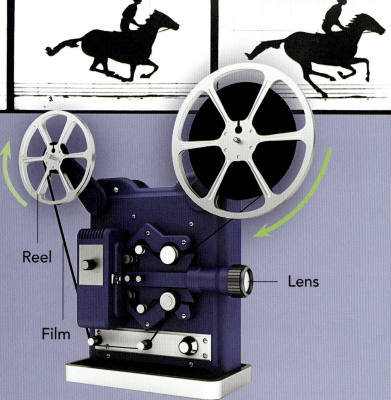

Reel

Lens

Film

Make your own flick book movie

A flick book works in the same way as a movie.

Here's how to make a mini-movie of somebody jumping up and down.

1 Get a notebook and draw a stick person, like the one here, on the last page.

2 On the page before, draw another person, just starting to jump up in the air.

3 Keep doing this until you have pictures of the person jumping up and down.

4 Flick through the pictures quickly. It will look like a movie of the person jumping.

Digital projectors

Modern movie theaters use digital projectors, which show at least 24 frames every second. This is much too fast for you to be able to see one frame changing to the next. This makes it look like one, moving picture.

- Scan the code to discover how to make your own moving pictures.
- For more links, go to **usborne.com/Quicklinks**

Micro mirrors

DMD™ chip

Most movie projectors contain three "digital micromirror devices," or DMD™s, which are microchips (see page 223), covered in thousands of tiny mirrors arranged in a grid.

Inside the projector, a lamp shines a beam of light through a colored filter – either red, blue or green – onto each DMD™.

The mirrors direct these colored lights to form the pixels that make up each movie frame.

This small digital projector is for watching movies at home. The light exits the projector through a curved lens, which can direct the light much wider, to show the frames larger than a TV screen.

Cooling fans stop the lamp from overheating.

Lens

Movie

221

Circuits

Household appliances, such as mixers, are powered by electricity. Plugging one into an electrical outlet and turning on the switch allows electricity to flow through the cable and around a circuit to make it work.

Switch

Mains cable

Beaters

Electricity flows from the mains cable into the circuits of this mixer, making the beaters turn.

- Scan the code to see how a simple circuit works.
- For more links, go to **usborne.com/Quicklinks**

Switches

A switch starts and stops the flow of electricity (current) around a circuit.

When the switch is off, it creates a gap, or break, in the circuit, so the current can't flow around.

Switch OFF

When the switch is on, the circuit is complete again, so the current can flow.

Switch ON

Switch OFF

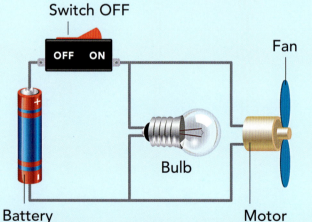

OFF   ON

Fan

Bulb

Battery

Motor

In this circuit, electricity comes from a battery, which is connected to a switch, a light bulb and a motor that turns a fan.

Switch ON

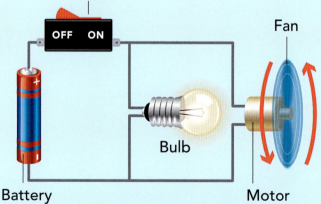

OFF   ON

Fan

Bulb

Battery

Motor

When the switch is on, an electrical current flows from the battery around the circuit, powering the light and the fan.

How a hairdryer works

When you turn on a hairdryer, electricity flows up the wires in the cable, around a circuit to a heating element, which becomes red hot.

Electricity also flows to the motor, turning the fan. The fan sucks air in through small holes (vents) and pushes it forward over the heating element, which heats up the air as it blows past.

In this picture you can see inside a hairdryer.

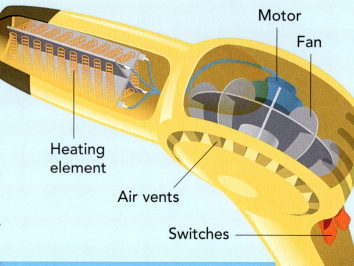

Motor

Fan

Heating element

Air vents

Switches

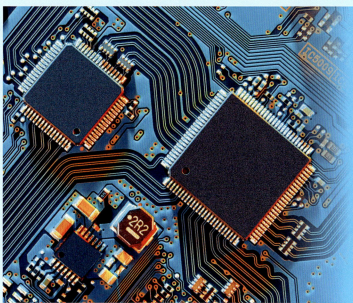

Microchips

Microchips, or "integrated circuits," are very small, flat pieces of a material called silicon, covered in tiny circuits that work together on a circuit board. They can be used to store information or carry out simple functions, or for more advanced tasks.

Microprocessors

Microprocessors are in many electrical devices, from calculators to aircraft navigation systems. They can carry out many complicated tasks, all on a single microchip.

Appliances such as dishwashers and ovens often have a small digital display screen, which is controlled by a microprocessor.

The digital display on this washing machine can be used to set the length of a wash cycle.

Computers

Computers can be used to do all kinds of things, from helping save lives to flying space rockets. They can store lots of information and do certain tasks very quickly.

- Scan the code to discover some of the things computers do.
- For more links, go to **usborne.com/Quicklinks**

Coding and programs

Computers use sets of instructions, called programs, to carry out particular tasks. Writing instructions for computers is known as coding.

Sometimes there might be an error in the code of a program, which is called a "bug," and means the program won't work exactly as it is supposed to.

Hardware and software

Computer monitors, laptops, keyboards and other parts that you can touch are called hardware. The programs that run on computers are called software.

These children are writing a computer program to control a small car.

The internet

The internet is a vast global network of shared data (information). It contains millions of websites, which are pages of information that form the "World Wide Web."

You can look at internet data on devices such as smartphones, anywhere there is a signal.

Going "online"

You can connect to the internet in different ways.

Mobile devices can use "cellular data," in a similar way to how phone calls are made (see page 227).

Broadband internet comes into a building through an underground cable which is plugged into a router inside.

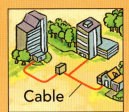

Cable

Routers and Wi-Fi

Routers send and receive radio signals wirelessly (see page 227) to internet-enabled devices nearby, such as TVs, computers or smartphones. This is known as connecting via "Wi-Fi."

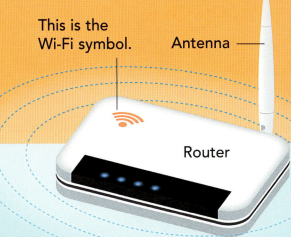

This is the Wi-Fi symbol.

Antenna

Router

Moving information

Images, videos and other online content can be downloaded (copied) onto your device so that you can look at them when you don't have an internet connection.

You can upload pictures, videos and other files to online storage spaces known as "The Cloud."

Streaming

Streaming is when you watch or listen to a program over the internet instead of downloading it.

Digital communication

Radio waves can be used to transmit (send) invisible signals. Digital radio signals can carry information. Many devices, including radios, TVs and cell phones, send and receive digital radio signals.

Broadcasting

TV studios and radio stations make programs to be broadcast at a certain time, for people to tune in to. The sounds and pictures are turned into digital information and transmitted through the air as radio signals.

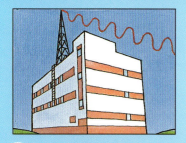

1 TV and radio programs are sent out as digital radio signals to a transmitter tower. They travel quickly through the air.

2 Transmitter towers pick up the signals and send them in all directions. This is called broadcasting.

3 Radio signals from a transmitter tower can travel a long way to reach lots of homes at once.

TV antenna

4 Antennae receive the signals and pass them to TVs or radios, which convert the information back into pictures and/or audio.

Towers like this can send signals over long distances.

Making a call

When you make a call on a cell phone, it sends out radio signals, which are picked up by the nearest cell phone tower.

Cell phone towers are linked to base stations, which receive incoming radio signals and direct them to where they need to go.

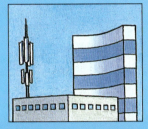

The base station sends your call out to the cell phone tower closest to the phone you are calling. The tower delivers your call to the phone as radio signals.

- Scan the code to explore how a cell phone works.
- For more links, go to **usborne.com/Quicklinks**

These headphones connect to a music player or cell phone without wires.

Wireless

Radio waves can also be used to transmit information between a smartphone and other digital devices that are nearby, without using a cable to connect them. You could listen to audio on a phone through wireless headphones, for example.

GPS

Some radio signals come from spacecraft called satellites, which orbit (travel around) the Earth. This is how a Global Positioning System (GPS) works. A navigation satellite receiver measures how long it takes for radio signals to travel from multiple satellites to receivers on the ground, to help it pinpoint locations.

GPS helps drivers plan a route.

Manufacturing

Manufacturing is the process of making lots of things at once using machines, often in a factory. Factories have production lines, which use step-by-step processes to turn ingredients or parts into finished items, called products.

This factory worker is using machines to manufacture chocolates. They travel on a moving surface called a conveyor belt.

Batch production

Some products, such as food, are manufactured in batches. Mixed ingredients go through each step in the production line together to make a final product. Often there is a human operator by each machine, and parts of the process are regularly inspected by people to check they have been carried out correctly. Follow the numbers to see how bread is manufactured.

- Scan the code to watch a factory production line in action.
- For more links, go to **usborne.com/Quicklinks**

1 The bread ingredients are poured into a mixing machine and churned around together. This creates a sticky, stretchy dough.

2 A machine slices the dough into equal chunks, which fall onto a conveyor belt. As the chunks move along, other machines shape and roll each one into a ball.

3 The smooth balls drop into baking pans. The dough is left to rest and rise, before the pans are transported into large ovens to bake.

4 The baked loaves are tipped out onto a conveyor belt, cooled, then passed under a slicing machine. Another machine packages them up, to be sent to stores.

Mass production

Some products, such as cars, are mass produced. They have lots of separate parts that are made in different areas of the factory, and then the complete car is put together at the end, on an assembly line. Often special robots are used to do each task.

Assembly lines like this produce only one type of car. Using a production line of robots, a factory can produce many cars each day.

Automation

Machines used in manufacturing are programmed to repeat their specific tasks over and over again on their own, which is called automation. This makes mass manufacturing much quicker.

Prototyping

Mass-produced products need to be designed and tested before they are manufactured. A single example of the product, called a prototype, can be made to test the design. Prototyping machines are programmed to turn the digital design drawing into a scale model.

This 3D printer uses a tool called an extruder, which pushes out melted plastic. As the tool traces the design over and over again, the liquid plastic hardens and builds up in layers to create a 3D object.

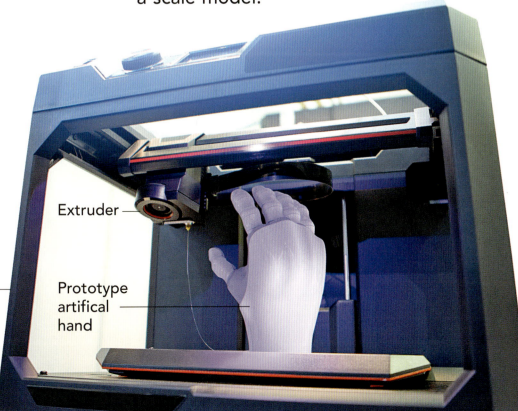

Extruder

Construction chamber

Prototype artifical hand

Construction

There are lots of types of construction vehicles. Many have moving mechanical parts that are controlled by changing pressure inside narrow tubes.

- Scan the code to see construction vehicles at work.
- For more links, go to **usborne.com/Quicklinks**

Diggers use a large metal bucket to dig holes in the ground.

Metal piston rod

Hinges allow the arm to move.

Spinning body

This is the digger's arm.

These crawler tracks help the digger grip.

Teeth

The bucket's metal teeth cut into the earth, helping it dig.

Digging

A digger works using a hydraulics system, involving liquid pressure. Metal rods with pistons at the end fit tightly into oil-filled cylinders. The force of oil moving in and out of the cylinders pushes the pistons up and down. This pulls and pushes the rods, making the bucket move.

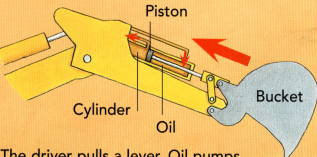

Piston

Cylinder

Oil

Bucket

The driver pulls a lever. Oil pumps into the bottom (and out of the top) of a cylinder. This pushes the piston up, pulling the bucket up.

The driver pushes the lever. Oil pumps into the top (and out of the bottom) of the cylinder. This pushes the piston down, pushing the bucket down.

Heavy machinery

These are some of the other vehicles and equipment that are used on construction sites.

Construction drills move using pneumatics (say "new-matics"). This is similar to hydraulics, but uses the pressure of compressed air instead of liquid.

Pneumatic drill

Crane trucks often have extendable legs, which help them to stay steady when lifting something.

Extending boom arm

Stabilizing legs

Concrete

Concrete mixers have a rotating drum, which mixes the concrete. If concrete stays still too long, it will set (harden).

Bulldozers push loads around the construction site.

Road rollers flatten large areas of concrete to make roads.

Lifting

Tower cranes have counterweights on the back to balance out the weight of their load, so that they don't fall over. They often use hydraulics systems to extend higher.

Trolley

Counter-weights

Cab

Hydraulic ram

Hook

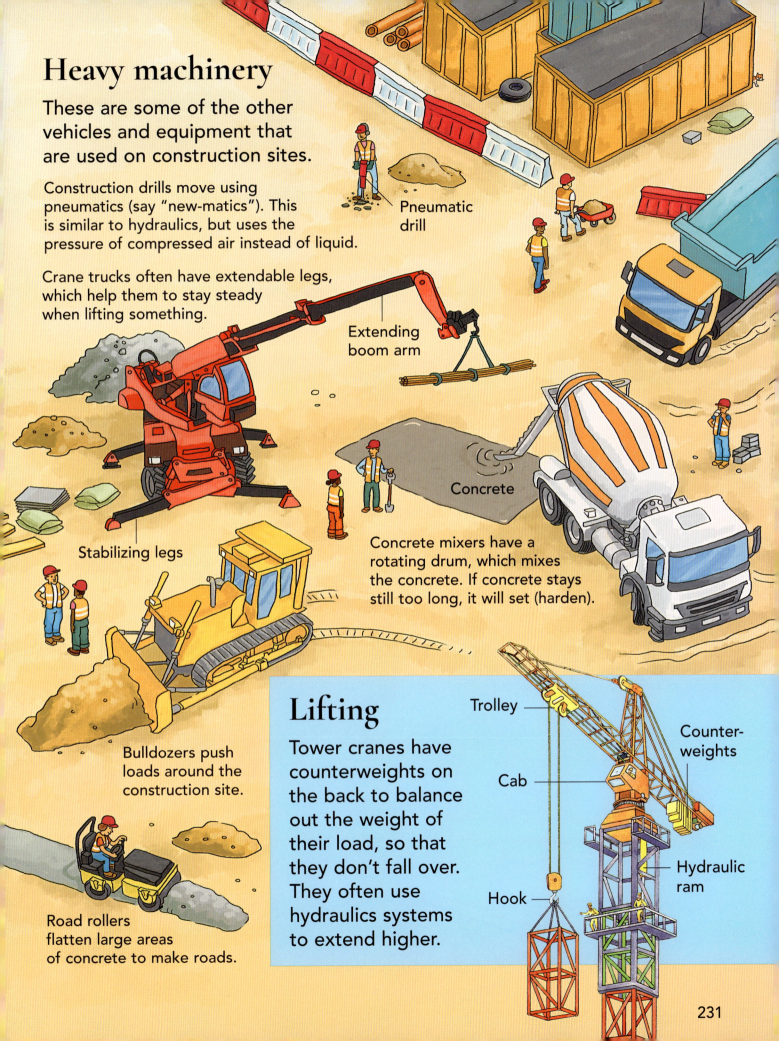

Refrigerators

A refrigerator stays cool by pumping a liquid called a refrigerant through pipes. Food stays fresh longer if it is kept in a fridge.

Keeping cool

When you get wet, your skin cools down as it dries. This is because the water turns into a gas, or evaporates. As liquid evaporates, it absorbs heat. This is what keeps a fridge cool. Follow the numbers on the big picture on the right to see how.

1 Refrigerant liquid is pumped into the evaporator coil. It starts to evaporate.

The light inside

The light inside a fridge comes on whenever you open the door. When you shut the door, it presses against a switch, turning the light off.

When the fridge door opens, the switch pops up, and the light comes on.

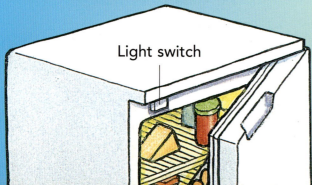

Light switch

This cutaway shows the inside of a fridge, so you can see how it works. The red arrows show heat leaving the back of the fridge.

Evaporator coil

2 As it evaporates, the refrigerant absorbs heat from the food and air in the fridge.

Condenser coil

3 The refrigerant gas goes into a condenser coil, where it turns back into a liquid (condenses). It lets off heat into the air outside.

Pump

Microwave ovens

A microwave oven can heat up food much more quickly than a normal oven can. To do this, it uses invisible waves called microwaves.

- Scan the code to see how a microwave oven works.
- For more links, go to **usborne.com/Quicklinks**

Hot and cold

Everything in the world is made up of very tiny parts, called atoms (see page 190), that are much too small to see. When something gets hot, it's because the atoms in it are moving quickly.

When something is cold, the atoms in it move slowly.

In something hot, the atoms move more quickly.

Bouncing waves

A microwave is a kind of radio wave. Microwaves can travel through the air and through water. Food contains water, so microwaves can travel through it. When they do this, they make all the atoms move around more quickly. This heats the food up.

A part called a magnetron makes the microwaves.

Part of this microwave oven has been cut away so that you can see inside.

Microwaves are invisible, but the green arrows show how they travel. They bounce off the oven's metal walls.

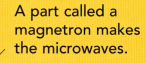

This turntable slowly spins around so the microwaves go into all parts of the food.

Plumbing

The water you use in your home probably comes from a place called a reservoir. Linked-up water pipes carry it to toilets, taps and radiators around the house. This is called plumbing.

Reservoirs are enormous human-made lakes. Water is stored in them until it is needed.

Heat pumps

Many homes are heated using a furnace or boiler. Using electricity instead, like in a heat pump, can be better for the environment (see page 44). An air source heat pump takes in air from outside and uses it to warm up a store of water in a home, using a process like a refrigerator in reverse (see page 232).

From the water tank, the hot water travels along pipes to radiators and taps. Cold water returns along pipes to the water tank to be heated again.

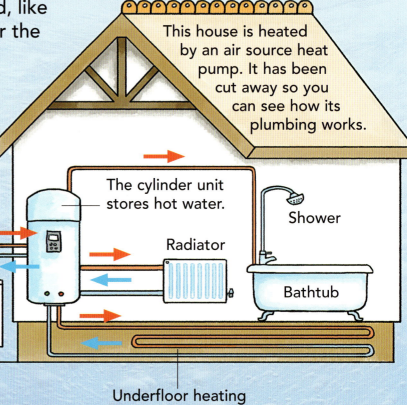

This house is heated by an air source heat pump. It has been cut away so you can see how its plumbing works.

The cylinder unit stores hot water.

Outside air

Radiator

Shower

Bathtub

Air source heat pump

Underfloor heating

Ground source heat pumps take heat from the ground. They are useful in places where the air can be very cold all year, because the ground stays warmer.

- Scan the code to find out more about heat pumps.
- For more links, go to **usborne.com/Quicklinks**

Around the bend

Water for flushing a toilet is stored in a tank called a cistern. Here's what happens when you flush.

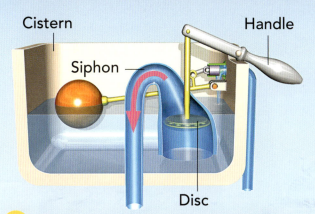

Cistern

Siphon

Handle

Disc

1 When you push the handle, the disc lifts up. This pushes water over the top of the siphon. As the water falls, it sucks the rest of the water with it.

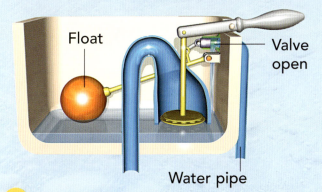

Float

Valve open

Water pipe

2 As the cistern empties, the disc drops, and a float, shaped like a ball, drops too. This pulls a valve out of the pipe so more water flows into the cistern.

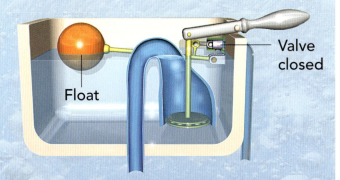

Valve closed

Float

3 As the cistern fills again, the float rises. When it is high enough, the float pushes the valve back into the pipe. This stops any more water from getting in.

When you flush a toilet, the water carries the waste around the bend and down the drain.

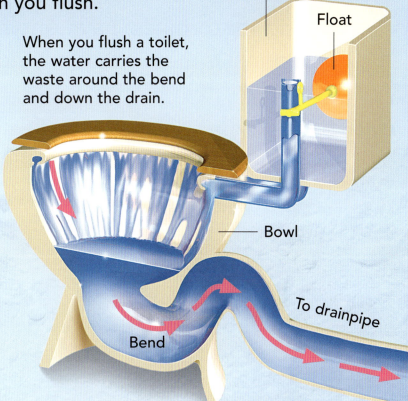

Cistern

Float

Bowl

To drainpipe

Bend

Down the drain

Dirty water and waste from toilets flow through underground pipes to places called sewage plants. At a sewage plant, all the dirt and waste is removed, so that the water can be used again.

This is a sewage plant from above. Each dark circle is an enormous tank full of dirty water.

Wheels and engines

Cars and other vehicles, such as trucks, vans and motorbikes, have engines in them to make them go. Many need fuel to make the engines work.

This type of car is called a MINI COOPER S. Parts of it have been cut away so you can see inside.

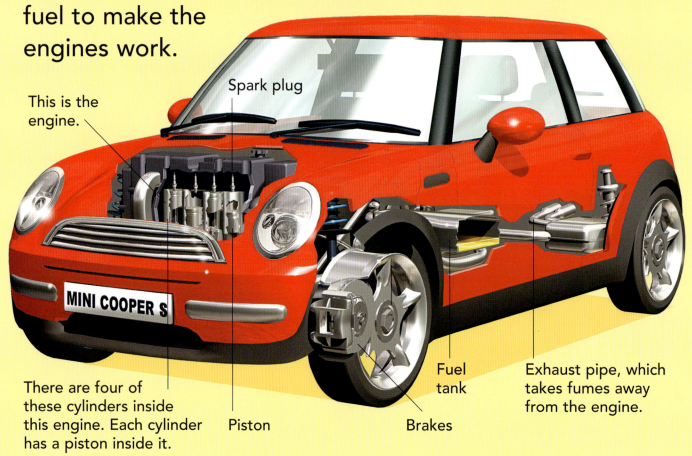

Spark plug

This is the engine.

MINI COOPER S

There are four of these cylinders inside this engine. Each cylinder has a piston inside it.

Piston

Fuel tank

Brakes

Exhaust pipe, which takes fumes away from the engine.

How does the engine work?

Air

Injector

Fuel spray

Cylinder

Piston

Crankshaft

A piston inside the cylinder moves down, sucking air and fuel into the cylinder.

Air and fuel mix

The piston then moves up again. This squashes the air and the fuel together.

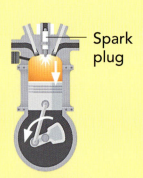

Spark plug

The spark plug ignites the fuel. It burns with a bang, pushing the piston down and creating fumes.

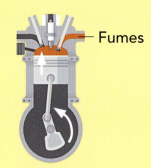

Fumes

The piston moves up, pushing the fumes out of the cylinder to the exhaust pipe.

How the wheels turn

The pistons in an engine are connected to a pole called the crankshaft. As they go up and down, they turn the crankshaft, which makes the driveshafts turn. The driveshafts make the front wheels go round.

- Scan the code to see how a car engine works.
- For more links, go to **usborne.com/Quicklinks**

The whole car is pulled along by the front wheels.

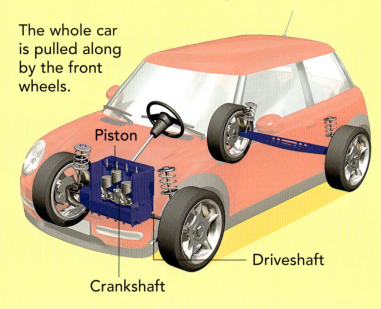

Piston

Crankshaft

Driveshaft

Disc brakes

Cars have disc brakes to make them slow down or stop.

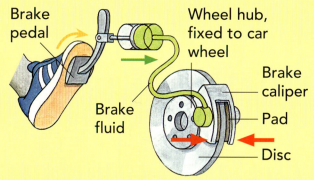

Brake pedal

Wheel hub, fixed to car wheel

Brake caliper

Pad

Brake fluid

Disc

Pressing the brake compresses hydraulic fluid (see page 230), making the calipers squeeze the pads onto the discs. This creates friction and slows the car down.

Bicycles

Bicycles don't need engines, only pedals, which turn the front gear wheel. This pulls the chain around.

The chain pulls the rear gear wheel, which turns the back wheel. The front wheel turns as the bike moves.

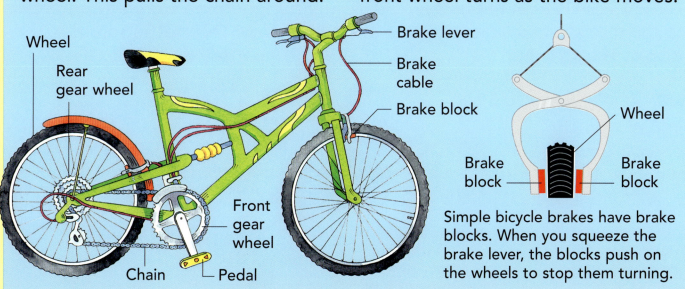

Wheel

Rear gear wheel

Brake lever

Brake cable

Brake block

Wheel

Brake block

Brake block

Front gear wheel

Chain

Pedal

Simple bicycle brakes have brake blocks. When you squeeze the brake lever, the blocks push on the wheels to stop them turning.

Electric vehicles (EVs)

Electric cars, trucks and bikes work using motors connected to batteries, instead of a fuel-powered engine, or pedal power alone.

- Scan the code to find out more about electric vehicles.
- For more links, go to **usborne.com/Quicklinks**

Electric vehicles need to be charged regularly. This is a charging station in the Netherlands, with a solar-paneled roof.

Battery power

Electric cars and trucks have large batteries that power all parts of the vehicle.

When you turn on an EV, an electric current travels from the battery to the motor and makes it spin. The spinning motor turns electrical energy into movement energy, powering the vehicle.

Saving some for later

As the vehicle moves, some movement energy goes back into the battery to be stored as potential energy. This makes sure the battery doesn't go flat as quickly while the vehicle is traveling.

This cutaway shows inside an EV car.

Charging socket

Battery

Electric motor

A motor makes the wheels turn.

Energy moves from the battery to the motor (and back).

238

Artificial intelligence (AI)

Artificial intelligence is technology that allows a computer to "think" like a human and solve problems itself, without human help. AI can be used for lots of things, from writing stories and songs to driving a car.

Algorithms

An algorithm is like a flowchart used by AI software to do a task, such as choose a song for you. For example, the AI is given data – the type of music you like. It follows the steps of the flowchart – browsing songs that fit the description – to achieve the best result.

The more data AI software receives, the better its results. With more data and practice, it learns how to do something better. Just like a human.

Smart speakers in your home are an example of AI.

- Scan the code for more about AI and how a computer "thinks."
- For more links, go to usborne.com/Quicklinks

Self-driving vehicles

Some electric cars, trucks and buses can be controlled using AI, which tells the vehicle what to do instead of a driver.

These vehicles have lots of sensors and cameras on them, which act like electronic eyes. The vehicle moves or stops based on the AI software making decisions about what it can "see," just like a human driver.

Camera

This is a driverless bus in Australia. Can you see the cameras that help it drive?

Trains

Trains move along specially built tracks to take people and things from one place to another. They often travel huge distances: the longest train track in the world is over 5,500 miles (9,000km) long.

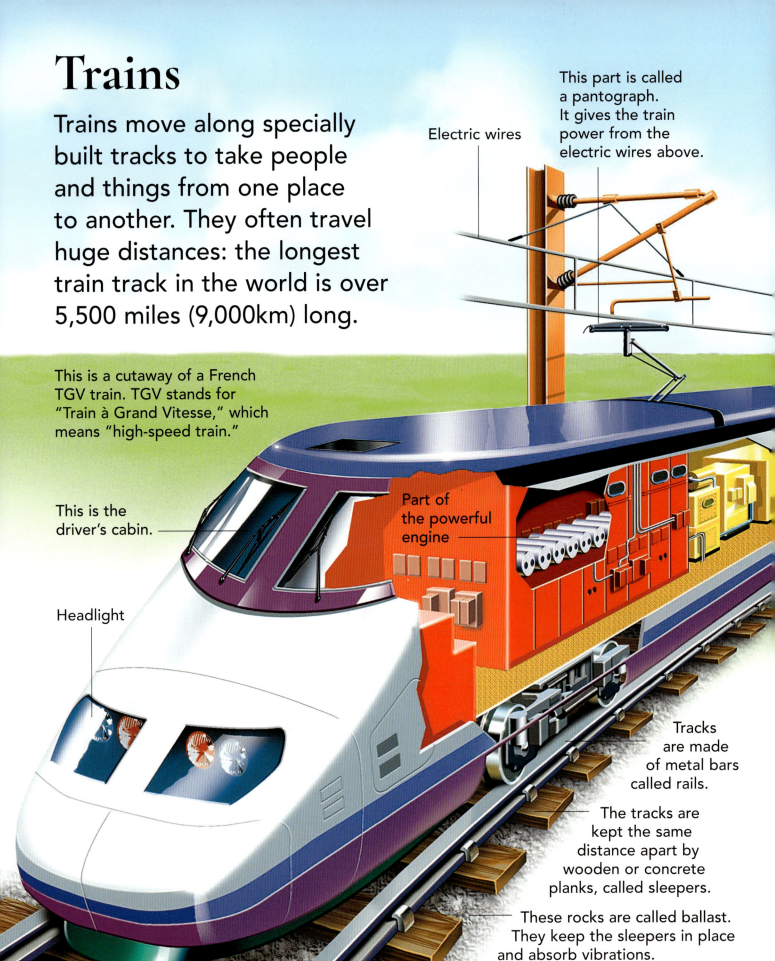

This part is called a pantograph. It gives the train power from the electric wires above.

Electric wires

This is a cutaway of a French TGV train. TGV stands for "Train à Grand Vitesse," which means "high-speed train."

This is the driver's cabin.

Part of the powerful engine

Headlight

Tracks are made of metal bars called rails.

The tracks are kept the same distance apart by wooden or concrete planks, called sleepers.

These rocks are called ballast. They keep the sleepers in place and absorb vibrations.

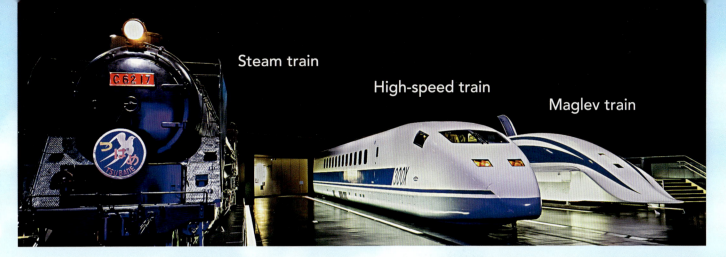

Steam train

High-speed train

Maglev train

This photo shows how the shape of trains has changed from the first steam trains. The curved front of a modern train allows it to push through the air more quickly. Some maglev trains can travel at more than 370mph (600km/h).

The sections of a train are called cars or carriages.

Getting faster

Scientists are always looking for ways to make faster trains. Maglev trains don't even touch the rail. They use magnets to push them through the air.

In the driving seat

The train driver sits in a cabin, called the control car, at the front of the train. The picture below shows the controls inside the cabin of a TGV train.

- Scan the code to see how trains have changed through time.
- For more links, go to **usborne.com/Quicklinks**

This button stops the train very quickly in an emergency.

This lever controls the speed of the train.

This shows how fast the train is going.

The driver can talk to the controller on this radio.

Planes

Flying in a plane is a very fast way to travel. Planes are able to fly because they have powerful engines and specially shaped wings.

Takeoff

A plane's wings are more curved on the top than on the bottom. This shape is called an airfoil. Follow the numbers below to see how it helps a plane take off and fly.

Engine

These arrows show how the air flows.

1 The plane's powerful engines make it go forward very quickly. Air rushes past the wings.

2 Because of the airfoil shape, air flows faster over the tops of the wings than underneath them.

3 The air under the wing pushes up more than the air on top of it pushes down. This lifts the plane up.

Make a wing

See how air flowing fast over one side of a piece of paper makes it lift, like a plane's wing. You will need:

a piece of very thin paper, 6in x 2in

1. Hold the short side of the paper to your lips, letting it hang down.

2. Blow across the top of the paper. It will lift up into the air.

Stunt planes, like this biplane, can do tricks in the air.

Steering the plane

Planes have parts on their wings and tails that can move. To make the plane go in different directions, the pilot uses the controls to move these parts.

- Scan the code for more about how planes fly.
- For more links, go to **usborne.com/Quicklinks**

To make the plane climb, the pilot tilts the elevators up. This makes the tail go down, so the nose goes up.

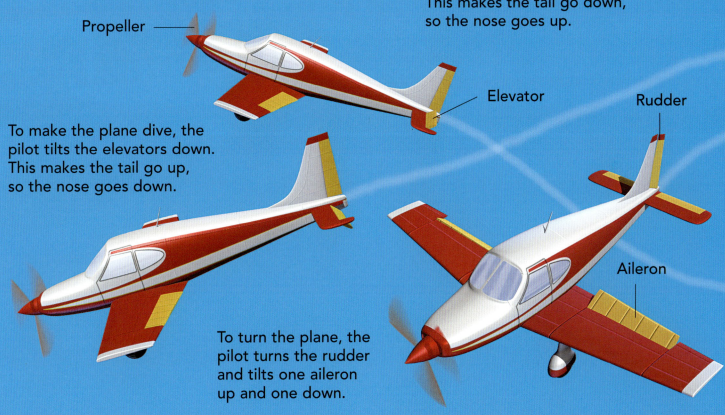

Propeller

Elevator

Rudder

Aileron

To make the plane dive, the pilot tilts the elevators down. This makes the tail go up, so the nose goes down.

To turn the plane, the pilot turns the rudder and tilts one aileron up and one down.

Flight control

The pilot controls the plane from the cockpit at the front. There are many dials that give the pilot information. The control panel of some planes looks like this.

This dial shows how high in the sky the plane is flying.

This dial shows the direction in which the plane is flying.

The pilot moves these controls to steer the plane.

243

Ships and boats

Ships and boats are often used for carrying people or heavy things around the world. Big boats are called ships. Some, like this cruise ship, can hold up to 7,000 passengers.

In this picture of a cruise ship, some parts have been cut away so you can see inside.

The funnel is like a big chimney.

Lifeboats like this can be used in emergencies.

A ship's back is called its stern.

Huge propellers push the ship forward.

Large engines power the propellers.

- Scan the code to see some of the world's biggest cruise ships.
- For more links, go to **usborne.com/Quicklinks**

How do boats float?

If you could put an enormous lump of metal that weighed the same as a boat into the sea, it would sink. A boat can float because it is hollow, and because of its special shape. You can find more about how things float on pages 204–205.

When a boat is in water, it pushes downward. The water pushes back, which makes the boat float. This is called upthrust (see page 204).

Make your own boat

Try this to see how a boat's shape makes it float. You will need:

a large bowl of water; a lump of modeling clay

1. Take the clay and roll it into a ball. Put it in the bowl of water. It will sink.

2. Cup the clay in one hand. Use your thumb to make it into a boat shape.

3. Put the clay in the water again. This time its shape will help it float.

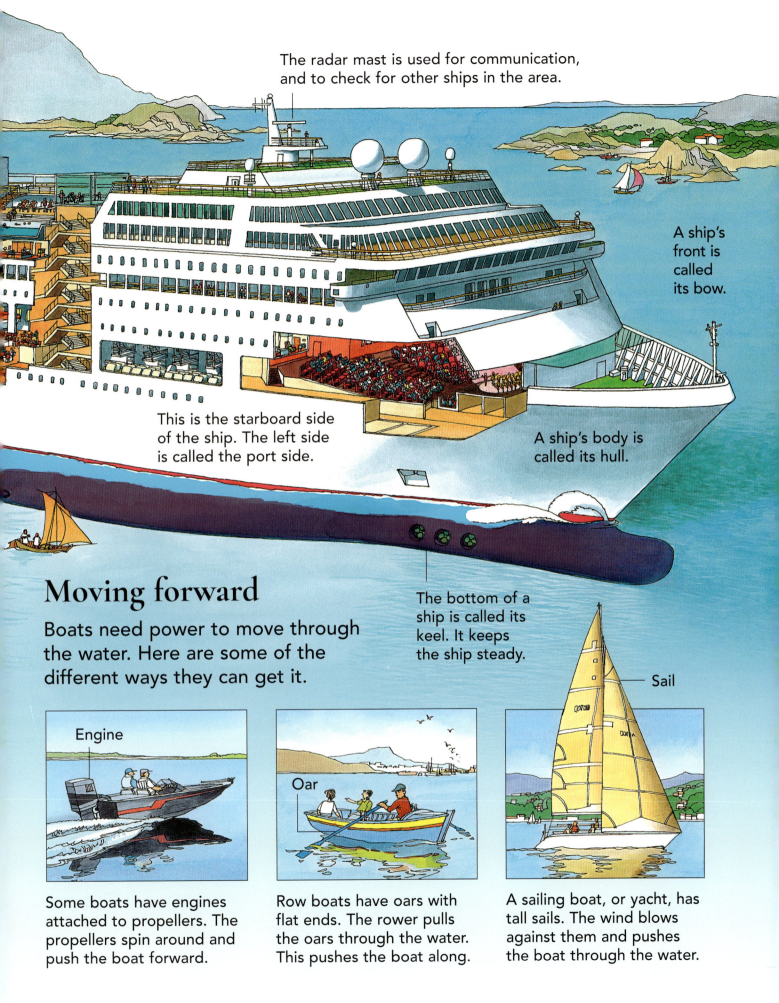

The radar mast is used for communication, and to check for other ships in the area.

A ship's front is called its bow.

This is the starboard side of the ship. The left side is called the port side.

A ship's body is called its hull.

Moving forward

Boats need power to move through the water. Here are some of the different ways they can get it.

The bottom of a ship is called its keel. It keeps the ship steady.

Sail

Engine

Oar

Some boats have engines attached to propellers. The propellers spin around and push the boat forward.

Row boats have oars with flat ends. The rower pulls the oars through the water. This pushes the boat along.

A sailing boat, or yacht, has tall sails. The wind blows against them and pushes the boat through the water.

Submersibles and submarines

Exploring the deep ocean is difficult, because it is so dark and cold. Scientists use underwater craft, called submarines and submersibles, to explore the depths.

This picture shows the Deep Flight I submersible in use.

This picture shows a submersible, called Deep Flight I, shown from above. Part of it has been cut away so you can see inside.

Fixed wings kept the submersible steady in the water.

Bottles filled with oxygen allowed the pilot to breathe.

Deep Flight I got its power from ten batteries (five along each side).

Propellers spun around quickly, pushing the submersible forward.

DEEP FLIGHT

Electric motors turned the propellers.

Powerful lights helped the pilot see clearly.

The pilot guided the submersible using these hand controls.

The very front part of the submersible was see-through, so the pilot could look around.

Going down

Deep Flight I used its wings to go up and down, but big submarines rise and sink in a different way.

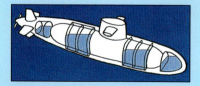

To dive down, tanks inside a submarine fill with water. This makes it heavy, so it sinks.

To come up, the water is pumped out. This makes the submarine lighter, so it rises.

- Scan the code to join scientists and dive into unexplored seas.
- For more links, go to usborne.com/Quicklinks

Space

Amazing space

Space is full of amazing sights. Some you can see with your own eyes, or with a telescope or binoculars. Here are some of the things you can find out about in this book.

Stars

A star is a blazing ball of very hot gas. The Sun is a star.

These bright dots are new stars being made from clouds of dust.

- Scan the code to take a trip into space.
- For more links, go to **usborne.com/Quicklinks**

Planets

A planet is an enormous ball of rock or gas which orbits, or travels around, a star. A group of planets orbiting a star is known as a solar system.

Some planets have rings. This is the planet Saturn with some of its rings.

This large blue planet is Neptune.

Moons

A moon is a natural object in space which orbits something other than a star. Most planets have moons.

This is Io, one of Jupiter's moons.

Comets

Comets are balls of dirty ice, which fly around in space. Sometimes they crash into planets.

This bright white shape is a comet and its tail.

Galaxies

Galaxies are huge groups of stars. Our Sun (and the rest of our Solar System) is in a galaxy called the Milky Way. Scientists think there are billions of galaxies in space.

Above is a galaxy called Messier 81. It has millions of stars.

Spacecraft

Rockets have been going into space since 1957. They have taken people as far as the Moon. Spacecraft without people in them have visited distant planets such as Uranus and Neptune.

This is the Saturn 5 rocket. It was used to send people to the Moon.

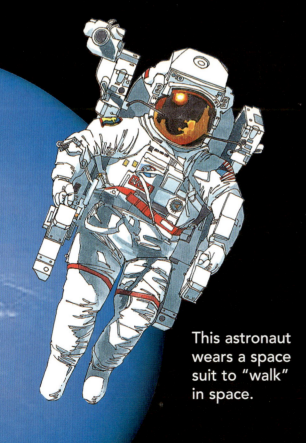

This astronaut wears a space suit to "walk" in space.

Astronauts

People who travel into space are called astronauts or cosmonauts. They have to train for many years before their trip.

The moving sky

Everything in the Universe, from individual moons to entire solar systems and galaxies, is moving. Even if you are sitting very still to read this book, you are moving with the Earth at a tremendous speed as it travels through space.

Spinners

All planets and moons spin around. The time it takes a planet to do one full turn is called a day. It takes the Earth 24 hours to spin around once.

The photo on the left was made over several hours. The position of the stars has changed in the sky because the Earth is turning.

Orbits

As they spin, planets and moons move through space in huge, near circular paths called orbits. It is hard to see them moving as they seem to travel slowly, but the Earth is actually orbiting the Sun at 19 miles (30km) per second.

The yellow lines and arrows in the pictures on the right show the paths Earth and the Moon take in their orbits.

The Sun

Earth's orbit

A planet orbits around a star.

Earth

The Moon's orbit

A moon orbits around a planet.

Gravity

Planets stay in orbit around the Sun, instead of flying off into space, because of gravity. Gravity is a force that pulls all the objects in the Universe toward each other.

- Scan the code for more about space telescopes and to see amazing photos of the Universe.
- For more links, go to **usborne.com/Quicklinks**

Space telescopes

Since the 1960s, scientists have put more than 100 telescopes into space. Outside the haze and pollution of Earth's atmosphere*, they can take very clear pictures.

Saturn, taken by the Hubble telescope

Across the Universe

The James Webb Space Telescope (JWST) is the largest telescope ever launched into space. Unlike most space telescopes, the JWST orbits the Sun, not the Earth. The JWST "sees" a kind of light which human eyes can't see, called infrared light. This means it can sense light from stars at the furthest reaches of the Universe.

The top part of the JWST is the telescope. It uses mirrors to focus the light from distant stars.

The bottom part is the spacecraft. It holds everything the telescope needs to work and to move around in space.

Primary mirror

Secondary mirror

Sensitive scientific instruments and cameras are behind the primary mirror.

This flap helps keep the spacecraft steady.

These solar panels use energy from the Sun to make electricity to power the telescope.

This is an antenna. It sends information to scientists back on Earth, and receives their instructions.

The sunshield protects the telescope from the Sun's heat and light. It has five layers, each the size of a tennis court.

*See page 9 for more about Earth's atmosphere.

251

A walk in space

Space is deadly. There is no air to breathe, so outside a spacecraft, an astronaut must wear an outfit called a space suit to stay alive. Space suits are like body-sized spaceships with their own air and water supplies.

Walk to work

Astronauts make space walks to repair satellites, build space stations or check the outside of their spaceships. On these pages you can see two American astronauts making a space walk.

- Scan the code to watch an astronaut go on a space walk.
- For more links, go to **usborne.com/Quicklinks**

A space suit has several very thin but strong layers. These protect the astronaut from tiny meteoroids and the heat and cold of space.

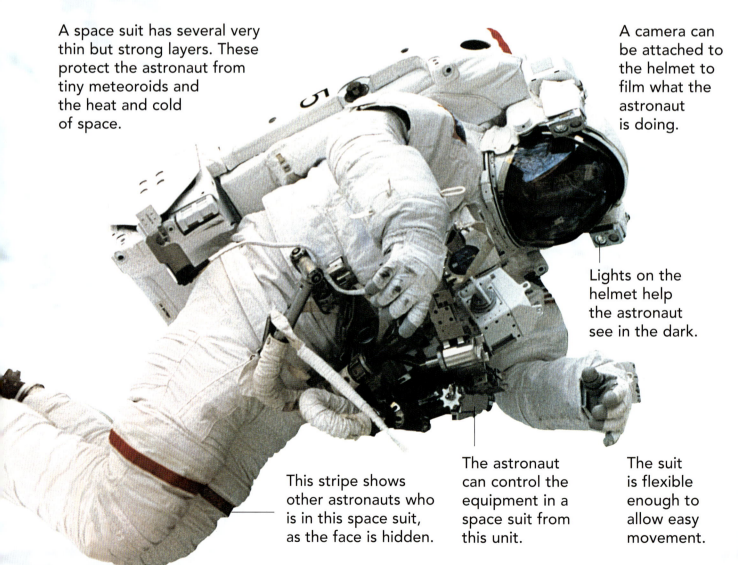

A camera can be attached to the helmet to film what the astronaut is doing.

Lights on the helmet help the astronaut see in the dark.

This stripe shows other astronauts who is in this space suit, as the face is hidden.

The astronaut can control the equipment in a space suit from this unit.

The suit is flexible enough to allow easy movement.

Survival equipment

Here is some of the equipment astronauts need to stay alive and comfortable outside their spaceships. Sometimes space walks can last for five hours or more.

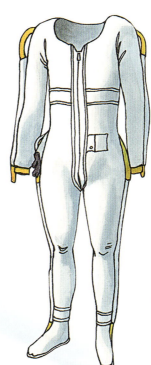

The shiny golden visor of this helmet protects against blinding, bright sunlight.

This cap holds a radio microphone and earpiece in place.

A drink bag has a tube which goes straight to the astronaut's mouth.

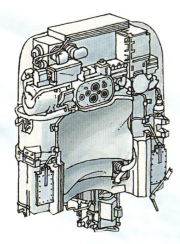

This is the Portable Life Support System. It contains air for the astronaut to breathe.

This outfit is worn next to the body. It has tubes of water which the astronaut can make hot or cold, to warm up or cool down.

Padded gloves have rubber fingertips so the astronaut can feel things more easily.

Boiling and freezing

When astronauts on a space walk face the Sun, its rays are hotter than boiling water. But when their spaceships travel around the dark side of the Earth, temperatures drop way below freezing.

The International Space Station takes about 92 minutes to go around the Earth.

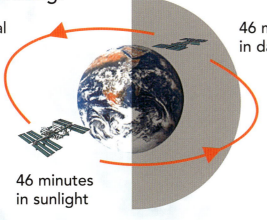

46 minutes in darkness

46 minutes in sunlight

Living in space

Space stations are homes in space where astronauts study the Earth and do experiments. People can live in them for many months at a time. The first space station was set up over 50 years ago.

The ISS

This is the International Space Station (ISS). It floats 250 miles (400km) above the Earth with up to seven people on board. The first crew arrived in 2000. A spacecraft takes each crew up and back to Earth. Crew members may live on board for up to six months at a time.

This is the inside of a laboratory where scientists can do tests to see how things behave in space.

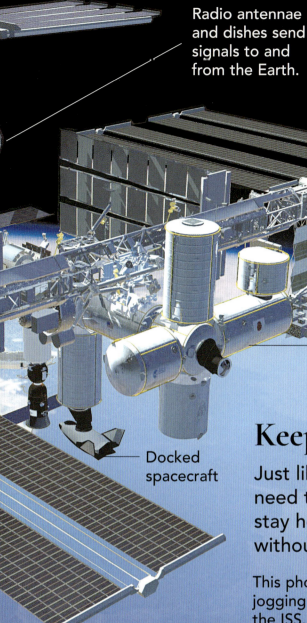

Radio antennae and dishes send signals to and from the Earth.

Criss-cross steel tubes hold the station together.

These are solar panels. They make energy by collecting heat from the Sun, and turning it into electricity.

Crew members live here and carry out experiments. There are 16 layers in the walls that keep heat or cold out, and stop meteoroids from getting in.

Docked spacecraft

Keeping fit

Just like on Earth, astronauts need to exercise each day to stay healthy. But exercising without gravity can be tricky.

This photo shows an astronaut jogging on a treadmill aboard the ISS. He is strapped down so he doesn't float away.

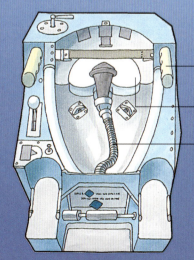

Space toilet

The picture on the right shows what a space toilet looks like. It is tricky to use.

- Scan the code to explore the ISS and find out how to live in space.
- For more links, go to **usborne.com/Quicklinks**

Handle for the astronaut to hold on to

Seat

Air sucks waste through this tube.

Urine is cleaned and turned back into water. Solid waste is frozen and returned to Earth.

Satellites and probes

Satellites and space probes are spacecraft with no people in them. Instead, scientists control them from Earth. Most satellites and probes have cameras or other kinds of viewing equipment.

Above is the Sentinel-5P satellite. It studies Earth's atmosphere and air quality.

Satellites

Some satellites look down on Earth, and others look out into space. Some types send television pictures, phone signals or the internet around the world. Others are used to help with navigation.

This is the SOHO satellite, which looks at the atmosphere of the Sun. It is also used to find out about the solar wind (see page 264).

Solar panels

- Scan the code for more about space probes and their amazing journeys.
- For more links, go to **usborne.com/Quicklinks**

Launched in 1977, the Voyager 2 space probe passed Neptune in 1989. It is now outside the Solar System.

Space probes

Space probes do similar jobs to satellites, but instead of orbiting the Earth, they visit other planets. All the planets in our Solar System have been visited by probes.

Voyager 2 probe

COBE satellite

Space views

Below are two pictures taken by satellites. Special cameras are used to show particular details, which can also be made clearer with computers.

A big picture

A satellite named COBE took the picture below. It is the first temperature map of the entire Universe.

ERS picture showing a hole in the atmosphere over Antarctica.

SOHO picture showing the outer edge of the Sun's surface.

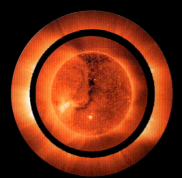

Parts of space are hotter than others. The pink and blue areas show different temperatures.

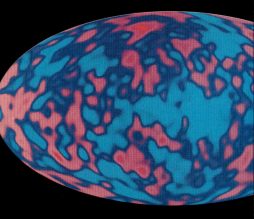

Is anyone out there?

Ever since people first began to study the stars, they have wondered whether there is life in space. At the moment, we don't know. Some astronomers think we will find evidence of alien life before the end of the century.

Reaching out

Four spacecraft that launched in the 1970s are now heading out of our Solar System. Two Pioneer probes each carry a picture of people and a map that shows where Earth is.

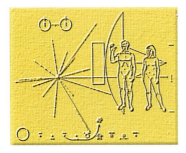

The Pioneer map and picture

Two Voyager probes each carry a disc with sounds and pictures of Earth. If aliens ever find the probes, they may be able to learn about life on Earth.

The Voyager disc

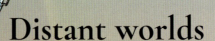

Pioneer probe

Voyager probe

Distant worlds

Planets beyond our Solar System are called exoplanets. Scientists think there could be as many exoplanets as there are stars. Powerful radio telescopes, such as FAST in China, search the skies near these planets, looking for signs of alien life.

FAST is the largest single radio telescope in the world.

Life on Europa?

Europa, one of Jupiter's moons, has an icy surface. Under it there may be a cold, dark sea. Scientists think they may find life there. The Europa Clipper mission, launched in 2024, aims to find out more about what could be under Europa's surface.

This illustration shows the Europa Clipper space probe arriving at Europa. This is due to happen in 2030.

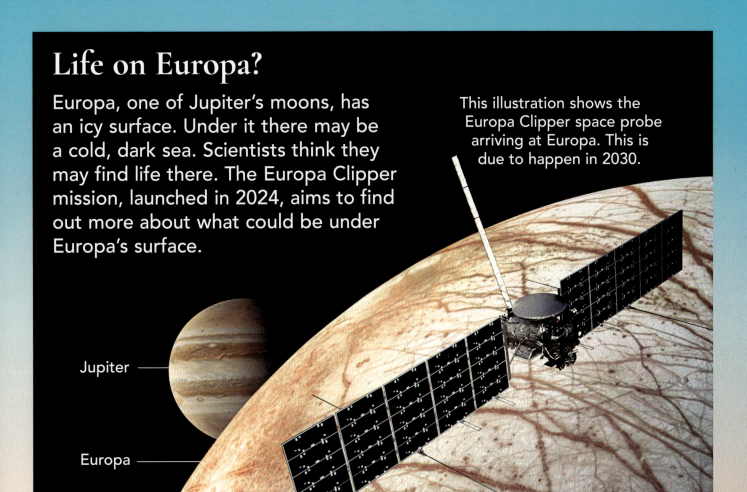

Jupiter

Europa

- Scan the code for more about the search for alien life.
- For more links, go to **usborne.com/Quicklinks**

Aliens often look like this in movies, but they're unlikely to look like this in reality.

What could aliens look like?

If we do find life in space, it may not look very interesting. It could be slime or moss, rather than intelligent beings with arms, legs and heads.

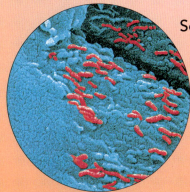

Some scientists think germ-like blobs (shown in red), found in a rock from Mars, show life once existed there.

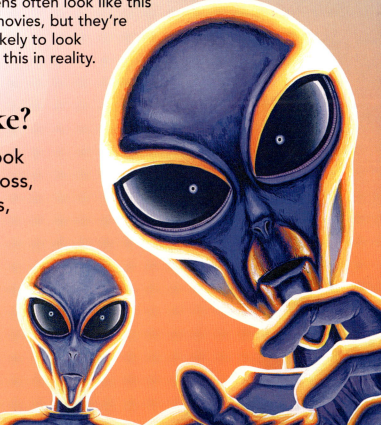

The Moon

The Moon travels around the Earth, just like the Earth travels around the Sun. So far, the Moon is the only part of the Solar System that people have been able to visit.

Sea of Crises

The first lunar landing, the Apollo 11 mission, landed in the Sea of Tranquillity in 1969.

Sea of Tranquillity

The Moon's "seas" are actually dark patches of melted rock.

Sea of Serenity

The Apollo 15 mission landed near here in 1971.

Sea of Rains

Craters like this one were made by rocks from space crashing into the Moon.

Earth

If you were orbiting the Moon in a spaceship, this is how far away Earth would look.

When people went to the Moon between 1969 and 1972, it took their spaceships three days to get there.

What is the Moon like?

The Moon is very different from Earth. There is no air, no weather, and no life. It is a dreary, dusty place that is boiling hot by day and freezing at night. The surface is covered with saucer-shaped holes called craters. You can see some if you look at the Moon on a clear night. Some are so huge, a city the size of London could fit inside them.

Where did the Moon come from?

The Moon is about the same age as the Earth. Here is one idea about where it came from.

1. Soon after the Earth formed, a planet hit it.

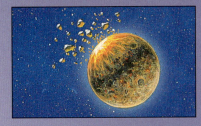

2. Rocks broke off and shot into space.

3. The rocks were held in orbit by Earth's gravity.

4. These rocks slowly formed into the Moon.

Moon landings

Between 1969 and 1972, people visited the Moon six times. More than 50 years later, some countries are starting new visits to the Moon, and there are even plans to set up a base there.

• Scan the code for more about Moon landings and exploration.

• For more links, go to **usborne.com/Quicklinks**

This spaceship is called a lunar module.

This is the Apollo 15 mission. See where they landed on the Moon on the opposite page.

There is no wind on the Moon. This flag has a rod sewn into it, to hold it out straight.

Electric rover

The Sun

The size of the Earth, compared to the Sun

Our Sun is a star. It is so big that it could hold over a million planets the size of Earth.

What is a star?

Stars are huge balls of blazing gas. The gases are constantly changing their structures to form new gases, which releases huge amounts of energy. This is what makes stars shine.

Sunlight is made by the Sun burning four million metric tons (tonnes) of hydrogen every second.

- Scan the code to find out about the Sun and see its fiery surface.
- For more links, go to **usborne.com/Quicklinks**

The solar wind

As well as light and heat, the Sun also sends out a stream of invisible specks, called particles, into space. This is called the solar wind. When the particles pass by the North and South Poles of Earth, they can make the air glow beautiful reds, blues, greens and purples.

When the solar wind lights up the sky in the north, it is known as the aurora borealis, or northern lights. In the south, it is called the aurora australis, or southern lights.

This is a solar prominence. It is a massive arch of hot gas, which reaches out into space like a huge, flaming tongue.

In this close-up of the Sun's surface, you can see jets of gas called coronal loops.

—— Facula

—— Sunspot

Solar surface

The Sun's surface is called the photosphere. Its temperature is about 10,000°F (5,500°C). The dark areas are sunspots. They have a lower temperature of around 6,500°F (3,600°C).

The Goldilocks zone

Life exists on Earth because our planet is just the right distance from the Sun for water to be a liquid, rather than ice or a gas. Scientists call this the Goldilocks zone, after the fairy tale.

Mars is too cold.

Venus is too hot.

Sun

Earth is just right.

Sometimes, white areas appear on the surface of the Sun. These are called faculae. The temperature here is even higher than that of the rest of the Sun.

Mercury and Venus

Mercury and Venus are the two planets closest to the Sun. Both are small and very hot. Mercury has almost no atmosphere, but Venus is covered with a thick layer of gas.

Tiny Mercury

Mercury is a tiny planet. Billions of years ago, many rocks crashed into it, so its surface is covered with lots of craters. Because it is so close to the Sun, it has the shortest year of any planet. Mercury takes just 88 Earth days to travel around the Sun.

Mercury is a third of the size of Earth, but is almost as heavy. It has a core of dense metal. This makes up nearly three-quarters of its inside.

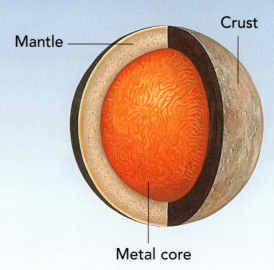

Mantle

Crust

Metal core

Four billion years ago, an enormous meteorite crashed into Mercury. It made a massive crater called the Caloris Basin. This is more than 950 miles (1,525km) across.

Mercury

Sweltering Venus

Venus is the nearest planet to us. Although it is farther away from the Sun than Mercury, its surface is actually hotter. This is because it has a thick atmosphere of carbon dioxide gas, which traps the Sun's heat and keeps it from escaping back into space.

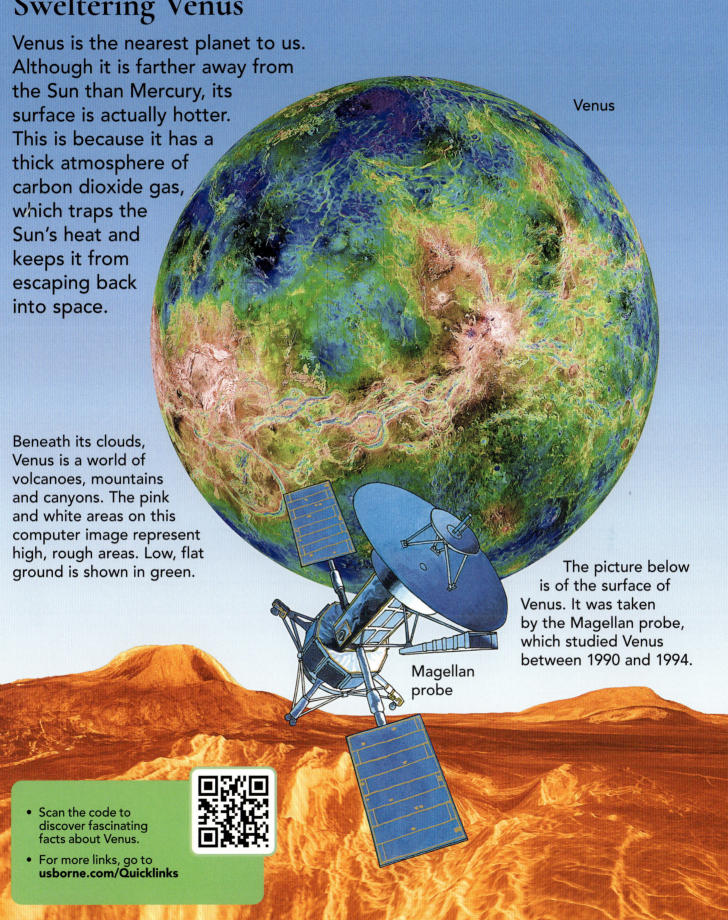

Venus

Beneath its clouds, Venus is a world of volcanoes, mountains and canyons. The pink and white areas on this computer image represent high, rough areas. Low, flat ground is shown in green.

The picture below is of the surface of Venus. It was taken by the Magellan probe, which studied Venus between 1990 and 1994.

Magellan probe

- Scan the code to discover fascinating facts about Venus.
- For more links, go to **usborne.com/Quicklinks**

Mars

If you were standing on Mars, being there would be a little like being on Earth. There is a bright sky during the day, and you could see thin clouds, morning mists and light frosts. But Mars is a lot colder than our planet.

Mars in detail

Mars is half the size of Earth. It is covered mainly with rocks and dust. Most of it looks like a great big desert. It has a thin atmosphere of poisonous gas.

- Scan the code to see what rovers do on Mars.
- For more links, go to **usborne.com/Quicklinks**

Mars

This is a polar ice cap where water has frozen into a huge field of ice.

These marks are great fields of dark dust. They are blown around by fierce storms.

This is a volcano called Olympus Mons.

This is a volcano called Ascraeus Mons.

This is a huge canyon called the Valles Marineris.

The Viking 1 space probe visited Mars in 1976. It sent down the first craft to land on the surface.

Volcanoes and canyons

Mars has some very interesting features. There are several volcanoes. The biggest one is called Olympus Mons. It is the largest in the Solar System. It rises 15 miles (25km) above the surface of Mars. There are also huge canyons and dried-up water channels.

Channel

The Olympus Mons volcano seen by a visiting space probe

The Valles Marineris canyon is a huge crack along one side of the planet. It is so long it would stretch across the whole of the USA.

Astronomers think that channels like this were made by running water, which has now frozen or leaked away.

Mars rovers

Many probes have landed on Mars. Some, known as rovers, can move around. Rovers conduct experiments and send images back to Earth.

This is a "selfie" taken by the Perseverance rover on the surface of Mars. You can see one of the rock sample tubes on the ground beside it.

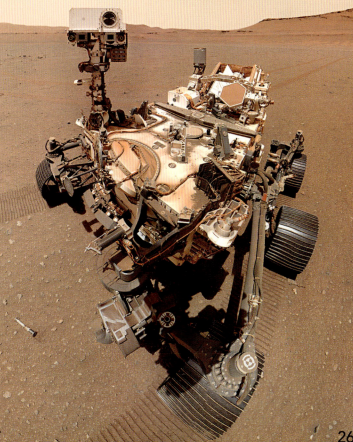

Life on Mars?

Nothing lives on Mars now, but it is possible that there was life on Mars a very long time ago. The Perseverance rover, which landed on Mars in 2021, is looking for any signs of that life. It is also collecting rock samples and leaving them to be picked up by a future mission, so that they can be taken to Earth and studied more closely.

Jupiter and Saturn

Farther from the Sun, beyond the Asteroid Belt*, lie four huge planets. The largest of these are Jupiter and Saturn. They are mostly made from thick atmospheres of gas, and are known as gas giants.

Jupiter

Jupiter is the biggest planet in the Solar System and has at least 95 moons. It also has the shortest day. It takes only 9 hours and 50 minutes to spin around once. Jupiter is a stormy planet. Swirling clouds of gas race around it, in dark and light bands.

The Great Red Spot is a storm that is wider than the Earth.

A probe from the Galileo space probe parachuted into Jupiter's gassy atmosphere in 1995.

Jupiter

- Scan the code to explore facts about Saturn and its rings.
- For more links, go to usborne.com/Quicklinks

Saturn

Saturn is the second biggest planet in the Solar System. Many broad rings of rock and ice orbit around it. Saturn is very light. If you could put it in a huge swimming pool, it would float there.

Saturn

Saturn's moons

Saturn has 274 moons, and there may be more. Titan is the largest. It has a thick atmosphere.

Here you can see how big Titan is compared to the planet Mercury and to Earth's moon.

Titan

Mercury

Earth's moon

Ring leader

Some planets are orbited by rings of ice, dust and rocks. Saturn has the widest rings of any planet in our Solar System. Some rocks in the rings are as big as a house, while others are smaller than a pebble. Scientists think the objects in Saturn's rings came from some of its moons, millions of years ago. You can see what might have happened below.

Two moons collided with each other.

They broke into billions of pieces.

The pieces stayed in Saturn's orbit.

Eventually, they formed Saturn's rings.

Uranus and Neptune

Uranus and Neptune are huge icy planets, known as ice giants. Both are around four times wider than Earth, and both have rings, like Saturn. They are hard to spot in the night sky, but you can see them with a telescope.

Uranus

This planet spins on its side. Its outer surface is cloaked by a thin mist, which wraps around a surface of thick gases and icy fluid. Farther inside, Uranus has a small core of solid rock.

Uranus has 28 moons that we know of. Here are some of them.

Puzzle moon

One of Uranus's moons, Miranda, looks like a huge jigsaw puzzle. Some scientists believe that, millions of years ago, it broke into pieces. Gradually time and gravity put it back together.

Uranus

Umbriel

Oberon

Titania

Ariel

Miranda

This is what Miranda's surface looks like now.

A comet may have crashed into Miranda.

Miranda's pieces drifted back together.

Miranda slowly put itself back into one piece.

Neptune

Neptune has the worst storms in the Solar System. Winds of 1,250mph (2,000km/h) whip methane clouds around the planet.

Neptune has 16 moons. One, named Triton, is a frozen world. Huge jets of gas have been seen shooting out from below its thin surface of ice. Some scientists believe they are caused by volcano-like eruptions from below the surface.

Triton orbits in the opposite direction from all of Neptune's other moons.

Triton

Neptune

Voyager 2

The longest year

Neptune is the furthest planet from the Sun. It takes 165 Earth years for Neptune to complete one full orbit around the Sun.

- Scan the code to watch a video about the ice giants Uranus and Neptune.
- For more links, go to **usborne.com/Quicklinks**

Visitor from Earth

The Voyager 2 space probe visited Uranus and Neptune in 1986 and 1989. The probe took 12 years to get to Neptune from Earth.

The Kuiper Belt and beyond

Beyond Neptune lies a huge ring of icy rocks known as the Kuiper Belt. These drifting rocks did not merge into one of the planets when the Solar System was formed.

Dwarf planets

Dwarf planets are like small planets, but they don't have enough gravity to clear other objects from their paths. We know of five dwarf planets in our Solar System: Ceres, Pluto, Haumea, Makemake and Eris. All of them except Ceres are in the Kuiper Belt.

Ceres

Pluto

Launched in 2006, the New Horizons space probe reached Pluto in 2015.

Ceres is part of the Asteroid Belt (see page 276). It was thought to be an asteroid until 2006, when it was renamed at the same time as Pluto.

The ninth planet?

For a long time, Pluto was thought of as the ninth planet in our Solar System. After the discovery of Eris and Makemake, scientists argued about the difference between a planet and a dwarf planet. In 2006, it was agreed that Pluto was not a planet, but a dwarf planet.

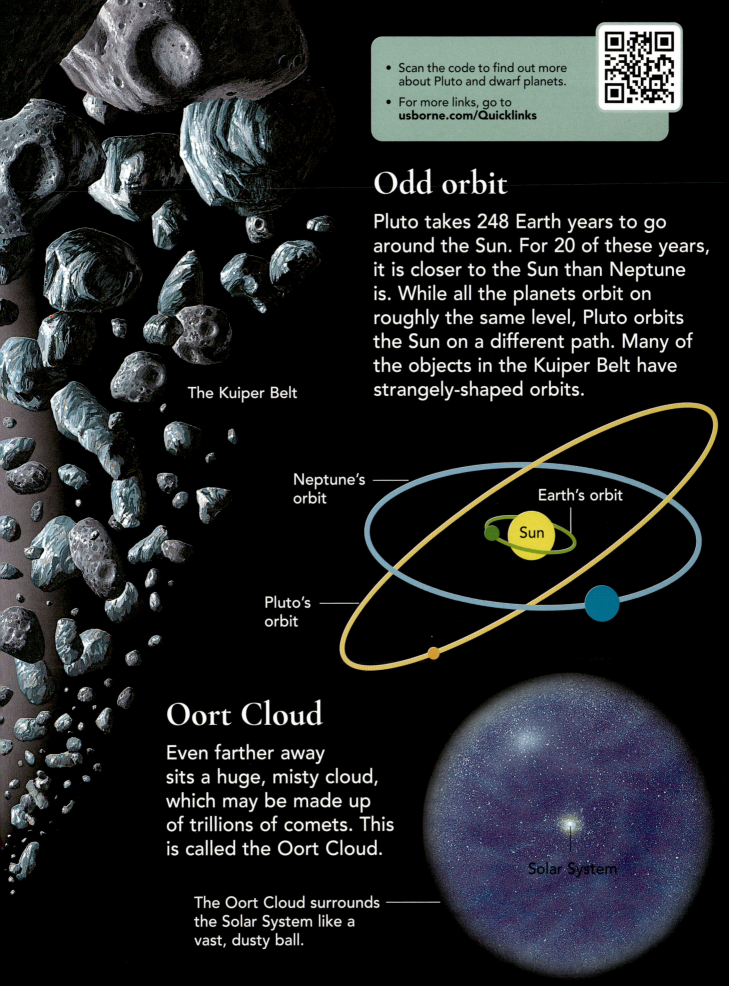

- Scan the code to find out more about Pluto and dwarf planets.
- For more links, go to **usborne.com/Quicklinks**

Odd orbit

Pluto takes 248 Earth years to go around the Sun. For 20 of these years, it is closer to the Sun than Neptune is. While all the planets orbit on roughly the same level, Pluto orbits the Sun on a different path. Many of the objects in the Kuiper Belt have strangely-shaped orbits.

The Kuiper Belt

Neptune's orbit

Earth's orbit

Sun

Pluto's orbit

Oort Cloud

Even farther away sits a huge, misty cloud, which may be made up of trillions of comets. This is called the Oort Cloud.

Solar System

The Oort Cloud surrounds the Solar System like a vast, dusty ball.

Space rocks

Our Solar System isn't just the Sun, the planets, and their moons. There are countless asteroids, meteoroids and comets flying around in it too.

Asteroids

Asteroids are big lumps of rocks and metal. Between Mars and Jupiter lies a large band of them, called the Asteroid Belt. The biggest one, named Vesta, is about 330 miles (530km) across. Some asteroids even have their own moons.

Meteoroids that burn up in the sky are called meteors or shooting stars.

Meteoroids that hit a planet are called meteorites.

Below is a photo of a huge crater in Arizona, USA. It was caused by a meteorite.

Meteoroids

Meteoroids are smaller pieces of rock from space. Many are no bigger than a grain of sand, but lots are larger. A few are as big as houses. Most burn up in the atmosphere as they fall to Earth, but some are too big to burn, and cause damage when they reach Earth.

This is part of the Asteroid Belt. Some of the rocks it contains are as big as small moons.

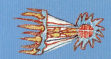

Comets

Comets are large balls of ice and dust. They come in from the outer edge of the Solar System to circle the Sun. Once past Jupiter, the heat from the Sun begins to melt the outer layer of the comet, and the solar wind blows a trail of gas and dust behind it.

Part of the Bayeux Tapestry shows people looking at a comet in 1066.

Deep Impact

Scientists have developed special space probes to find out more about comets. One, called Deep Impact, visited a comet called Tempel 1. The probe blasted a hole in the comet, took photographs and collected some of the dust and ice from the blast.

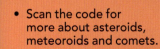

This picture shows the comet Hale-Bopp when it passed by the Earth in 1997.

A comet far away from the Sun has no tail. It is just a solid block of dirty ice.

Closer to the Sun, the outside begins to melt, and forms a trail of gas and dust.

By the time it flies by Earth, the comet's tail is glowing. This makes it easy to spot.

- Scan the code for more about asteroids, meteoroids and comets.

- For more links, go to **usborne.com/Quicklinks**

Galaxies

Galaxies are collections of billions of stars held together by gravity. There are billions of galaxies in the Universe.

The Milky Way

The Sun is one of the 100 billion stars that make up a galaxy called the Milky Way. The Milky Way is a spiral-shaped galaxy, and it is about 100,000 light years across. It is not the biggest galaxy in the Universe, but it is much larger than many others. Like most galaxies, it is spinning around a central hub.

The middle of the Milky Way is hidden by great clouds of dust.

If you could see the Milky Way from the side, it would look like a flat plate with a bulge in the middle.

Astronomers think the Sun and our Solar System are here.

A long trip

It takes 225 million years for the Milky Way to spin all the way around. The last time our Solar System was in the same place in space as it is now, dinosaurs roamed the Earth.

- Scan the code to explore our galaxy, the Milky Way.
- For more links, go to **usborne.com/Quicklinks**

Radio view

Everything in space gives off radio waves, which radio telescopes can "see." The picture on the right is from a radio telescope. It shows the big bulge in the middle of our galaxy.

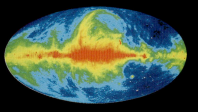

The red patch in this picture shows where most of the stars are in the Milky Way.

Galaxy shapes

Not all galaxies look the same. There are several different shapes a galaxy might be. You can see three of them below.

This type is known as an irregular galaxy. It doesn't have any real shape at all.

This oval-shaped type is called an elliptical galaxy.

This type is a barred spiral galaxy.

How many galaxies?

A hundred years ago, astronomers thought the Milky Way was the only galaxy in the Universe. But over the last century, telescopes and radio telescopes have detected many millions of other galaxies.

This photograph shows some more newly discovered galaxies. Before this picture was taken, astronomers thought there was nothing in this part of space.

Looking at the night sky

Although many of the pictures in this section were taken using powerful telescopes, you can still see some amazing things in the night sky with only your eyes. Here are just a few of them.

A spiral galaxy

Milky Way

The Moon

Betelgeuse, an old star

Hyades, a star cluster

These three stars are Orion's Belt – part of the Orion constellation.

Sirius, the brightest star in the sky

These are some of the things you may be able to see without a telescope.

The Moon

The clearest sight in the night sky is the Moon. You can see it shining brightly in the darkness because it is lit up by light from the Sun. As the Moon orbits the Earth, it seems to change shape.

New Moon

When no light shines on the Moon, it is impossible to see it.

Waxing Moon

Gradually, a sliver of light returns. The Moon appears to grow.

Full Moon

Once every 28 days, all of one side of the Moon is lit by the Sun's light.

Waning Moon

As the Moon moves in its orbit, less light falls on it. It seems to shrink.

- Scan the code for tips about looking at the night sky.
- For more links, go to **usborne.com/Quicklinks**

Stars

A clear night sky is full of stars. There are certain patterns you can look for. These patterns are called constellations, and there are 88 altogether.

This is a star pattern called Orion. Ancient people thought this shape looked like a hunter. The three stars that make up his waist are known as Orion's Belt.

Above is a photograph of part of the constellation Orion. His arms, club and shield are not shown in this picture.

The Milky Way

This is what the Milky Way looks like on a very clear night. You can see it at certain times of the year if you are away from city lights.

Space words

alien a living thing from another world.

asteroid a rock orbiting the Sun. There are thousands of them in a part of the Solar System called the Asteroid Belt.

astronaut someone who goes into space.

atmosphere a layer of gases that surrounds a planet or a star.

cluster a group of space objects gathered together, such as stars or galaxies.

comet a chunk of dirty ice orbiting the Sun which can form a long tail as it melts.

core the middle of a planet, moon, star or other space object.

crater a hollow on the surface of a planet, moon or asteroid, caused by something hitting it, such as a meteorite.

day the time it takes a planet or moon to spin all the way around.

galaxy a group of hundreds of millions of stars all held together by gravity.

gravity a force that pulls objects toward other objects.

meteor a meteoroid that burns up in a planet's atmosphere. Also called a shooting star.

meteorite a meteoroid that hits the surface of a planet or moon.

meteoroid dust, or small chunks of rock, in orbit around the Sun.

moon a natural object that orbits a planet, dwarf planet or asteroid.

orbit the path of an object in space, as it travels around another object.

planet a huge ball of rock or gas, which travels around a star.

rocket a type of engine in a spacecraft which uses exploding fuel to make it move.

satellite 1) something in space which orbits something else. 2) an uncrewed spacecraft which orbits the Earth.

solar system a group of planets and other objects all orbiting a star.

spacecraft (also called spaceship) a vehicle that is used for space travel. If it has no people in it, it is uncrewed.

space probe an uncrewed spacecraft that collects information about objects in space.

space station a large spacecraft orbiting the Earth, where astronauts learn about living and working in space.

space walk when an astronaut in a space suit leaves a spacecraft and floats in space.

star a huge ball of blazing gas.

Universe everything in space.

year the length of time it takes a planet to travel around its star. Earth's year lasts 365 days.

- Scan the code to explore space with videos, facts and activities.
- For more links, go to **usborne.com/Quicklinks**

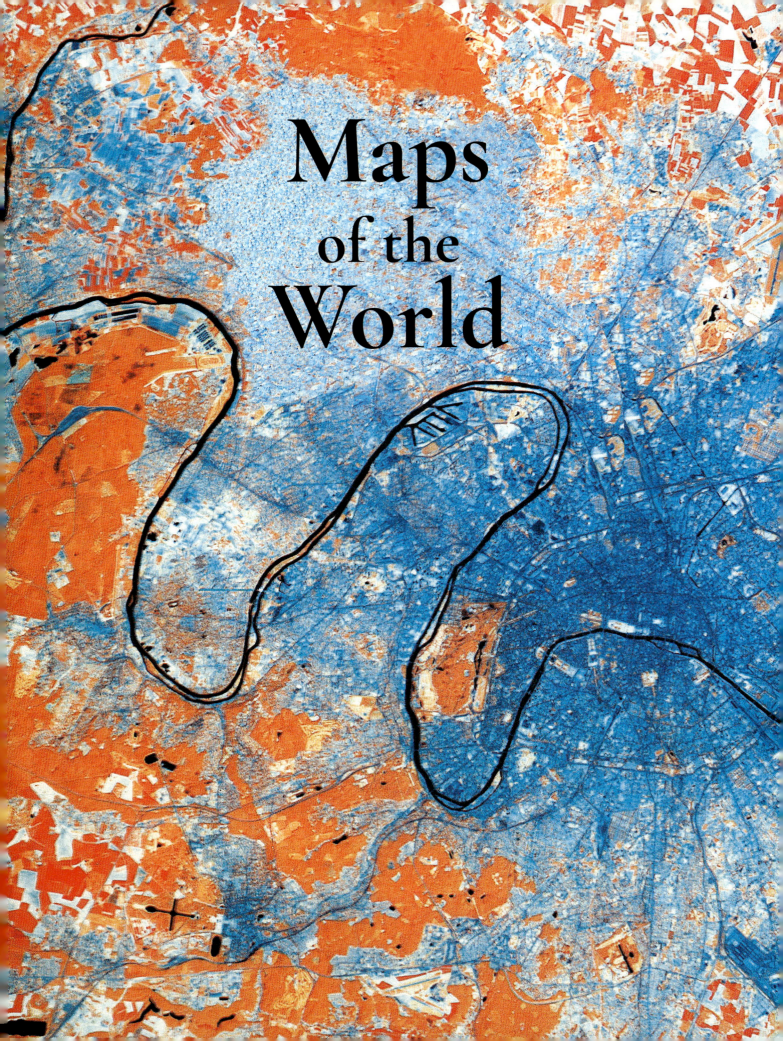

Maps
of the
World

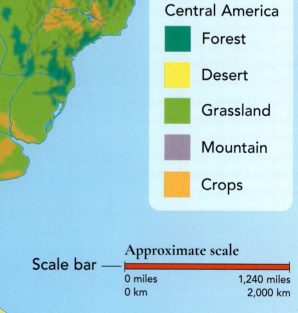

About maps

A map is a picture that shows a particular area of the world. Places are usually shown as you would see them from above, and much smaller than in real life. A map could show the whole world or just one street.

This map shows what the land in South and Central America is covered with.

What will you see on a map?

Maps are designed to be easy to understand. Colors and symbols on a map all mean different things. A key tells you what they all stand for.

The size of a map compared with the area it shows is called its scale. Some maps show this with a scale bar. This is a line that tells you how many miles or kilometers are represented by a certain distance on the map.

Which way is up?

The Earth doesn't have a top and a bottom, but north is usually shown at the top of maps. Some maps have a symbol to show which way is north.

Key to map of South and Central America

- ■ Forest
- ■ Desert
- ■ Grassland
- ■ Mountain
- ■ Crops

Approximate scale

Scale bar ——

0 miles — 1,240 miles
0 km — 2,000 km

This compass symbol shows which way is north (N), south (S), east (E) and west (W).

Kinds of maps

A map can show features of an area in a clear, simple way. There are lots of different kinds of maps. Here are three of them.

Political maps show countries or states. They often show the names of important cities and towns.

Physical maps show natural features such as mountains, rivers and lakes. They usually have a key.

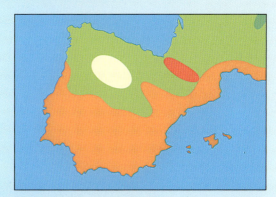

Thematic maps show various types of information, such as which types of plants grow in which regions.

Dividing lines

Map makers divide up the Earth with imaginary lines. These are numbered in degrees (°) and minutes (') to help us measure distances and find places on a map. There are two sets of lines. They are called latitude and longitude.

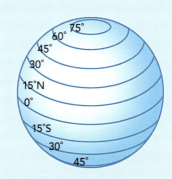

Lines of latitude run around the globe. They are the same distance apart.

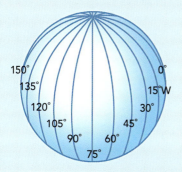

Lines of longitude run from the North Pole to the South Pole.

Here is a drawing of the Earth showing the North Pole and the main lines of latitude and longitude.

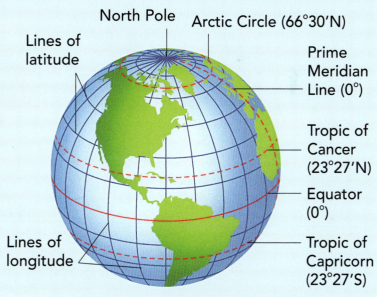

The South Pole is at the bottom of the globe, but you can't see it here.

- Scan the code to watch a video about lines of latitude and longitude.
- For more links, go to **usborne.com/Quicklinks**

The world's environments

This map shows the seven continents of the world and its different types of land, or environments, such as desert or mountain.

- Scan the code to explore some of the world's environments.
- For more links, go to **usborne.com/Quicklinks**

Approximate scale

0 miles	1,860 miles
0 km	3,000 km

Key to map of the world's environments

- **Forest**
- **Grassland**
- **Desert**
- **Mountain (only high mountains are shown)**
- **Tundra (frozen ground with few or no trees)**
- **Ice (areas where there is always ice)**
- **Crops (land used for growing plants for people and animals to eat)**
- **Sea**
- **Lake**
- **River**
- ▲ **Mountain peak**

ARCTIC OCEAN

Svalbard
North Cape
Novaya Zemlya
Barents Sea
Kara Sea
Severnaya Zemlya
Laptev Sea
New Siberian Islands
East Siberian Sea
Arctic Circle
Bering Sea
Sea of Okhotsk
Kamchatka Peninsula

S i b e r i a

Ob
Yenisey
Lena
Verkhoyansk Range
Amur

EUROPE
Danube
Black Sea
Mount Elbrus ▲
Caspian Sea
Ural Mountains
Aral Sea
A S I A
Altai Mountains
Gobi Desert
Japan
Honshu
PACIFIC OCEAN
Tropic of Cancer

Mediterranean Sea
Libyan Desert
Nile
Arabia
Red Sea
Rub al Khali (Empty Quarter)
H i m a l a y a s
Mount Everest
Ganges
China
Yangtze
East China Sea
Taiwan

Sahel
Arabian Sea
India
Bay of Bengal
Mekong
South China Sea
Luzon
Philippines
Micronesia

AFRICA
Ethiopian Highlands
Cape Comorin (Kanyakumari)
Sri Lanka
Mindanao
Equator

Lake Victoria
Kilimanjaro ▲
Seychelles
Sumatra
Borneo
Celebes
New Guinea
Mount Wilhelm ▲
Solomon Islands
Melanesia

Zambezi
Comoro Islands
INDIAN OCEAN
Java Sea
Java
Arafura Sea
Coral Sea
Fiji Islands

Madagascar
Mauritius
Great Sandy Desert
New Caledonia
Tropic of Capricorn

Kalahari Desert
AUSTRALIA
Great Barrier Reef
Great Dividing Range

Cape of Good Hope
Great Victoria Desert
Tasman Sea
New Zealand
North Island (Te Ika-a-Māui)

Tasmania
South Island (Te Waipounamu)

Kerguelen Islands

SOUTHERN OCEAN

Antarctic Circle

A N T A R C T I C A
Ross Sea

20° E 40° 60° 80° 100° 120° 140° 160° 180° 80° 60° 40° 20° N 0° 20° S 40° 60° 80°

Countries of the world

This map shows the different countries that make up each continent.

Approximate scale

0 miles	1,860 miles
0 km	3,000 km

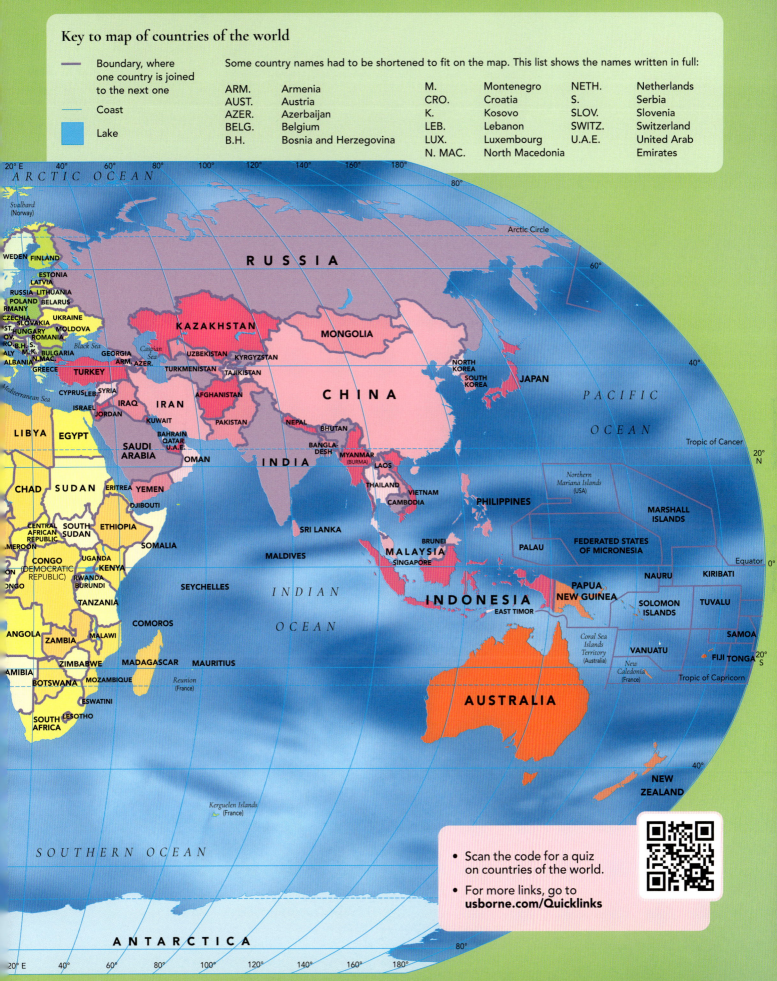

• Scan the code for a quiz on countries of the world.

• For more links, go to usborne.com/Quicklinks

North America

This continent includes three very large countries – Canada, the USA, and Mexico. It also covers Greenland, the Caribbean, and the countries in the land that joins South America.

PACIFIC OCEAN

Approximate scale

0 miles	620 miles
0 km	1,000 km

Key to map of North America

- ■ Capital city
- ○ Major city or town
- ── Boundary (where one country joins another one)
- ── River

Raccoons are found mainly in North and Central America. They usually sleep in trees during the day and come out at night to feed.

- Scan the code for a video tour of North America.
- For more links, go to **usborne.com/Quicklinks**

Arctic Circle

ARCTIC OCEAN

Bering Strait

Queen Elizabeth Islands

Point Barrow

Beaufort Sea

Parry Islands

Bering Sea

Yukon

Alaska (USA)

▲ Denali

○ Anchorage

Victoria Island

Mackenzie

Great Bear Lake

Gulf of Alaska

Great Slave Lake

CANADA

Lake Athabasca

Reindeer Lake

○ Vancouver

○ Calgary

○ Winnipe

R O C K Y   M O U N T A I N S

Great Plains

○ Seattle

Columbia

Missouri

Great Salt Lake

San Francisco ○

U N I T E D   S T A T E S

California

Colorado

○ Denver

Los Angeles ○

○ Phoenix

Ciudad Juarez ○

Texa

Lower California

○ Hermosillo

Rio Grande

Hawaiian Islands (USA)

Tropic of Cancer

○ Monterrey

MEXICO

○ Guadalajara

Mexico City ■

○ Acapulco

290

GREENLAND
(Denmark)

Baffin Bay

Baffin Island

Nuuk

Cape Farewell

Labrador Sea

Hudson Bay

Labrador Peninsula

Newfoundland

St. John's

Quebec

ke Winnipeg

Lake Superior

St. Lawrence

Quebec

Nova Scotia

Montreal

Halifax

Ottawa

Great Lakes

Lake Huron

Minneapolis

Toronto *Lake Ontario*

Boston

Lake Michigan

Detroit *Lake Erie*

New York

Chicago Pittsburgh

Philadelphia

OF AMERICA

St. Louis Cincinnati

Washington, D.C.

ATLANTIC OCEAN

nsas City

Ohio

Appalachian Mountains

Cape Hatteras

Arkansas

Atlanta

Bermuda (UK)

las

Mississippi

Florida

Sargasso Sea

Tropic of Cancer

Houston

New Orleans

Gulf of Mexico

Miami

THE BAHAMAS

Nassau

Havana

Puerto Rico (USA)

ST. KITTS AND NEVIS

Merida

CUBA

DOMINICAN REPUBLIC

ANTIGUA AND BARBUDA

HAITI

Guadeloupe (France)

Yucatan Peninsula

Port-au-Prince

Santo Domingo

DOMINICA

Veracruz

Martinique (France)

JAMAICA Kingston

ST. LUCIA

BELIZE

ST. VINCENT AND THE GRENADINES

BARBADOS

GUATEMALA

Belmopan

GRENADA

HONDURAS

Caribbean Sea

TRINIDAD AND TOBAGO

Guatemala City

Tegucigalpa

Port of Spain

San Salvador

NICARAGUA

EL SALVADOR

Managua

San José Panama City

COSTA RICA PANAMA

This photograph of North America was taken from space by a satellite. The orange parts are deserts. The brown areas are the Rocky Mountains.

North America facts

Total land area
9,540,198 miles²

Biggest country
Canada 3,855,103 miles²

Smallest country
St. Kitts and Nevis 101 miles²

Biggest island
Greenland 836,330 miles²

Highest mountain
Denali, Alaska, USA 20,308ft

Longest river Mississippi/
Missouri, USA 3,740 miles

Biggest lake
Lake Superior, USA/Canada
31,699 miles²

Highest waterfall
Colonial Creek Falls,
Washington, USA 2,568ft

Biggest desert
Great Basin Desert, USA
189,962 miles²

291

South America

South America stretches from just north of the Equator almost to Antarctica in the south. Brazil is the biggest of the twelve countries in South America.

Key to map of South America

- ■ Capital city
- ○ Major city or town
- ▬ Boundary (where one country joins another one)
- ── River

Approximate scale

0 miles	620 miles
0 km	1,000 km

Toucans live in the rainforests of South America. They use their long, jagged beaks to pick and eat fruit from the trees.

Caribbean Sea

Maracaibo • ■ Caracas

VENEZUELA

Medellin •
■ Bogotá

Guiana Highlands

Cali ○ **COLOMBIA**

Orinoco

Equator

Galapagos Islands (Ecuador)

■ Quito
ECUADOR
Guayaquil

Negro

Amazon

Amazon Rainforest

Madeira

PERU

Ucayali

A N D E S

■ Lima

Lake Titicaca **BOLIVIA**

■ La Paz

Atacama Desert

■ Sucre

Lake Poopo

Tropic of Capricorn

CHILE

○ San Miguel de Tucuman

A N D E S

Aconcagua ▲

Cordoba ○

PACIFIC OCEAN

Rosario

■ Santiago

ARGENTINA

Pampas

Patagonia

Punta Arenas *Strait of Magellan*

Tierra del Fuego

Cape Horn

Drake Passage

Georgetown
Paramaribo
UYANA
Cayenne
SURINAME
FRENCH
GUIANA
(France)

Equator

Salbina Reservoir

Amazon

anaus

Xingu

Belem

Tucurui Reservoir

Fortaleza

B R A Z I L

Tocantin

Sobradinho
Reservoir

Recife

Plateau of
Mato Grosso

Brazilian Highlands

São Francisco

Salvador

Brasilia

Goiania

Belo Horizonte

Parana

Furnas
Reservoir

Rio de Janeiro

ARAGUAY

São Paulo

Tropic of Capricorn

Asunción

Curitiba

Porto Alegre

ATLANTIC

OCEAN

URUGUAY

Montevideo

Buenos Aires

Falkland Islands
(UK)

This is what South America looks like from space. The gray, mottled patch on the left-hand side is the Andes mountain range.

South America facts

Total land area
6,888,063 miles²

Biggest country
Brazil 3,287,612 miles²

Smallest country
Suriname 63,251 miles²

Biggest island
Tierra del Fuego 18,302 miles²

Highest mountain
Aconcagua, Argentina 22,838ft

Longest river
Amazon, Brazil 4,000 miles

Biggest lake
Lake Maracaibo, Venezuela
5,100 miles²

Highest waterfall
Angel Falls, on the Churun River,
Venezuela 3,212ft

Biggest desert
Patagonian Desert, Argentina
259,847 miles²

- Scan the code to explore South America's countries, landscapes and wildlife.
- For more links, go to **usborne.com/Quicklinks**

Asia

Asia is the world's biggest continent, covering thousands of miles. It stretches from the Arctic Circle to the Equator, and from the Ural Mountains in western Russia to Japan in the east.

ARCTIC OCEAN

Arctic Circle

Novaya Zemlya

Barents Sea

Kara Sea

Norilsk

Arkhangelsk

St. Petersburg

Moscow

Nizhniy Novgorod

Kazan

Ural Mountains

Ob

Yenisey

R U S S

Volga

Samara

Yekaterinburg

Chelyabinsk

Irtysh

Ob

Omsk

Novosibirsk

Mediterranean Sea

Istanbul

Izmir

Ankara

TURKEY

Black Sea

Rostov

Astrakhan

Caucasus Mountains

GEORGIA

Tbilisi

ARMENIA

Yerevan

Caspian Sea

Aqtobe

KAZAKHSTAN

Astana

Altai Mountains

CYPRUS

Nicosia

AZERBAIJAN

Baku

Aral Sea

Lake Balkhash

LEBANON

Beirut

SYRIA

Damascus

Tabriz

TURKMENISTAN

UZBEKISTAN

Almaty

Urumqi

Gaza

ISRAEL

Euphrates

Tigris

Ashgabat

Tashkent

Bishkek

KYRGYZSTAN

Jerusalem (disputed)

Amman

JORDAN

Baghdad

Tehran

Mashhad

Dushanbe

TAJIKISTAN

West Bank

IRAQ

Basra

IRAN

AFGHANISTAN

Kabul

Islamabad

Kunlun Mountai

Plateau of Tibet

Lhasa

Syrian Desert

KUWAIT

Shiraz

Kandahar

HIMALAYAS

Medina

SAUDI ARABIA

BAHRAIN

QATAR

Abu Dhabi

PAKISTAN

Delhi

NEPAL

Mount Everest

Jeddah

Mecca

Riyadh

UNITED ARAB EMIRATES

Muscat

New Delhi

Kathmandu

BHUTAN

Red Sea

The Gulf

Rub al Khali (Empty Quarter)

Karachi

Indus

Thar Desert

Ganges

Varanasi

BANGLADESH

Dhaka

Sanaa

YEMEN

OMAN

Arabian Sea

Nagpur

INDIA

Kolkata (Calcutta)

Bay of Bengal

Aden

Mumbai (Bombay)

Socotra (Yemen)

Bengaluru (Bangalore)

Chennai (Madras)

Cape Comorin (Kanyakumari)

SRI LANKA

MALDIVES

Colombo

Sri Jayawardenepura Kotte

Malé

Equator

INDIAN OCEAN

Key to map of Asia

- ■ Capital city
- ○ Major city or town
- — Boundary (where one country joins another one)
- -- Disputed boundary
- — River

Approximate scale

| 0 miles | 620 miles |
| 0 km | 1,000 km |

Giant pandas live in bamboo forests in the high mountains of western China. There are fewer than 2,000 giant pandas left in the wild.

- Scan the code to visit the continent of Asia.
- For more links, go to usborne.com/Quicklinks

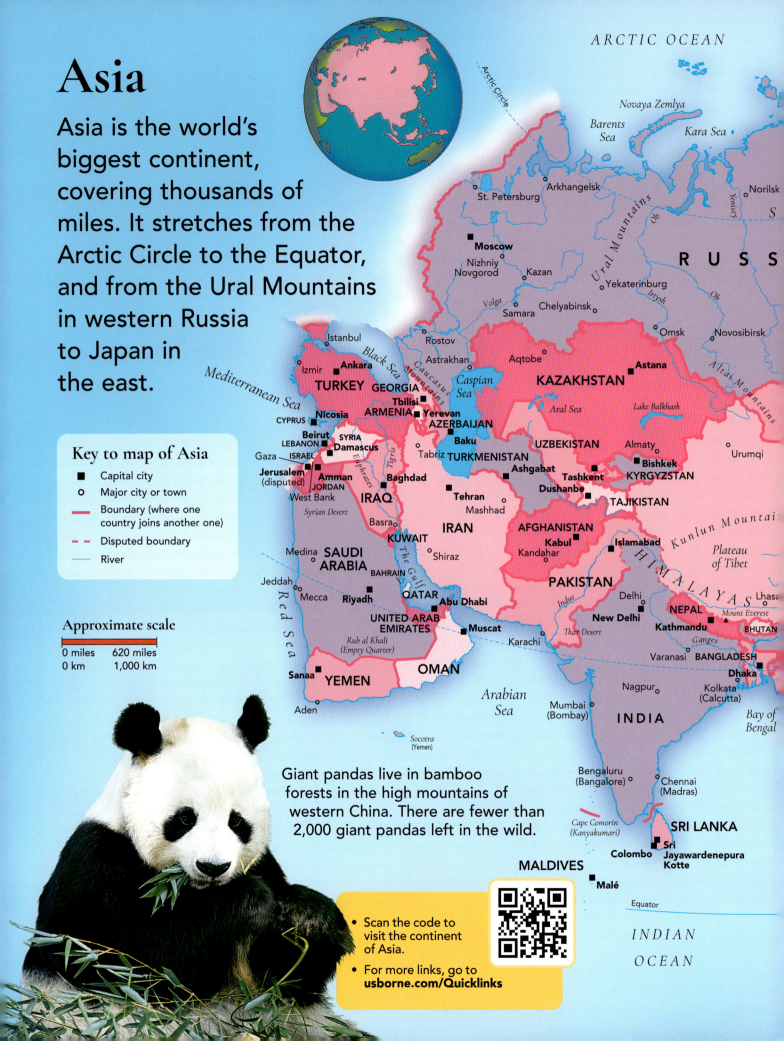

East Siberian Sea

Bering Sea

Laptev Sea

Arctic Circle

Anadyr

Verkhoyansk Range

Lena

S i b e r i a

Okhotsk

Yakutsk

Kamchatka Peninsula

Petropavlovsk-Kamchatskiy

Sea of Okhotsk

A

Lena

Irkutsk

Lake Baikal

Komsomolsk

Amur

Ulan Bator ■

MONGOLIA

Qiqihar

Hokkaido

Sapporo

Gobi Desert

Shenyang

NORTH KOREA

Sea of Japan

JAPAN

Tokyo ■

Beijing ■

Baotou

Pyongyang ■

Seoul ■

Osaka

Honshu

Hiroshima

SOUTH KOREA

Yellow

Xian

East China Sea

C H I N A

Shanghai

Hangzhou

Chongqing

Yangtze

Fuzhou

Taipei

Tropic of Cancer

Kunming

Taiwan

Hong Kong

PACIFIC OCEAN

Irrawaddy

YANMAR (BURMA)

y Pyi Taw ■

Hanoi ■

Hainan

Luzon

LAOS

Vientiane ■

South China Sea

PHILIPPINES

Yangon

Mekong

THAILAND

VIETNAM

Manila ■

Philippine Sea

Bangkok ■

CAMBODIA

Phnom Penh ■

Ho Chi Minh City (Saigon)

Mindanao

Davao

Equator

MALAYSIA

BRUNEI

Medan

Kuala Lumpur ■

Putrajaya ■

New Guinea

SINGAPORE

Borneo

Celebes

Banda Sea

Sumatra

I N D O N E S I A

Palembang

Java Sea

Ujung Pandang

Arafura Sea

Jakarta ■

Surabaya

Dili ■

EAST TIMOR

Java

Timor Sea

The white streaks across the middle of this satellite photograph of Asia are the snowy peaks of mountain ranges.

Asia facts

Total land area
17,196,187 miles^2

Biggest country
Russia (total area)
6,592,772 miles^2
Asiatic Russia 4,934,694 miles^2

Smallest country
Maldives 116 miles^2

Biggest island
Borneo 288,869 miles^2

Highest mountain
Mount Everest, Himalayas
29,032ft

Longest river
Yangtze, China 3,915 miles

Biggest lake
Caspian Sea, western Asia
149,190 miles^2

Highest waterfall
Kadamaian Falls, Malaysia
2,300ft

Biggest desert
Arabian Desert (the name
given to the deserts of
Saudi Arabia) 899,618 miles^2

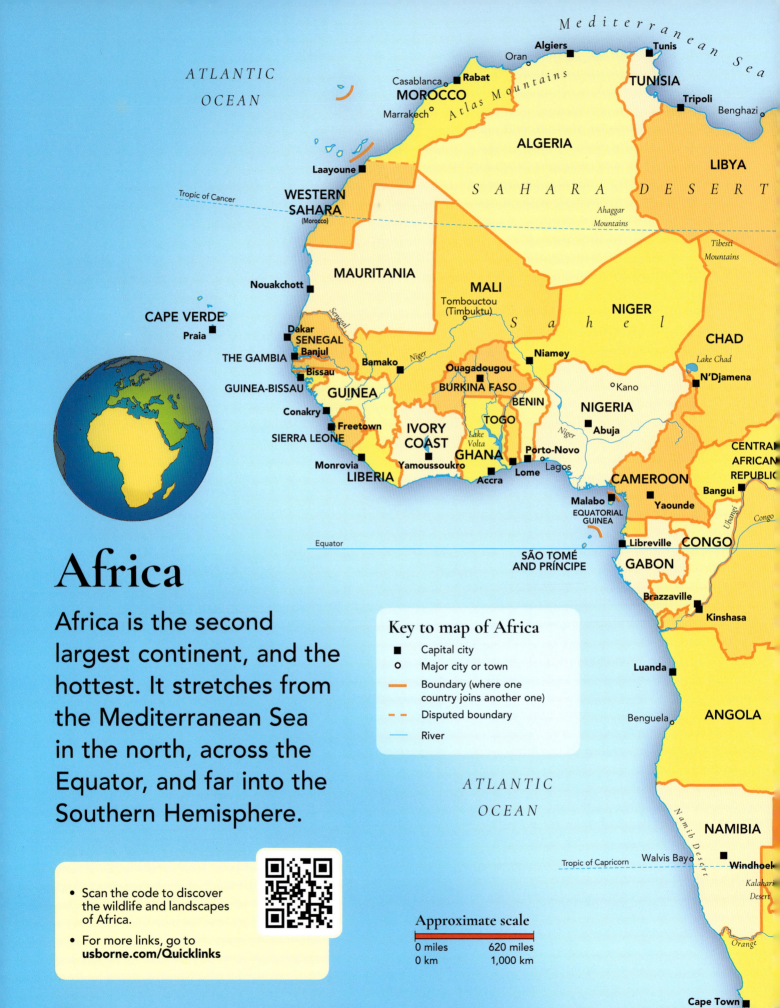

ATLANTIC OCEAN

Mediterranean Sea

Oran ■ Algiers ■ Tunis
Casablanca ■ **Rabat** **TUNISIA** ■ Tripoli
MOROCCO *Atlas Mountains* Benghazi
Marrakech

ALGERIA **LIBYA**

S A H A R A   D E S E R T

Tropic of Cancer *Ahaggar Mountains*
WESTERN SAHARA *Tibesti Mountains*
(Morocco)

Laayoune ■

MAURITANIA **MALI** **NIGER**
Tombouctou (Timbuktu) **CHAD**
Nouakchott ■ *S a h e l*
Lake Chad
CAPE VERDE ■ N'Djamena
Praia ■ Niamey ■
Dakar ■ **SENEGAL** Kano °
THE GAMBIA Banjul ■ Bamako ■ **BURKINA FASO** **NIGERIA**
Bissau ■ Ouagadougou ■
GUINEA-BISSAU **GUINEA** **BENIN** Abuja ■
TOGO *Niger*
Conakry ■ **IVORY COAST** **CENTRAL AFRICAN REPUBLIC**
Freetown ■ Lake Volta **GHANA** Porto-Novo ■ Bangui ■
SIERRA LEONE Yamoussoukro ■ Lome ■
Monrovia ■ Accra ■ Lagos **CAMEROON**
LIBERIA Malabo ■ Yaounde ■
EQUATORIAL GUINEA *Ubangi* *Congo*
Libreville ■ **CONGO**
Equator **SÃO TOMÉ AND PRÍNCIPE** **GABON**
Brazzaville ■
Kinshasa ■

Africa

Africa is the second largest continent, and the hottest. It stretches from the Mediterranean Sea in the north, across the Equator, and far into the Southern Hemisphere.

Key to map of Africa

■	Capital city
○	Major city or town
—	Boundary (where one country joins another one)
– –	Disputed boundary
—	River

ATLANTIC OCEAN

Luanda ■
Benguela **ANGOLA**

Namib Desert **NAMIBIA**

Tropic of Capricorn Walvis Bay ° Windhoek ■
Kalahari Desert

Cape Town ■
Cape of Good Hope

- Scan the code to discover the wildlife and landscapes of Africa.
- For more links, go to **usborne.com/Quicklinks**

Approximate scale

0 miles	620 miles
0 km	1,000 km

The pale brown areas on this satellite picture show how much of Africa is desert. The Sahara Desert is at the top of the continent.

Alexandria
Cairo
Suez
Libyan Desert
EGYPT
Aswan
Tropic of Cancer
Al Jawf
Lake Nasser
Nile
Port Sudan
Red Sea
SUDAN
Khartoum
ERITREA
Asmara
El Obeid
Blue Nile
Lake Tana
DJIBOUTI
Djibouti
White Nile
Ethiopian Highlands
SOUTH SUDAN
Addis Ababa
Juba
ETHIOPIA
SOMALIA
UGANDA
Lake Turkana
Kisangani
Kampala
KENYA
Mogadishu
Equator
Lake Victoria
Nairobi
CONGO
Kigali
RWANDA
Gitega
Bujumbura
BURUNDI
Mwanza
Kilimanjaro
Mombasa
Victoria
DEMOCRATIC
REPUBLIC)
Lake Tanganyika
Dodoma
Dar es Salaam
SEYCHELLES
TANZANIA
INDIAN OCEAN
Lubumbashi
COMOROS
Moroni
Ndola
Lake Nyasa (Lake Malawi)
ZAMBIA
Lilongwe
Lusaka
Zambezi
MALAWI
Lake Kariba
Nampula
Harare
MOZAMBIQUE
Toamasina
ZIMBABWE
Beira
Antananarivo
Bulawayo
MAURITIUS
Mozambique Channel
Port Louis
OTSWANA
MADAGASCAR
Gaborone
Pretoria (Tshwane)
Maputo
Tropic of Capricorn
ohannesburg
Mbabane
Lobamba
ESWATINI
Bloemfontein
Maseru
LESOTHO
UTH
Durban
RICA
Drakensberg
Gqeberha (Port Elizabeth)

Africa facts

Total land area
11,723,992 miles²

Biggest country
Algeria 919,595 miles²

Smallest country
Seychelles 176 miles²

Biggest island
Madagascar 226,665 miles²

Highest mountain
Kilimanjaro, Tanzania 19,341ft

Longest river
River Nile 4,132 miles

Biggest lake
Lake Victoria, Tanzania 26,828 miles²

Highest waterfall
Tugela Falls, South Africa 3,110ft

Biggest desert
Sahara, North Africa
3,552,140 miles²

This lion's sandy brown coat helps it blend in with its surroundings in its dry African grassland home.

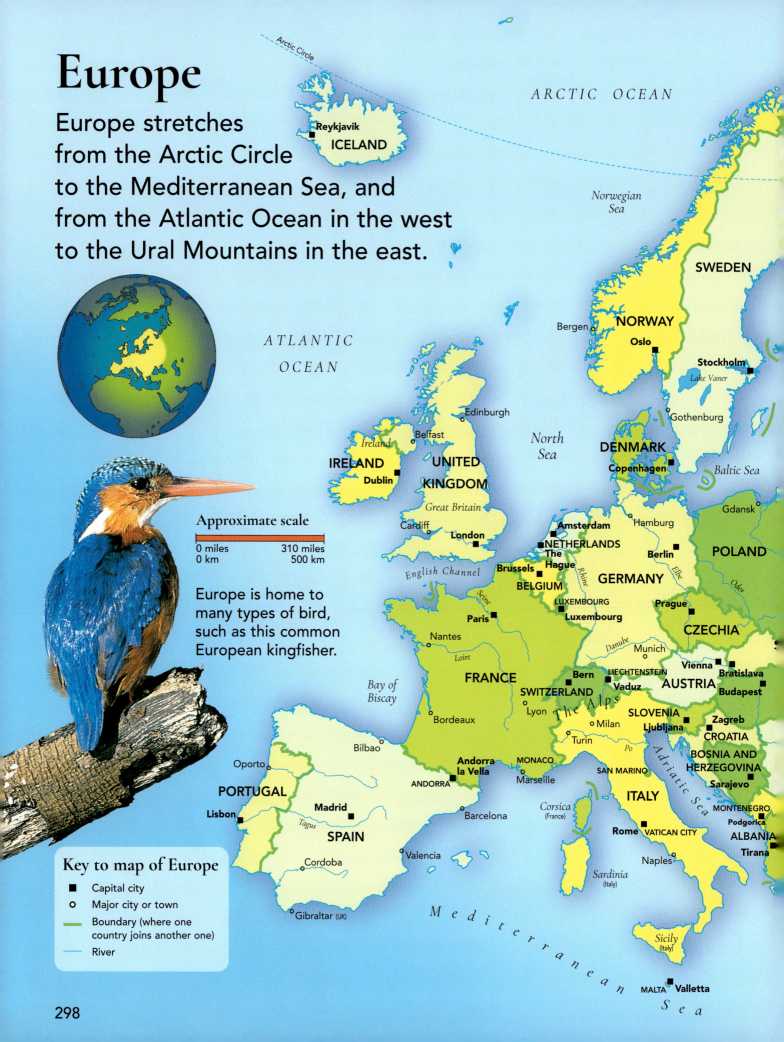

Europe

Europe stretches from the Arctic Circle to the Mediterranean Sea, and from the Atlantic Ocean in the west to the Ural Mountains in the east.

Europe is home to many types of bird, such as this common European kingfisher.

Approximate scale

| 0 miles | 310 miles |
| 0 km | 500 km |

Arctic Circle

ARCTIC OCEAN

ATLANTIC OCEAN

Norwegian Sea

North Sea

Baltic Sea

English Channel

Bay of Biscay

Mediterranean Sea

Adriatic Sea

Reykjavik
ICELAND

SWEDEN

NORWAY
Bergen
Oslo
Stockholm
Lake Vaner
Gothenburg

Edinburgh
Belfast
Ireland
IRELAND
Dublin
UNITED KINGDOM
Great Britain
Cardiff
London

DENMARK
Copenhagen

Hamburg
Gdansk
POLAND
Amsterdam
NETHERLANDS
The Hague
Berlin
Brussels
BELGIUM
GERMANY
Rhine
Elbe
Oder
Prague
CZECHIA
LUXEMBOURG
Luxembourg
Paris
Seine
Nantes
Loire
FRANCE
Danube
Munich
Vienna
Bratislava
Budapest
Bern
LIECHTENSTEIN
Vaduz
AUSTRIA
SWITZERLAND
Lyon
The Alps
Milan
SLOVENIA
Ljubljana
Zagreb
CROATIA
Turin
Po
Bordeaux
Andorra la Vella
MONACO
ANDORRA
Marseille
SAN MARINO
BOSNIA AND HERZEGOVINA
Sarajevo
Oporto
Bilbao
Corsica (France)
ITALY
MONTENEGRO
Podgorica
ALBANIA
Tirana
PORTUGAL
Madrid
Tagus
Lisbon
SPAIN
Rome
VATICAN CITY
Barcelona
Cordoba
Valencia
Sardinia (Italy)
Naples
Gibraltar (UK)
Sicily (Italy)
MALTA
Valletta

Key to map of Europe

- ■ Capital city
- ○ Major city or town
- ▬ Boundary (where one country joins another one)
- ～ River

North Cape

Barents Sea

Murmansk

Kola Peninsula

Arctic Circle

Pechora

Ural Mountains

Ukhta

pland

Oulu

Arkhangelsk

FINLAND

Northern Dvina

RUSSIA

Lake Onega

Perm

elsinki

St. Petersburg

Cherepovets

Tallinn

Rybinsk Reservoir

Volga

ESTONIA

Lake Ladoga

Kama

Nizhniy Novgorod

Kazan

LATVIA

Riga

Moscow

Samara

THUANIA

Tula

Vilnius

SIA

Minsk

Don

Volga

BELARUS

Voronezh

rsaw

Kyiv

Kharkiv

Volgograd

Lviv

UKRAINE

Dnieper

Volga

Astrakhan

VAKIA

Donetsk

Don

Carpathian Mountains

Dnipropetrovsk

Rostov

MOLDOVA

NGARY

Chisinau

Odesa

Sea of Azov

Caspian Sea

Cluj-Napoca

ROMANIA

Crimean Peninsula

grade

Bucharest

Caucasus Mountains

RBIA

Danube

Black Sea

Mount Elbrus

stina

BULGARIA

VO

Sofia

Skopje

NORTH

ACEDONIA

REECE

Aegean Sea

Athens

Crete
(Greece)

Europe facts

Total land area
3,930,520 miles²

Biggest country
Russia (total area)
6,592,772 miles²
European Russia
1,658,077 miles²

Smallest country
Vatican City   0.17 miles²

Biggest island
Great Britain   80,823 miles²

Highest mountain
Mount Elbrus, Russia   18,510ft

Longest river
Volga   2,294 miles

Biggest lake
Lake Ladoga, Russia
6,834 miles²

Highest waterfall
Vinnufossen, Norway   2,838ft

Biggest desert
There are no true
deserts in Europe.

- Scan the code to
  explore different
  European countries.

- For more links, go to
  usborne.com/Quicklinks

This satellite photograph
of Europe shows how
the continent joins on
to Asia at the right. The
white patch at the top
of the picture is the ice
that covers the Arctic.

Australia

Australia is the smallest continent. It is part of the region of Oceania, which also includes New Zealand and Papua New Guinea, as well as thousands of small islands in the Pacific Ocean.

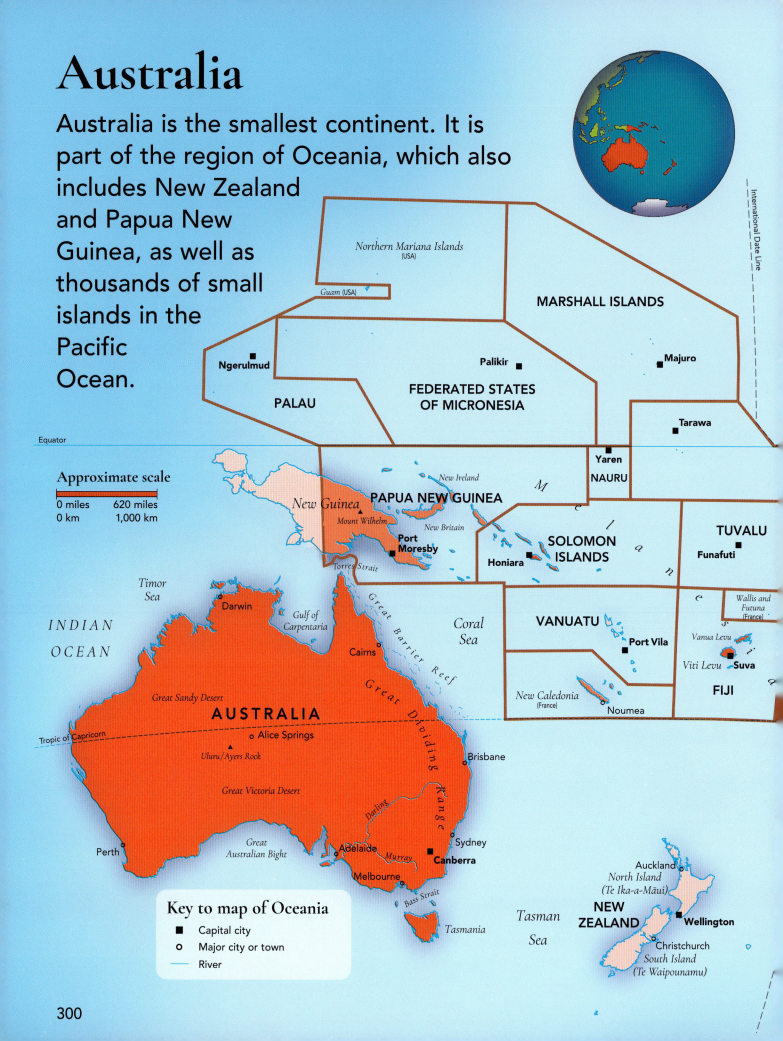

International Date Line

Northern Mariana Islands (USA)

Guam (USA)

MARSHALL ISLANDS

Ngerulmud ■

Palikir ■

Majuro ■

PALAU

FEDERATED STATES OF MICRONESIA

Tarawa ■

Equator

Yaren ■

NAURU

Approximate scale

0 miles	620 miles
0 km	1,000 km

New Ireland

M
e
l
a
n
e
s
i
a

TUVALU

New Guinea

Mount Wilhelm ▲

PAPUA NEW GUINEA

New Britain

Port Moresby ■

SOLOMON ISLANDS

Honiara ■

Funafuti ■

Wallis and Futuna (France)

Torres Strait

Timor Sea

Darwin ●

Gulf of Carpentaria

Cairns ●

Coral Sea

VANUATU

Port Vila ■

Vanua Levu

Viti Levu

Suva ■

INDIAN OCEAN

Great Sandy Desert

Great Barrier Reef

FIJI

Great Dividing Range

Tropic of Capricorn

AUSTRALIA

● Alice Springs

Uluru/Ayers Rock ▲

New Caledonia (France)

Noumea ●

Great Victoria Desert

Brisbane ●

Darling

Perth ●

Great Australian Bight

Adelaide ●

Murray

Sydney ●

Canberra ■

Melbourne ●

Bass Strait

Tasmania

Tasman Sea

Auckland ●

North Island (Te Ika-a-Māui)

NEW ZEALAND

Wellington ■

Christchurch ●

South Island (Te Waipounamu)

Key to map of Oceania

- ■ Capital city
- ○ Major city or town
- — River

Oceania facts

Total land area
3,306,733 miles²

Biggest country
Australia 2,968,402 miles²

Smallest country
Nauru 8 miles²

Biggest island (after Australia)
New Guinea 317,144 miles²

Highest mountain
Mount Wilhelm, Papua New Guinea 14,793ft

Longest river
Murray/Darling River, Australia 2,310 miles

Biggest lake
Lake Eyre, Australia 3,668 miles²

Highest waterfall
Sutherland Falls on the Arthur River, New Zealand 1,903ft

Biggest desert
Great Victoria Desert, Australia 134,653 miles²

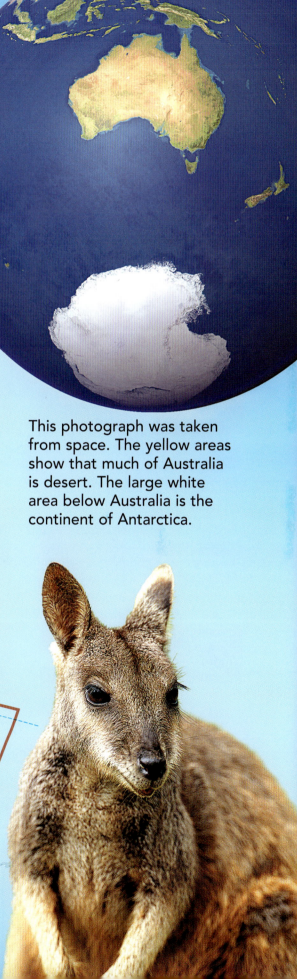

This photograph was taken from space. The yellow areas show that much of Australia is desert. The large white area below Australia is the continent of Antarctica.

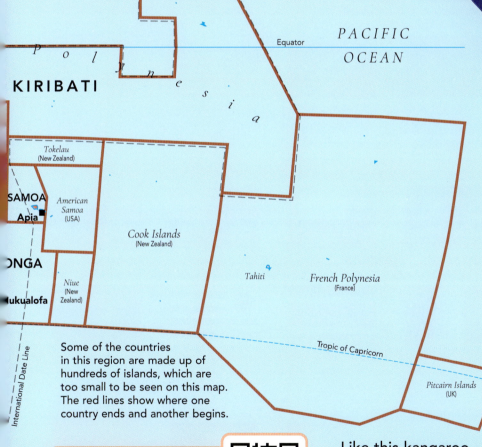

PACIFIC
OCEAN

Equator

P o l y n e s i a

KIRIBATI

Tokelau
(New Zealand)

SAMOA
Apia

American Samoa
(USA)

Cook Islands
(New Zealand)

ONGA

Niue
(New Zealand)

Nukualofa

Tahiti

French Polynesia
(France)

Tropic of Capricorn

Pitcairn Islands
(UK)

International Date Line

Some of the countries in this region are made up of hundreds of islands, which are too small to be seen on this map. The red lines show where one country ends and another begins.

- Scan the code to take a trip to Australia and Oceania.
- For more links, go to **usborne.com/Quicklinks**

Like this kangaroo, many mammals in Australia are marsupials. This means that they carry their babies in a pouch.

Flags of the world

North America

Antigua and Barbuda

Bahamas, The

Barbados

Belize

Canada

Costa Rica

Cuba

Dominica

Dominican Republic

El Salvador

Grenada

Guatemala

Haiti

Honduras

Jamaica

Mexico

Nicaragua

Panama

St. Kitts and Nevis

St. Lucia

St. Vincent and the Grenadines

Trinidad and Tobago

United States of America

South America

Argentina

Bolivia

Brazil

Chile

Colombia

Ecuador

Guyana

Paraguay

Peru

Suriname

Uruguay

Venezuela

Asia

Afghanistan

Armenia

Azerbaijan

Bahrain

Bangladesh

Bhutan

Brunei

Cambodia

China

East Timor

Georgia

India

Asia (continued)

 Indonesia

 Iran

 Iraq

 Israel

 Japan

 Jordan

 Kazakhstan

 Kuwait

 Kyrgyzstan

 Laos

 Lebanon

 Malaysia

 Maldives

 Mongolia

 Myanmar (Burma)

Nepal

 North Korea

 Oman

 Pakistan

 Philippines

 Qatar

 Russia

 Saudi Arabia

 Singapore

 South Korea

 Sri Lanka

 Syria

 Tajikistan

 Thailand

 Turkey

 Turkmenistan

 United Arab Emirates

 Uzbekistan

 Vietnam

 Yemen

Africa

 Algeria

 Angola

 Benin

 Botswana

 Burkina Faso

 Burundi

 Cameroon

Cape Verde

Central African Republic

Chad

Comoros

Congo

Congo (Democratic Republic)

Djibouti

Egypt

Equatorial Guinea

Eritrea

Eswatini

Africa (continued)

Ethiopia

Gabon

Gambia, The

Ghana

Guinea

Guinea-Bissau

Ivory Coast (Côte d'Ivoire)

Kenya

Lesotho

Liberia

Libya

Madagascar

Malawi

Mali

Mauritania

Mauritius

Morocco

Mozambique

Namibia

Niger

Nigeria

Rwanda

Sao Tome and Principe

Senegal

Seychelles

Sierra Leone

Somalia

South Africa

South Sudan

Sudan

Tanzania

Togo

Tunisia

Uganda

Zambia

Zimbabwe

Europe

Albania

Andorra

Austria

Belarus

Belgium

Bosnia and Herzegovina

Bulgaria

Croatia

Cyprus

Czechia

Denmark

Estonia

Finland

France

Germany

Greece

Hungary

Iceland

Europe (continued)

Ireland

Italy

Kosovo

Latvia

Liechtenstein

Lithuania

Luxembourg

Malta

Moldova

Monaco

Montenegro

Netherlands

North Macedonia

Norway

Poland

Portugal

Romania

Russia

San Marino

Serbia

Slovakia

Slovenia

Spain

Sweden

Switzerland

Turkey

Ukraine

United Kingdom

Vatican City

Changing flags

Flags of the world change frequently. New flags are designed as new countries are born, or their situation changes.

For example, in 1994, there were important changes to the way South Africa was run. All adults in the country were allowed to vote in free elections for the first time. To celebrate this, a new flag was designed.

South African flag until 1994

South African flag from 1994

- Scan the code for a quiz about flags of the world.
- For more links, go to **usborne.com/Quicklinks**

Oceania

Australia

Federated States of Micronesia

Fiji

Kiribati

Marshall Islands

Nauru

New Zealand

Palau

Papau New Guinea

Samoa

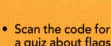
Solomon Islands

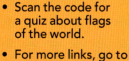
Tonga

Tuvalu

Vanuatu

Earth facts and records

The oceans

Ocean	Area in miles²	Deepest point in ft
Pacific Ocean	65,144,000	35,840
Atlantic Ocean	32,870,000	27,487
Indian Ocean	27,243,000	23,907
Southern Ocean	8,479,000	24,383
Arctic Ocean	6,007,000	18,212

This map shows the Earth's continents and oceans.

Highest mountains in each continent

Continent	Mountain	Other name	Height in ft	Location
Asia	Mount Everest	Chomolungma	29,035	Nepal/China
South America	Mount Aconcagua	Cerro Aconcagua	22,840	Argentina
North America	Denali	Mount McKinley	20,310	USA
Africa	Mount Kilimanjaro	Oldoinyo Oibor	19,340	Tanzania
Europe	Mount Elbrus	Gora Elbrus	18,510	Russia
Antarctica	Vinson Massif	Mount Vinson	16,050	Antarctica
Australia	Mount Kosciuszko	Kunama Namadgi	7,310	Australia

Climate records

Location	Notes
Death Valley, USA	Hottest recorded temperature on Earth: 134°F (1913)
Vostok, Antarctica	Coldest recorded temperature on Earth: −128.6°F (1983)
Mawsynram, India	Wettest place on Earth: 476.4 inches average rainfall per year
Arica, Chile	Driest place on Earth: 0.03 inches of rain per year, on average

Angel Falls is over three times as high as the Eiffel Tower in Paris, France.

- Scan the code to investigate more records and facts about Earth.
- For more links, go to **usborne.com/Quicklinks**

Deepest and highest

The deepest cave ever explored is Veryovkina Cave, in the country of Georgia. It is 1.4 miles deep.

The highest waterfall is Angel Falls in Venezuela. It is 3,212ft high.

Space facts

Comparing planet sizes

Distances across planets are given in miles.

Venus
7,512

Mars
4,221

Mercury
3,032

Earth
7,926

Jupiter
88,846

Saturn
74,897

Neptune
30,775

Uranus
31,763

- Scan the code to explore all sorts of space facts.
- For more links, go to **usborne.com/Quicklinks**

Solar System facts

Name of planet	Distance from the Sun	Time taken to orbit the Sun	Time it takes to spin once
Mercury	38 million miles	88 days	59 days
Venus	67 million miles	224.7 days	243 days
Earth	93 million miles	365.25 days	23 hours, 56 minutes
Mars	142 million miles	687 days	24 hours, 37 minutes
Jupiter	484 million miles	11.9 years	9 hours, 50 minutes
Saturn	890 million miles	29.4 years	10 hours, 34 minutes
Uranus	1,781 million miles	84 years	17 hours, 14 minutes
Neptune	2,805 million miles	165 years	15 hours, 58 minutes

Stars much larger than the Sun are called giant stars. Arcturus is a red giant. It is 25 times wider than our Sun.

Star types

Stars are huge balls of blazing gas. Our Sun is a star – one of billions in the Universe. It looks the biggest because it is the closest.

Any stars similar in size to our Sun, or smaller, are called dwarf stars. The Sun is a yellow dwarf.

The hottest, brightest stars are blue.

Compared to other stars, red stars are cooler and dimmer.

Sun

The biggest known stars are called supergiants. Rigel is a blue supergiant over 75 times wider than the Sun.

Animal and plant records

The biggest...

Living thing	A seagrass meadow in Shark Bay, Australia	Area 77 miles²	The whole plant is connected by underground shoots.
Animal	Blue whale	Length 98ft	Longer than a tennis court – the largest animal of all time
Land animal	African elephant	Weight 15,000lb	A newborn African elephant weighs more than many adult humans.
Bird (flightless)	Ostrich	Height 9ft	Lives in Africa
Bird (flying)	Wandering albatross	Wingspan 12ft	Migrates up to 75,000 miles a year
Reptile	Saltwater crocodile	Length 23ft	Lives in Australia and Southern Asia
Spineless animal	Colossal squid	Weight 1,091lb	Has the biggest eyes of any animal – the size of basketballs
Insect	Giant wētā	Weight 2.5oz	Lives in New Zealand
Tree (tallest)	"Hyperion," a coast redwood	Height 380ft	Grows in California, USA

Comparing animal sizes

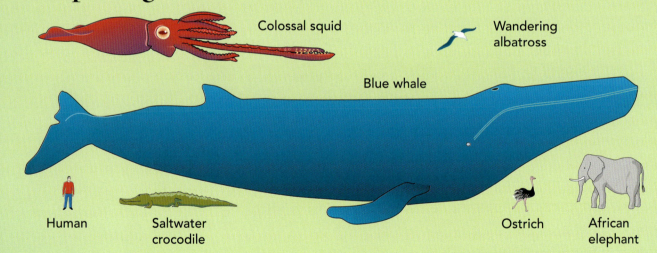

Colossal squid

Wandering albatross

Blue whale

Human

Saltwater crocodile

Ostrich

African elephant

The smallest...

Living thing	Mycoplasma genitalium	Length 0.0003mm	A germ living in the human body
Insect	Fairyfly male	Length 0.127mm	A tiny wasp from Costa Rica
Fish	Spinyhead seadevil male	Length 6.2mm	A minute male anglerfish
Reptile	Nano-chameleon	Length 13.5mm	Lives in Madagascar
Mammal	Bumblebee bat	Length 30mm	Lives in Thailand
Bird	Bee hummingbird	Length 55mm	Lives in Cuba

The oldest...

Living thing	Neptune seagrass	Age 100,000 years (or more)	An ancient meadow of this seagrass grows under the Mediterranean Sea, south of Ibiza
Tree	Bristlecone pine	Age 5,075+ years	Grows in the White Mountains of California, USA
Sea creature	Antarctic sponge	Age 1,550 years	Grows slowly in the cold Southern Ocean
Land animal	"Jonathan," a giant tortoise	Age 193+ years	Jonathan was born in the Seychelles in about 1832. He now lives on the island of St. Helena.

The rarest...

Bird	Kākāpō	Native to New Zealand, fewer than 250 are left
Land mammal	Northern white rhino	Only two females exist, at a conservancy in Kenya
Sea mammal	Vaquita porpoise	Fewer than 10 are left, around the coast of Mexico
Fish	Devils Hole pupfish	These only live in Death Valley National Park, Nevada
Tree	Three Kings Kaikomako	Just one remains in the wild, in New Zealand

The fastest...

Animal (over a short distance)	Cheetah	62mph
Animal (over a long distance)	Pronghorn (American antelope)	35mph
Swimmer	Sailfish	68mph
Bird	Peregrine falcon, while diving	200mph

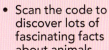

- Scan the code to discover lots of fascinating facts about animals.
- For more links, go to **usborne.com/Quicklinks**

Giant tortoises are some of the longest-living animals in the world. This one is from Galapagos Islands, north-west of South America.

Map index

This is an index of the **countries** named on the maps and their *capital cities.*

Index

Acknowledgments

Every effort has been made to trace and acknowledge ownership of copyright. If any rights have been omitted, the publishers offer to rectify this in any subsequent editions following notification. The publishers are grateful to the following organizations and individuals for their contributions and permission to reproduce copyright material:

(t = top, m = middle, b = bottom, l = left, r = right, Alamy = Alamy Stock Photo, DV = Digital Vision, SPL = Science Photo Library)

Cover: tl © Mark Carwardine/naturepl, tm © Images of Africa Photobank/Alamy, tr © Puwadol Jaturawutthichai/Alamy, ml © Wirestock/Dreamstime.com, m © Sigive/Dreamstime.com, mr © Maximilian Weinzierl/Alamy, bl © Glenda Powers/Dreamstime.com, bm © Aphelleon/Dreamstime.com, br © Kittipong Jirasukhanont/Alamy; p1 © Judy Unger/Photodisc/Getty Images; p2–3 © Solvin Zankl/Nature Picture Library/SPL; p7 © Dinodia Photos/Alamy; p8–9b © DV; p9tr © DV; p10 ml, bl © DV; p11 r, b © DV; p12 bg, ml, mr © DV; p12bl © Richard Hamilton Smith/Getty Images; p12br © DV; p14 tl, tr © DV; p14tm © Douglas Peebles/Corbis Documentary/Getty Images; p15r © NOAA/Dept of Commerce; p16–17bg © Corbis; p16 ml, bl © DV; p16m © Corbis; p16mr © DV; p17 © Leo McGilly/Alamy; p20bl © Joseph Sohm/The Image Bank/Getty Images; p22 t, bl © DV; p23tl © FLPA/Alamy; p23b © DV; p25tr © Karind/Alamy; p26–27bg © DV; p27tl © Ian Walker/Eye Ubiquitous; p31br © Ron Watts/Image Bank/Getty Images; p35bm © Steve Raymer/The Image Bank/Getty Images; p36–37bg © DV; p36ml © Gary Braasch/Corbis Historical/Getty Images; p40–41bg © DV; p45bl © imageBROKER.com GmbH & Co. KG/Alamy; p45bm © Chinch Gryniewicz/Bridgeman Images; p45br © DV; p46 bg, ml © DV; p47b © DV; p49b © NOAA/Department of Commerce; p50br © DV; p51 © DV; p52tr © Stockbyte; p52br © DV; p53bl © DV; p53br © Kim Taylor/Warren Photographic; p54tl © Professor P. Motta/Department of Anatomy/University "La Sapienza", Rome/SPL; p55m © Dr Linda Stannard/UCT/SPL; p55br © Fadil Aziz/Alamy; p56tr © DV; p56 m, bl © DV; p57 tr, br © DV; p58l © Karl Ammann/naturepl; p59tr © Jack Fields/Corbis; p60l © Karl Ammann/Corbis; p61b © Winifred Wisniewski; FLPA/Corbis; p62tr © George Lepp/Corbis; p63br © Wolfgang Kaehler/Corbis; p65r © Suzi Eszterhas/Minden/naturepl.com; p66r © Uwe Walz/Corbis; p67tr © DV; p67br © Jonathan Smith/Cordaiy Photo/Corbis; p68tl © Image Source/Jupiter Images/Getty Images; p68br © Heather Angel/Natural Visions; p69br © Westend61/SuperStock; p70–71bg © DV; p70bl © Jane Burton/Warren Photographic; p71mr © blickwinkel/Alamy; p72l © Geoff du Feu; p73br © Mick Martin; p78–79bg © Pacific Stock/Bruce Coleman; p78mr © Stuart Westmorland/Corbis Documentary/Getty Images; p78bl © Franco Banfi/WaterF/age fotostock/SuperStock; p80tr © SeaTops/Alamy; p82–83t © Francois Gohier/ardea.com; p83mr © 123rf; p87tr © Paul A. Souders/Stone/Getty Images; p87br © Gary W. Carter/Getty Images; p89bl © Kim Taylor/Bruce Coleman Collection; p90–91bg © Bob Krist; p91mr © DV; p92l © Tony Watson/Alamy; p93 © Mehau Kulyk/SPL; p95tr © National Cancer Institute/SPL; p95b © BSIP SA/Alamy; p96bl © Dave Roberts/SPL; p99br © Juergen Berger, Max-Plank Institute/SPL; p100b © Mehau Kulyk/SPL; p101br © Gary Gay/Stock Connection Distribution/Alamy; p102tr © Dr G. Moscoso/SPL; p103tr © Laura Dwight Photography; p104–105bg © Rick Gomez/Integrity Productions; p106tl © Custom Medical Stock Photo/SPL; p106br © Dr Linda Stannard, Uct/SPL; p107tr © Biology Media/SPL; p107br © Custom Medical Stock Photo/SPL; p108tr © Karel Noppe/Dreamstime.com; p108bl © Laura Doss; p110b © SPL; p111tm © Image State/Alamy; p111br © David Young-Wolff; p112bl © Peter Cade/Stone/Getty Images; p113tr © Biophoto Associates/SPL; p114bg © Salisbury dept of Clinical radiology/SPL; p115 © Gianni Dagli Orti/Shutterstock; p116b © Trustees of the Natural History Museum; p117b © Roger Harris/SPL; p118–119bg © DIOMEDIA/DeAgostini/G. DAGLI ORTI; p119b © George Roos, Peter Arnold Inc./SPL; p120tr © The Trustees of the British Museum; p120bl © Mattpix/Alamy; p122tr © Leemage/Corbis Historical/Getty Images; p122b © Michael Runkel/robertharding; p123tl © The Trustees of the British Museum; p123r © Royal Albert Memorial Museum, Exeter, Devon/Bridgeman Art Library; p123bl © DIOMEDIA/DeAgostini/G. DAGLI ORTI; p124b © Sorin Colac/Alamy; p125bl © Michael Holford; p126bl © National Museums & Galleries of Wales; p127mr © PRISMA ARCHIVO/Alamy; p128tl © The Vikings, Britain's oldest Dark Age re-enactment society; p129br © Werner Forman Archive/Statens Historiska Museum, Stockholm; p130mr © The Trustees of the British Museum; p130b © Connect Images/Alamy; p131bl © Michael S. Lewis/Corbis Documentary/Getty Images; p133tr © The Art Archive/Shutterstock; p134tl © Alan Levy; p134b © Kevin Schafer/The Image Bank/Getty Images; p135tl © Werner Forman Archive/British Museum, London; p136tl © JLBvdWOLF/Alamy; p137tl © Martha Avery/Corbis Historical/Getty Images; p137ml © Martha Avery/Corbis Historical/Getty Images; p137tr © The Art Archive/Shutterstock; p138tr © Adam Woolfitt/Robert Harding; p138bl Detail from a portrait of Henry VIII by Hans Holbein/Galleria Nazionale d'Arte Antica, Rome/Photo Scala, Florence; p139t © SuperStock/SuperStock; p140tl © Eurasia/robertharding; p141br © DIOMEDIA/DeAgostini/G. DAGLI ORTI; p142tr © robertharding/Alamy; p142b © Image State/Alamy; p143tr © Gala/SuperStock; p143bl © Lebrecht Authors/Bridgeman Images; p144tr © FL Historical 31/Alamy; p144bl © Valentyn Volkov/Alamy; p145br © North Wind Picture Archives/Alamy; p146bl © Ashley Cooper/Alamy; p149tr © Malcolm Haines/Alamy; p150tl © The Imperial War Museum, London; p150mr © Hulton-Deutsch Collection/Corbis Historical/Getty Images; p150b © Bettmann/Getty Images; p151bl © Science History Images/Alamy; p152tr © Science History Images/Alamy; p152bl © Phillip Harrington/Alamy; p153tr © Ian Dagnall/Alamy; p153bl © Dom Slike/Alamy; p154l © DV; p155 © Galen Rowell/Corbis; p156–157bg © Penny Tweedle/Image Bank Unreleased/Getty Images; p156bl © DV; p157tl © Laura Dwight Photography; p158b © Britstock-IFA/HAGA; p159t © Mira/Alamy; p159br © Joanna Kearney/Alamy; p160–161bg © Patrick Bachelder/Alamy; p161ml © Jeremy Horner/Corbis Documentary/Getty Images; p162tr © Shutterstock; p162b © Peter Turnley/Corbis Historical/Getty Images; p163tr © Sean Pavone/Dreamstime.com; p163bl © Peter Turnley/Corbis Premium Historical/Getty Images; p163br © The History Emporium/Alamy; p164b © Reed Kaestner; p165b © Julia Waterlow/Eye Ubiquitous; p166tr © Smallredgirl/Dreamstime.com; p166br © blickwinkel/Alamy; p167tr © Zoonar GmbH/Alamy; p167br © Stock Connection Blue/Alamy; p168tr © Jane & Arthur Klonsky; p170tr © Kevin R. Morris/Bohemian Nomad Picture Makers/The Image Bank/Getty Images; p171mr © Owaki - Kulla/The Image Bank/Getty Images; p171b © Peter Bowater/Alamy; p172–173bg © Wally McNamee/Corbis Historical/Getty Images; p173mr © Rex Features; p173bm © Wally McNamee/Getty Images; 174tr © Askoldsb/Dreamstime.com; p175tl © North Wind Picture Archives/Alamy; p175br © Sjors737/Dreamstime.com; p176tl © Rudolph Staechelin Foundation, Chateau de Malmaison, Paris, France/Lauros-Giraudon, Paris/SuperStock; p176bl © Images-USA/Alamy; p177b © Jon Arnold Images Ltd/Alamy; p178tr © Michael Turner/Dreamstime.com; p178bl © Elliott Franks/ArenaPAL/

With thanks to:
Louise Baxter and Paul I'Anson at MINI UK (Wheels and engines), Vincent Deloménie, Centre audiovisuel SNCF (Trains), Christopher Denne (Cameras), Tim Milbourne (Computers, The internet), Balfour Knox (Plumbing), Albert Milbourne (Wheels and engines), Andy Hart, UK SNCF society (Trains), Shipmate Flags, Vlaardingen, The Netherlands, Hawkes Ocean Technologies (H.O.T.) for their permission to feature the Deep Flight I submersible in this book. Special thanks to Bob Whiteaker for help with the Deep Flight I diagram on page 246.

Additional consultancy: Dr. Tom Weston (Science) and Mark Champkins (Technology)

Additional design and editorial: Sam Baer, Verinder Bhachu, Sharon Cooper, Kate Fearn, Georgina Hooper, Tom Lalonde, Vici Leyhane, Laura Parker, Fiona Patchett, Jane Rigby, Leonard Le Rolland, Andrea Slane and Nicky Wainwright

Additional illustrations: Sophie Allington, John Barber, Verinder Bhachu, Gary Bines, Isabel Bowring, Trevor Boyer, Andy Burton, Michèle Busby, Nicola Butler, Kuo Kang Chen, Adam Constantine, Pam Cornfield, Richard Cox, Gary Cross, David Cuzik, Jon Davis, Tony Gibson, Robert Gilmore, Rebecca Hardy, Nicholas Hewetson, Inklink Firenze, Ian Jackson, Colin King, Steven Kirk, Adam Linley, Rachel Lockwood, Chris Lyon, Philip Nicholson, Alex Pang, Justine Peek, Maurice Pledger, Leonard Le Rolland, Chris Shields, Guy Smith, Treve Tamblin, Mike Wheatley, Graham White, John Woodcock and David Wright